THE WORKS OF SHAKESPEARE

EDITED FOR THE SYNDICS OF THE
CAMBRIDGE UNIVERSITY PRESS
BY
JOHN DOVER WILSON

THE SECOND PART OF THE
HISTORY OF HENRY IV

THE SECOND PART OF THE HISTORY OF HENRY IV

CAMBRIDGE
AT THE UNIVERSITY PRESS
1971

PUBLISHED BY
THE SYNDICS OF THE CAMBRIDGE UNIVERSITY PRESS

Bentley House, 200 Euston Road, London, NW1 2DB
American Branch: 32 East 57th Street, New York, N.Y. 10022

ISBNs:
0 521 07533 5 *clothbound*
0 521 09476 3 *paperback*

First edition 1946
* Reprinted 1953
1961
1965
First paperback edition 1968
Reprinted 1971

* Places where editorial changes or additions intro-
duce variants from the first edition are, where possible, marked by a date [1952] in square brackets.

First printed in Great Britain at the University Press, Cambridge
Reprinted in Great Britain by Hazell Watson & Viney Ltd,
Aylesbury, Bucks

CONTENTS

PREFATORY NOTE   PAGE vi

TO THE READER   vii

TITLE-PAGE OF THE QUARTO OF 1600 (reduced   1
     facsimile)

THE SECOND PART OF KING HENRY THE
     FOURTH   3

THE COPY FOR THE TEXTS OF 1600 AND 1623   115

NOTES ON 2 *HENRY IV*   124

GLOSSARY   216

PREFATORY NOTE

The *Introduction* to *Henry IV*, together with the *Stage-History* of its two Parts, is to be found at the beginning of the volume containing Part I.

TO THE READER

The following is a brief description of the punctuation and other typographical devices employed in the text, which have been more fully explained in the *Note on Punctuation* and the *Textual Introduction* to be found in *The Tempest* volume:

An obelisk (†) implies corruption or emendation, and suggests a reference to the Notes.

A single bracket at the beginning of a speech signifies an 'aside.'

Four dots represent a *full stop* in the original, except when it occurs at the end of a speech, and they mark a long pause. Original *colons* or *semicolons*, which denote a somewhat shorter pause, are retained, or represented as three dots when they appear to possess special dramatic significance. Similarly, significant *commas* have been given as dashes.

Round brackets are taken from the original, and mark a significant change of voice; when the original brackets seem to imply little more than the drop in tone accompanying parenthesis, they are conveyed by commas or dashes.

Single inverted commas (' ') are editorial; double ones (" ") derive from the original, where they are used to draw attention to maxims, quotations, etc.

The reference number for the first line is given at the head of each page. Numerals in square brackets are placed at the beginning of the traditional acts and scenes.

THE
Second part of Henrie

the fourth, continuing to his death,
and coronation of Henrie
the fift.

With the humours of sir Iohn Fal-
staffe, and swaggering
Pistoll.

As it hath been sundrie times publikely
acted by the right honourable, the Lord
Chamberlaine his seruants.

Written by William Shakespeare.

LONDON
Printed by V.S. for Andrew Wise, and
William Aspley.
1600.

The scene: England

CHARACTERS IN THE PLAY

RUMOUR, *the Presenter*
KING HENRY *the Fourth*
PRINCE HENRY, *afterwards crowned*
   King Henry V   *sons to*
PRINCE JOHN OF LANCASTER   *King Henry*
PRINCE HUMPHREY OF GLOUCESTER   *the Fourth*
PRINCE THOMAS OF CLARENCE

EARL *of* WARWICK
EARL *of* WESTMORELAND
EARL *of* SURREY (*mute*)
EARL *of* KENT (*mute*)   *of the king's party*
GOWER
HARCOURT
SIR JOHN BLUNT (*mute*)
LORD CHIEF JUSTICE
A Servant to the Lord Chief Justice

EARL *of* NORTHUMBERLAND
SCROOP, *Archbishop of York*
LORD MOWBRAY   *opposites against King*
LORD HASTINGS   *Henry the Fourth*
LORD BARDOLPH
SIR JOHN COLEVILE

TRAVERS *and* MORTON, *retainers to Northumberland*
EDWARD POINS, *gentleman-in-waiting to Prince Henry*

FALSTAFF
BARDOLPH
PISTOL   *irregular humourists*
PETO
A Page

SHALLOW ⎫
SILENCE ⎬ *country justices*

DAVY, *servant to Shallow*

FRANCIS *and another drawer*

FANG *and* SNARE, *a sergeant and his yeoman*

MOULDY ⎫
SHADOW ⎪
WART ⎬ *country soldiers*
FEEBLE ⎪
BULLCALF ⎭

LADY NORTHUMBERLAND

LADY PERCY

HOSTESS QUICKLY

DOLL TEARSHEET

EPILOGUE

*Lords and Attendants; a Porter, Beadles, three
Strewers of rushes.*

THE SECOND PART OF
KING HENRY IV

Warkworth. *Before the gate of Northumberland's castle*

Induction   '*Enter* RUMOUR, *painted full of tongues*'

Rumour. Open your ears; for which of you will stop
The vent of hearing when loud Rumour speaks?
I from the orient to the drooping west,
Making the wind my post-horse, still unfold
The acts commencéd on this ball of earth.
Upon my tongues continual slanders ride,
The which in every language I pronounce,
Stuffing the ears of men with false reports.
I speak of peace while covert enmity
Under the smile of safety wounds the world: 10
And who but Rumour, who but only I,
Make fearful musters and prepared defence,
Whiles the big year, swoln with some other grief,
Is thought with child by the stern tyrant war,
And no such matter? Rumour is a pipe
Blown by surmises, jealousies, conjectures,
And of so easy and so plain a stop
That the blunt monster with uncounted heads,
The still-discordant wav'ring multitude,
Can play upon it....But what need I thus   20
My well-known body to anatomize
Among my household? Why is Rumour here?
I run before King Harry's victory,
Who in a bloody field by Shrewsbury
Hath beaten down young Hotspur and his troops,
Quenching the flame of bold rebellion,
Even with the rebels' blood. But what mean I

To speak so true at first? my office is
To noise abroad that Harry Monmouth fell
30 Under the wrath of noble Hotspur's sword,
And that the king before the Douglas' rage
Stooped his anointed head as low as death.
This have I rumoured through the peasant towns
Between that royal field of Shrewsbury
And this worm-eaten hold of ragged stone,
Where Hotspur's father, old Northumberland,
Lies crafty-sick. The posts come tiring on,
And not a man of them brings other news
Than they have learned of me. From Rumour's tongues
40 They bring smooth comforts false, worse than true
        wrongs.   [*he goes*

[I. I.]   '*Enter the* LORD BARDOLPH'

L. Bardolph [*calls*]. Who keeps the gate here, ho?
        [*A Porter appears on the wall above the gate*
                                    Where is the earl?
Porter. What shall I say you are?
L. Bardolph.   Tell thou the earl
That the Lord Bardolph doth attend him here.
    Porter. His lordship is walked forth into the orchard,
Please it your honour knock but at the gate,
And he himself will answer.

    NORTHUMBERLAND *comes forth, hobbling upon
        a crutch and with his head muffled*

L. Bardolph.   Here comes the earl.
Northumberland. What news, Lord Bardolph? every
        minute now
Should be the father of some stratagem.

The times are wild, contention like a horse,
Full of high feeding, madly hath broke loose,   10
And bears down all before him.

  L. Bardolph.   Noble earl,
I bring you certain news from Shrewsbury.

  Northumberland. Good, an God will!

  L. Bardolph.   As good as heart can wish:
The king is almost wounded to the death,
And in the fortune of my lord your son
Prince Harry slain outright, and both the Blunts
Killed by the hand of Douglas, young Prince John
And Westmoreland and Stafford fled the field,
And Harry Monmouth's brawn, the hulk Sir John,
Is prisoner to your son: O, such a day,   20
So fought, so followed, and so fairly won,
Came not till now to dignify the times,
Since Caesar's fortunes!

  Northumberland.   How is this derived?
Saw you the field? came you from Shrewsbury?

  L. Bardolph. I spake with one, my lord, that came
      from thence,
A gentleman well bred and of good name,
That freely rend'red me these news for true.

TRAVERS approaches

  Northumberland. Here comes my servant Travers,
      whom I sent
On Tuesday last to listen after news.

  L. Bardolph. My lord, I over-rode him on the way,   30
And he is furnished with no certainties
More than he haply may retail from me.

  Northumberland. Now, Travers, what good tidings
      comes with you?

Travers. My lord, † Sir John Umfrevile turned
    me back
With joyful tidings, and, being better horsed,
Out-rode me. After him came spurring hard
A gentleman, almost forspent with speed,
That stopped by me to breathe his bloodied horse.
He asked the way to Chester, and of him
40 I did demand what news from Shrewsbury.
He told me that rebellion had bad luck,
And that young Harry Percy's spur was cold:
With that he gave his able horse the head,
And bending forward struck his arméd heels
Against the panting sides of his poor jade
Up to the rowel-head, and starting so
He seemed in running to devour the way,
Staying no longer question.
   Northumberland.   Ha? Again!
Said he young Harry Percy's spur was cold?
50 Of Hotspur Coldspur? that rebellion
Had met ill luck?
   L. Bardolph.   My lord, I'll tell you what—
If my young lord your son have not the day,
Upon mine honour, for a silken point
I'll give my barony. Never talk of it.
   Northumberland. Why should that gentleman that rode
    by Travers
Give then such instances of loss?
   L. Bardolph.   Who, he?
He was some hilding fellow, that had stol'n
The horse he rode on, and upon my life
Spoke at a venture. Look, here comes more news.

MORTON is seen drawing near

Northumberland. Yea, this man's brow, like to   60
 a title-leaf,
Foretells the nature of a tragic volume.
So looks the strond whereon the imperious flood
Hath left a witnessed usurpation....
Say, Morton, didst thou come from Shrewsbury?
 Morton. I ran from Shrewsbury, my noble lord,
Where hateful death put on his ugliest mask
To fright our party.
 Northumberland. How doth my son and brother?
Thou tremblest, and the whiteness in thy cheek
Is apter than thy tongue to tell thy errand.
Even such a man, so faint, so spiritless,   70
So dull, so dead in look, so woe-begone,
Drew Priam's curtain in the dead of night,
And would have told him half his Troy was burnt:
But Priam found the fire ere he his tongue,
And I my Percy's death ere thou report'st it.
This thou wouldst say, 'Your son did thus and thus,
Your brother thus; so fought the noble Douglas'—
Stopping my greedy ear with their bold deeds,
But in the end, to stop my ear indeed,
Thou hast a sigh to blow away this praise,   80
Ending with 'Brother, son, and all are dead.'
 Morton. Douglas is living, and your brother yet,
But for my lord your son...
 Northumberland. Why, he is dead.
See what a ready tongue suspicion hath!
He that but fears the thing he would not know,
Hath by instinct knowledge from others' eyes
That what he feared is chancéd...Yet speak, Morton.
Tell thou an earl his divination lies,

And I will take it as a sweet disgrace,
90 And make thee rich for doing me such wrong.
　Morton. You are too great to be by me gainsaid,
Your spirit is too true, your fears too certain.
　Northumberland. Yet, for all this, say not that
　　　Percy's dead.
I see a strange confession in thine eye,
Thou shak'st thy head, and hold'st it fear or sin
To speak a truth: if he be slain, say so.
The tongue offends not that reports his death,
And he doth sin that doth belie the dead,
Not he which says the dead is not alive.
100 Yet the first bringer of unwelcome news
Hath but a losing office, and his tongue
Sounds ever after as a sullen bell,
Remembered tolling a departing friend.
　L. Bardolph. I cannot think, my lord, your son is dead.
　Morton. I am sorry I should force you to believe
That which I would to God I had not seen,
But these mine eyes saw him in bloody state,
Rend'ring faint quittance, wearied and out-breathed,
To Harry Monmouth, whose swift wrath beat down
110 The never-daunted Percy to the earth,
From whence with life he never more sprung up.
In few, his death, whose spirit lent a fire
Even to the dullest peasant in his camp,
Being bruited once, took fire and heat away
From the best-tempered courage in his troops.
For from his mettle was his party steeled,
Which once in him abated, all the rest
Turned on themselves, like dull and heavy lead.
And as the thing that's heavy in itself,
120 Upon enforcement flies with greatest speed,
So did our men, heavy in Hotspur's loss,

Lend to this weight such lightness with their fear,
That arrows fled not swifter toward their aim
Than did our soldiers, aiming at their safety,
Fly from the field: then was that noble Worcester
Too soon ta'en prisoner, and that furious Scot,
The bloody Douglas, whose well-labouring sword
Had three times slain th' appearance of the king,
'Gan vail his stomach and did grace the shame
Of those that turned their backs, and in his flight,   130
Stumbling in fear, was took: the sum of all
Is that the king hath won, and hath sent out
A speedy power to encounter you, my lord,
Under the conduct of young Lancaster
And Westmoreland...This is the news at full.

   Northumberland. For this I shall have time enough
        to mourn.
In poison there is physic; and these news,
Having been well, that would have made me sick,
Being sick, have (in some measure) made me well:
And as the wretch whose fever-weak'ned joints,   140
Like strengthless hinges, buckle under life,
Impatient of his fit, breaks like a fire
Out of his keeper's arms; even so my limbs,
Weakened with grief, being now enraged with grief,
Are thrice themselves: hence therefore, thou nice crutch!
A scaly gauntlet now with joints of steel
Must glove this hand, and hence, thou sickly coif!
Thou art a guard too wanton for the head
Which princes, fleshed with conquest, aim to hit:
Now bind my brows with iron, and approach   150
The ragged'st hour that Time and Spite dare bring
To frown upon th'enraged Northumberland!
Let heaven kiss earth! now let not Nature's hand
Keep the wild flood confined! let Order die!

And let this world no longer be a stage
To feed contention in a ling'ring act;
But let one spirit of the first-born Cain
Reign in all bosoms, that, each heart being set
On bloody courses, the rude scene may end,
160 And darkness be the burier of the dead!

    L. Bardolph. This strainéd passion doth you wrong,
        my lord.

    Morton. Sweet earl, divorce not wisdom from your
        honour.
The lives of all your loving complices
Lean on your health, the which, if you give o'er
To stormy passion, must perforce decay.
You cast th'event of war, my noble lord,
And summed the account of chance, before you said
'Let us make head': it was your presurmise,
That, in the dole of blows, your son might drop:
170 You knew he walked o'er perils, on an edge,
More likely to fall in than to get o'er:
You were advised his flesh was capable
Of wounds and scars, and that his forward spirit
Would lift him where most trade of danger ranged.
Yet did you say 'Go forth'; and none of this,
Though strongly apprehended, could restrain
The stiff-borne action: what hath then befall'n,
Or what hath this bold enterprise brought forth,
More than that being which was like to be?
180   *L. Bardolph.* We all that are engagéd to this loss
Knew that we ventured on such dangerous seas
That if we wrought out life 'twas ten to one,
And yet we ventured for the gain proposed,
Choked the respect of likely peril feared,
And, since we are o'erset, venture again...
Come, we will all put forth body and goods.

Morton. 'Tis more than time: and, my most noble lord,
I hear for certain, and dare speak the truth,
The gentle Archbishop of York is up
With well-appointed powers; he is a man   190
Who with a double surety binds his followers.
My lord your son had only but the corpse,
But shadows and the shows of men, to fight:
For that same word, rebellion, did divide
The action of their bodies from their souls,
And they did fight with queasiness, constrained,
As men drink potions, that their weapons only
Seemed on our side; but, for their spirits and souls,
This word, rebellion, it had froze them up,
As fish are in a pond. But now the bishop   200
Turns insurrection to religion:
Supposed sincere and holy in his thoughts,
He's followed both with body and with mind;
And doth enlarge his rising with the blood
Of fair King Richard, scraped from Pomfret stones;
Derives from heaven his quarrel and his cause;
Tells them he doth bestride a bleeding land,
Gasping for life under great Bolingbroke;
And more and less do flock to follow him.

Northumberland. I knew of this before: but, to   210
    speak truth,
This present grief had wiped it from my mind.
Go in with me, and counsel every man
The aptest way for safety and revenge.
Get posts and letters, and make friends with speed;
Never so few, and never yet more need.   [*they go*

[1.2.]   *A street in London*

Enter SIR JOHN FALSTAFF, *hobbling with a stick; 'his*
     PAGE, *bearing his sword and buckler', following*

Falstaff. Sirrah, you giant, what says the doctor to
my water?

Page. He said, sir, the water itself was a good healthy
water, but for the party that owed it, he might have moe
diseases than he knew for.

Falstaff. Men of all sorts take a pride to gird at me:
the brain of this foolish-compounded clay-man is not
able to invent any thing that intends to laughter, more
than I invent or is invented on me. I am not only witty
10 in myself, but the cause that wit is in other men. I do
here walk before thee like a sow that hath overwhelmed
all her litter but one. If the prince put thee into my
service for any other reason than to set me off, why then
I have no judgement. Thou whoreson mandrake, thou
art fitter to be worn in my cap than to wait at my heels.
I was never manned with an agate till now: but I will
inset you neither in gold nor silver, but in vile apparel,
and send you back again to your master, for a jewel—the
juvenal, the prince your master, whose chin is not yet
20 fledge. I will sooner have a beard grow in the palm of
my hand than he shall get one off his cheek; and yet he
will not stick to say his face is a face royal: God may
finish it when he will, 'tis not a hair amiss yet: he may
keep it still at a face-royal, for a barber shall never earn
sixpence out of it; and yet he'll be crowing as if he had
writ man ever since his father was a bachelor. He may
keep his own grace, but he's almost out of mine, I can
assure him...What said Master Dommelton about the
satin for my short cloak and my slops?

Page. He said, sir, you should procure him better 30
assurance than Bardolph, he would not take his band
and yours, he liked not the security.

Falstaff. Let him be damned like the Glutton! pray
God his tongue be hotter! A whoreson Achitophel!
a rascally yea-forsooth knave! to bear a gentleman in
hand, and then stand upon security! The whoreson
smooth-pates do now wear nothing but high shoes, and
bunches of keys at their girdles, and if a man is through
with them in honest taking-up, then they must stand
upon security. I had as lief they would put ratsbane in 40
my mouth as offer to stop it with security. I looked a'
should have sent me two and twenty yards of satin, as
I am a true knight, and he sends me 'security'...Well, he
may sleep in security, for he hath the horn of abundance,
and the lightness of his wife shines through it, and yet
cannot he see, though he have his own lanthorn to light
him....Where's Bardolph?

Page. He's gone into Smithfield to buy your worship
a horse.

Falstaff. I bought him in Paul's, and he'll buy me a 50
horse in Smithfield; an I could get me but a wife in the
stews, I were manned, horsed, and wived.

The LORD CHIEF JUSTICE *approaches,*
with a servant

Page. Sir, here comes the nobleman that committed
the prince for striking him about Bardolph.

Falstaff. Wait close, I will not see him. [*whips down*
an alley, the Page after him]

L. Chief Justice. What's he that goes there?

Servant. Falstaff, an't please your lordship.

L. Chief Justice. He that was in question for the
robbery?

60 *Servant.* He, my lord. But he hath since done good
service at Shrewsbury, and, as I hear, is now going with
some charge to the Lord John of Lancaster.

L. Chief Justice. What, to York? Call him back again.

Servant. Sir John Falstaff!

Falstaff. Boy, tell him I am deaf.

Page. You must speak louder, my master is deaf.

L. Chief Justice. I am sure he is, to the hearing of any
thing good. Go, pluck him by the elbow. I must speak
with him.

70 *Servant* [*runs and takes him by the sleeve*]. Sir John!

Falstaff [*turns*]. What! a young knave, and begging!
Is there not wars? is there not employment? doth not
the king lack subjects? do not the rebels need soldiers?
Though it be a shame to be on any side but one, it is
worse shame to beg than to be on the worst side, were it
worse than the name of rebellion can tell how to make it.

Servant. You mistake me, sir.

Falstaff. Why, sir, did I say you were an honest man?
setting my knighthood and my soldiership aside, I had
80 lied in my throat, if I had said so.

Servant. I pray you, sir, then set your knighthood and
your soldiership aside, and give me leave to tell you,
you lie in your throat, if you say I am any other than an
honest man.

Falstaff. I give thee leave to tell me so! I lay aside that
which grows to me! If thou get'st any leave of me, hang
me. If thou tak'st leave, thou wert better be hanged.
You hunt counter, hence! avaunt!

[*the Lord Chief Justice comes up*

Servant [*bows*]. Sir, my lord would speak with you.

90 *L. Chief Justice.* Sir John Falstaff, a word with you.

Falstaff. My good lord! God give your lordship good
time of day, I am glad to see your lordship abroad, I

heard say your lordship was sick, I hope your lordship goes abroad by advice. Your lordship, though not clean past your youth, have yet some smack of age in you, some relish of the saltness of time, and I most humbly beseech your lordship to have a reverend care of your health.

L. Chief Justice. Sir John, I sent for you before your expedition to Shrewsbury.

Falstaff. An't please your lordship, I hear his majesty 100 is returned with some discomfort from Wales.

L. Chief Justice. I talk not of his majesty. You would not come when I sent for you.

Falstaff. And I hear, moreover, his highness is fallen into this same whoreson apoplexy.

L. Chief Justice. Well, God mend him! I pray you, let me speak with you.

Falstaff. This apoplexy, as I take it, is a kind of lethargy, an't please your lordship, a kind of sleeping in the blood, a whoreson tingling. 110

L. Chief Justice. What tell you me of it? be it as it is.

Falstaff. It hath it original from much grief, from study and perturbation of the brain. I have read the cause of his effects in Galen, it is a kind of deafness.

L. Chief Justice. I think you are fallen into the disease, for you hear not what I say to you.

Falstaff. Very well, my lord, very well—rather, an't please you, it is the disease of not listening, the malady of not marking, that I am troubled withal. 120

L. Chief Justice. To punish you by the heels would amend the attention of your ears, and I care not if I do become your physician.

Falstaff. I am as poor as Job, my lord, but not so patient. Your lordship may minister the potion of imprisonment to me, in respect of poverty, but how I

should be your patient to follow your prescriptions, the
wise may make some dram of a scruple, or indeed a
scruple itself.

130 *L. Chief Justice.* I sent for you, when there were
matters against you for your life, to come speak with me.

Falstaff. As I was then advised by my learned counsel
in the laws of this land service, I did not come.

L. Chief Justice. Well, the truth is, Sir John, you live
in great infamy.

Falstaff. He that buckles himself in my belt cannot
live in less.

L. Chief Justice. Your means are very slender, and
your waste is great.

140 *Falstaff.* I would it were otherwise, I would my means
were greater and my waist slenderer.

L. Chief Justice. You have misled the youthful prince.

Falstaff. The young prince hath misled me. I am the
fellow with the great belly, and he my dog.

L. Chief Justice. Well, I am loath to gall a new-healed
wound. Your day's service at Shrewsbury hath a little
gilded over your night's exploit on Gad's Hill, you may
thank th'unquiet time for your quiet o'er-posting that
action.

150 *Falstaff.* My lord!

L. Chief Justice. But since all is well, keep it so, wake
not a sleeping wolf.

(*Falstaff.* To wake a wolf is as bad as smell a fox.

L. Chief Justice. What, you are as a candle, the
better part burnt out.

Falstaff. A wassail candle, my lord, all tallow—if I did
say of wax, my growth would approve the truth.

L. Chief Justice. There is not a white hair on your
face, but should have his effect of gravity.

160 (*Falstaff.* His effect of gravy, gravy, gravy.

L. Chief Justice. You follow the young prince up and down, like his ill angel.

Falstaff. Not so, my lord, your ill angel is light, but I hope he that looks upon me will take me without weighing, and yet in some respects I grant I cannot go.... I cannot tell. Virtue is of so little regard in these coster-mongers' times that true valour is turned bear'ard: pregnancy is made a tapster, and his quick wit wasted in giving reckonings: all the other gifts appertinent to man, as the malice of this age shapes them, are not worth a 170 gooseberry. You that are old consider not the capacities of us that are young, you do measure the heat of our livers with the bitterness of your galls, and we that are in the vaward of our youth, I must confess, are wags too.

L. Chief Justice. Do you set down your name in the scroll of youth, that are written down old with all the characters of age? Have you not a moist eye? a dry hand? a yellow cheek? a white beard? a decreasing leg? an increasing belly? is not your voice broken? your wind short? your chin double? your wit single? and every 180 part about you blasted with antiquity? and will you yet call yourself young? Fie, fie, fie, Sir John!

Falstaff. My lord, I was born about three of the clock in the afternoon, with a white head and something a round belly. For my voice, I have lost it with hallooing and singing of anthems....To approve my youth further, I will not: the truth is, I am only old in judgement and understanding; and he that will caper with me for a thousand marks, let him lend me the money, and have at him. For the box of the ear that the prince gave you, 190 he gave it like a rude prince, and you took it like a sensible lord: I have checked him for it, and the young lion repents—[*aside*] marry, not in ashes and sackcloth, but in new silk and old sack.

L. Chief Justice. Well, God send the prince a better companion!

Falstaff. God send the companion a better prince! I cannot rid my hands of him.

L. Chief Justice. Well, the king hath severed you: 200 I hear you are going with Lord John of Lancaster against the Archbishop and the Earl of Northumberland.

Falstaff. Yea, I thank your pretty sweet wit for it... [*louder*] But look you, pray, all you that kiss my lady Peace at home, that our armies join not in a hot day! for, by the Lord, I take but two shirts out with me, and I mean not to sweat extraordinarily: if it be a hot day, and I brandish any thing but a bottle, I would I might never spit white again...There is not a dangerous action can peep out his head but I am thrust upon it. Well, I 210 cannot last ever, but it was alway yet the trick of our English nation, if they have a good thing, to make it too common. If ye will needs say I am an old man, you should give me rest: I would to God my name were not so terrible to the enemy as it is. I were better to be eaten to death with a rust than to be scoured to nothing with perpetual motion.

L. Chief Justice. Well, be honest, be honest, and God bless your expedition!

Falstaff. Will your lordship lend me a thousand pound 220 to furnish me forth?

L. Chief Justice. Not a penny, not a penny, you are too impatient to bear crosses: fare you well: commend me to my cousin Westmoreland.

[*he goes his way, the servant following*

Falstaff. If I do, fillip me with a three-man beetle... A man can no more separate age and covetousness than a' can part young limbs and lechery: but the gout galls the one, and the pox pinches the other; and so both the degrees prevent my curses. Boy!

Page. Sir?

Falstaff. What money is in my purse?   230

Page. Seven groats and two pence.

Falstaff. I can get no remedy against this consumption of the purse, borrowing only lingers and lingers it out, but the disease is incurable....Go bear this letter to my Lord of Lancaster, this to the prince, this to the Earl of Westmoreland, and this to old Mistress Ursula, whom I have weekly sworn to marry since I perceived the first white hair of my chin: about it, you know where to find me. [*Page goes*] A pox of this gout! or, a gout of this pox! for the one or the other plays the rogue with 240 my great toe. 'Tis no matter if I do halt, I have the wars for my colour, and my pension shall seem the more reasonable: a good wit will make use of any thing; I will turn diseases to commodity.   [*he limps off*

[I. 3.] *The Palace of the Archbishop of York*

Enter the ARCHBISHOP *of* YORK, HASTINGS, MOWBRAY, *and* LORD BARDOLPH

Archbishop. Thus have you heard our cause and known
　　our means,
And, my most noble friends, I pray you all,
Speak plainly your opinions of our hopes.
And first, lord marshal, what say you to it?

Mowbray. I well allow the occasion of our arms,
But gladly would be better satisfied
How in our means we should advance ourselves
To look with forehead bold and big enough
Upon the power and puissance of the king.

Hastings. Our present musters grow upon the file   10
To five and twenty thousand men of choice,
And our supplies live largely in the hope

Of great Northumberland, whose bosom burns
With an incenséd fire of injuries.

 L. Bardolph. The question then, Lord Hastings,
  standeth thus—
Whether our present five and twenty thousand
May hold up head without Northumberland.

 Hastings. With him, we may.

 L. Bardolph.   Yea, marry, there's the point.
But if without him we be thought too feeble,
20 My judgement is, we should not step too far
Till we had his assistance by the hand.
For in a theme so bloody-faced as this
Conjecture, expectation, and surmise
Of aids incertain should not be admitted.

 Archbishop. 'Tis very true, Lord Bardolph, for indeed
It was young Hotspur's cause at Shrewsbury.

 L. Bardolph. It was, my lord; who lined himself
  with hope,
Eating the air on promise of supply,
Flatt'ring himself in project of a power
30 Much smaller than the smallest of his thoughts,
And so, with great imagination
Proper to madmen, led his powers to death,
And, winking, leaped into destruction.

 Hastings. But, by your leave, it never yet did hurt
To lay down likelihoods and forms of hope.

 L. Bardolph. Yes, if this present quality of war—
Indeed the instant action, a cause on foot—
Lives so in hope, as in an early spring
We see th'appearing buds; which to prove fruit
40 Hope gives not so much warrant as despair
That frosts will bite them. When we mean to build,
We first survey the plot, then draw the model,
And when we see the figure of the house,

Then must we rate the cost of the erection,
Which if we find outweighs ability,
What do we then, but draw anew the model
In fewer offices, or at least desist
To build at all? Much more, in this great work
(Which is almost to pluck a kingdom down
And set another up) should we survey   50
The plot of situation and the model,
Consent upon a sure foundation,
Question surveyors, know our own estate,
How able such a work to undergo,
To weigh against his opposite; or else
We fortify in paper and in figures,
Using the names of men instead of men:
Like one that draws the model of an house
Beyond his power to build it; who, half through,
Gives o'er, and leaves his part-created cost   60
A naked subject to the weeping clouds,
And waste for churlish winter's tyranny.

  Hastings. Grant that our hopes (yet likely of fair birth)
Should be still-born, and that we now possessed
The utmost man of expectation,
I think we are a body strong enough,
Even as we are, to equal with the king.

    L. Bardolph. What, is the king but five and
      twenty thousand?

    Hastings. To us no more, nay, not so much,
      Lord Bardolph.

For his divisions, as the times do brawl,   70
Are in three heads, one power against the French,
And one against Glendower; perforce a third
Must take up us: so is the unfirm king
In three divided, and his coffers sound
With hollow poverty and emptiness.

Archbishop. That he should draw his several
    strengths together
And come against us in full puissance,
Need not be dreaded.

  Hastings.   If he should do so,
He leaves his back unarmed, the French and Welsh
80 Baying him at the heels: never fear that.

  L. Bardolph. Who is it like should lead his forces
    hither?

  Hastings. The Duke of Lancaster and Westmoreland:
Against the Welsh, himself and Harry Monmouth:
But who is substituted 'gainst the French,
I have no certain notice.

  Archbishop.   Let us on;
And publish the occasion of our arms.
The commonwealth is sick of their own choice,
Their over-greedy love hath surfeited:
An habitation giddy and unsure
90 Hath he that buildeth on the vulgar heart.
O thou fond many, with what loud applause
Didst thou beat heaven with blessing Bolingbroke,
Before he was what thou wouldst have him be!
And being now trimmed in thine own desires,
Thou, beastly feeder, art so full of him,
That thou provok'st thyself to cast him up.
So, so, thou common dog, didst thou disgorge
Thy glutton bosom of the royal Richard,
And now thou wouldst eat thy dead vomit up,
100 And howl'st to find it. What trust is in these times?
They that, when Richard lived, would have him die,
Are now become enamoured on his grave:
Thou, that threw'st dust upon his goodly head,
When through proud London he came sighing on
After th' admiréd heels of Bolingbroke,

Criest now 'O earth, yield us that king again,
And take thou this!' O thoughts of men accursed!
Past and to come seems best; things present, worst.

Mowbray. Shall we go draw our numbers, and set on?
Hastings. We are time's subjects, and time bids   110
be gone.   *[they go*

[2. 1.]   *Eastcheap. Near the Boar's Head Tavern*

Enter HOSTESS, *with Sergeant* FANG, *a large
villainous fellow*

Hostess. Master Fang, have you entered the action?
Fang. It is entered.
Hostess. Where's your yeoman? Is't a lusty yeoman?
will a' stand to't?
Fang [roars]. Sirrah! Where's Snare?
Hostess. O Lord, ay! good Master Snare.

Yeoman SNARE, *a starved bloodhound, shuffles up*

Snare. Here, here.
Fang. Snare, we must arrest Sir John Falstaff.
Hostess. Yea, good Master Snare, I have entered him
and all.   10
Snare. It may chance cost some of us our lives, for he
will stab.
Hostess. Alas the day, take heed of him, he stabbed me
in mine own house, most beastly in good faith. A' cares
not what mischief he does, if his weapon be out. He will
foin like any devil, he will spare neither man, woman,
nor child.
Fang. If I can close with him, I care not for his
thrust.
Hostess. No, nor I neither, I'll be at your elbow.   20

Fang. An I but fist him once, an a' come but within my vice—

Hostess. I am undone by his going. I warrant you, he's an infinitive thing upon my score. Good Master Fang, hold him sure; good Master Snare, let him not 'scape. A' comes continuantly to Pie-corner (saving your manhoods) to buy a saddle, and he is indited to dinner to the Lubber's head in Lumbert street, to Master Smooth's the silkman. I pray you, since my exion is entered, and
30 my case so openly known to the world, let him be brought in to his answer. A hundred mark is a long one for a poor lone woman to bear, and I have borne, and borne, and borne, and have been fubbed off, and fubbed off, and fubbed off, from this day to that day, that it is a shame to be thought on. There is no honesty in such dealing, unless a woman should be made an ass, and a beast, to bear every knave's wrong....

Sir John Falstaff, Page, and Bardolph
come along the street

Yonder he comes, and that arrant malmsey-nose knave Bardolph with him. Do your offices, do your offices,
40 Master Fang and Master Snare, do me, do me, do me your offices.

Falstaff. How now? whose mare's dead? what's the matter?

Fang. Sir John, I arrest you at the suit of Mistress Quickly.

Falstaff. Away, varlets! Draw, Bardolph, cut me off the villain's head, throw the quean in the channel.

[*Bardolph draws, and a scuffle ensues*

Hostess. Throw me in the channel? I'll throw thee in the channel. Wilt thou? wilt thou? thou bastardly

rogue! Murder, murder! Ah, thou honey-suckle villain! 50
wilt thou kill God's officers and the king's? Ah, thou
honey-seed rogue! thou art a honey-seed, a man-queller,
and a woman-queller.

Falstaff. Keep them off, Bardolph.

Fang. A rescue! a rescue!   [*a crowd assembles*

Hostess. Good people, bring a rescue or two. [*the
Page attacks her*] Thou wot, wot thou? thou wot,
wot ta? do! do! thou rogue! do, thou hempseed!

[*she strikes at him and flees; Fang arrests Falstaff*

Page [*pursuing*]. Away, you scullion! you rampallian!
you fustilarian! I'll tickle your catastrophe.   60

'*Enter the* L. CHIEF JUSTICE *and his men*'

L. Chief Justice. What is the matter? keep the peace
here, ho!

Hostess. Good my lord, be good to me. I beseech you,
stand to me!

L. Chief Justice. How, now, Sir John? what are you
              brawling here?
Doth this become your place, your time and business?
You should have been well on your way to York.
Stand from him, fellow, wherefore hang'st upon him?

Hostess. O my most worshipful lord, an't please your
grace, I am a poor widow of Eastcheap, and he is 70
arrested at my suit.

L. Chief Justice. For what sum?

Hostess. It is more than for some, my lord, it is for all,
all I have. He hath eaten me out of house and home,
he hath put all my substance into that fat belly of his.
But I will have some of it out again, or I will ride thee
a-nights like the mare.

(*Falstaff.* I think I am as like to ride the mare, if I have
any vantage of ground to get up.

80 *L. Chief Justice.* How comes this, Sir John? Fie! what man of good temper would endure this tempest of exclamation? Are you not ashamed to enforce a poor widow to so rough a course to come by her own?

Falstaff. What is the gross sum that I owe thee?

Hostess. Marry, if thou wert an honest man, thyself and the money too: thou didst swear to me upon a parcel-gilt goblet, sitting in my Dolphin chamber, at the round table by a sea-coal fire, upon Wednesday in Wheeson week, when the prince broke thy head for 90 liking his father to a singing-man of Windsor, thou didst swear to me then, as I was washing thy wound, to marry me, and make me my lady thy wife. Canst thou deny it? did not goodwife Keech, the butcher's wife, come in then and call me gossip Quickly? coming in to borrow a mess of vinegar, telling us she had a good dish of prawns, whereby thou didst desire to eat some, whereby I told thee they were ill for a green wound? and didst thou not, when she was gone down stairs, desire me to be no more so familiarity with such poor people, saying 100 that ere long they should call me madam? and didst thou not kiss me, and bid me fetch thee thirty shillings? I put thee now to thy book-oath, deny it if thou canst.

Falstaff. My lord, this is a poor mad soul, and she says up and down the town that her eldest son is like you. She hath been in good case, and the truth is, poverty hath distracted her. But for these foolish officers, I beseech you I may have redress against them.

L. Chief Justice. Sir John, Sir John, I am well acquainted with your manner of wrenching the true 110 cause the false way: it is not a confident brow, nor the throng of words that come with such more than impudent sauciness from you, can thrust me from a level consideration: you have, as it appears to me, practised

upon the easy-yielding spirit of this woman, and made
her serve your uses both in purse and in person.

Hostess. Yea, in truth, my lord.

L. Chief Justice. Pray thee, peace. Pay her the debt
you owe her, and unpay the villainy you have done with
her. The one you may do with sterling money, and the
other with current repentance.　　120

Falstaff. My lord, I will not undergo this sneap without
reply. You call honourable boldness impudent sauciness:
if a man will make curtsy and say nothing, he is virtuous.
No, my lord, my humble duty remembered, I will not
be your suitor. I say to you, I do desire deliverance from
these officers, being upon hasty employment in the king's
affairs.

L. Chief Justice. You speak as having power to do
wrong. But answer in th'effect of your reputation, and
satisfy the poor woman.　　130

Falstaff. Come hither, hostess.　　　*[he takes her aside*

GOWER *comes up with a letter*

L. Chief Justice. Now, Master Gower, what news?

Gower. The king, my lord, and Harry Prince of Wales
Are near at hand—the rest the paper tells.

　　　　　[the L. Chief Justice reads the letter,
　　　　　　　　frowning the while

Falstaff. As I am a gentleman!

Hostess. Faith, you said so before.

Falstaff. As I am a gentleman. Come, no more words
of it.

Hostess. By this heavenly ground I tread on, I must be
fain to pawn both my plate and the tapestry of my 140
dining-chambers.

Falstaff. Glasses, glasses, is the only drinking—and for
thy walls, a pretty slight drollery or the story of the

Prodigal or the German hunting, in waterwork, is
worth a thousand of these bed-hangers and these fly-
bitten tapestries. Let it be ten pound, if thou canst...
Come, an 'twere not for thy humours, there's not a
better wench in England. Go, wash thy face, and draw
the action. Come, thou must not be in this humour with
150 me, dost not know me? Come, come, I know thou wast
set on to this.

Hostess. Pray thee, Sir John, let it be but twenty
nobles. I' faith, I am loath to pawn my plate, so God
save me, la.

Falstaff. Let it alone, I'll make other shift, you'll be
a fool still.

Hostess. Well, you shall have it, though I pawn my
gown. I hope you'll come to supper. You'll pay me all
together?

160 *Falstaff.* Will I live? [*aside to Bardolph*] Go, with her,
with her, hook on, hook on.

Hostess. Will you have Doll Tearsheet meet you at
supper?

Falstaff. No more words, let's have her.

> [*the Hostess goes off with Bardolph,*
> *Officers and Page following*

L. Chief Justice [*to Gower*]. I have heard better news.

Falstaff. What's the news, my lord?

L. Chief Justice [*to Gower*]. Where lay the king
to-night?

Gower. At Basingstoke, my lord.

170 *Falstaff.* I hope, my lord, all's well. What is the news,
my lord?

L. Chief Justice [*to Gower*]. Come all his forces back?

Gower. No, fifteen hundred foot, five hundred horse,
Are marched up to my lord of Lancaster,
Against Northumberland and the Archbishop.

Falstaff. Comes the king back from Wales, my noble
lord?

L. Chief Justice. [*to Gower*] You shall have letters of
me presently.

Come, go along with me, good Master Gower.

[*they turn to go*

Falstaff. My lord!   180

L. Chief Justice [*sharply*]. What's the matter?

Falstaff [*to Gower*]. Master Gower, shall I entreat
you with me to dinner?

Gower. I must wait upon my good lord here, I thank
you, good Sir John.

L. Chief Justice. Sir John, you loiter here too long,
being you are to take soldiers up in counties as you
go.

Falstaff [*to Gower*]. Will you sup with me, Master
Gower?   190

L. Chief Justice. What foolish master taught you these
manners, Sir John?

Falstaff. Master Gower, if they become me not, he
was a fool that taught them me....[*to the L. Chief Justice*]
This is the right fencing grace, my lord, tap for tap, and
so part fair.

L. Chief Justice. Now the Lord lighten thee! thou art
a great fool.   [*they go*

[2. 2.]   *London. A room in the Prince's house*

Enter PRINCE HENRY and POINS, *newly arrived
from Wales*

Prince [*flings himself down*]. Before God, I am exceeding weary.

Poins. Is't come to that? I had thought weariness durst
not have attached one of so high blood.

Prince. Faith, it does me, though it discolours the complexion of my greatness to acknowledge it...Doth it not show vilely in me to desire small beer?

Poins. Why, a prince should not be so loosely studied as to remember so weak a composition.

10 *Prince*. Belike then my appetite was not princely got, for, by my troth, I do now remember the poor creature, small beer. But indeed these humble considerations make me out of love with my greatness. What a disgrace is it to me to remember thy name! or to know thy face to-morrow! or to take note how many pair of silk stockings thou hast, viz. these, and those that were thy peach-coloured ones! or to bear the inventory of thy shirts—as, one for superfluity, and another for use! But that the tennis-court-keeper knows better than I, for it is 20 a low ebb of linen with thee when thou keepest not racket there, as thou hast not done a great while, because the rest of thy low countries have made a shift to eat up thy holland: and God knows whether those that bawl out the ruins of thy linen shall inherit his kingdom: but the midwives say the children are not in the fault, whereupon the world increases and kindreds are mightily strengthened.

Poins. How ill it follows, after you have laboured so hard, you should talk so idly! Tell me, how many good 30 young princes would do so, their fathers being so sick as yours at this time is?

Prince. Shall I tell thee one thing, Poins?

Poins. Yes faith, and let it be an excellent good thing.

Prince. It shall serve among wits of no higher breeding than thine.

Poins. Go to, I stand the push of your one thing that you will tell.

Prince. Marry, I tell thee, it is not meet that I should be sad now my father is sick, albeit I could tell to thee, 40 as to one it pleases me for fault of a better to call my friend, I could be sad, and sad indeed too.

Poins. Very hardly, upon such a subject.

Prince. By this hand, thou thinkest me as far in the devil's book as thou and Falstaff for obduracy and persistency. Let the end try the man. But I tell thee, my heart bleeds inwardly that my father is so sick, and keeping such vile company as thou art hath in reason taken from me all ostentation of sorrow.

Poins. The reason?   50

Prince. What wouldst thou think of me if I should weep?

Poins. I would think thee a most princely hypocrite.

Prince. It would be every man's thought, and thou art a blessed fellow to think as every man thinks; never a man's thought in the world keeps the road-way better than thine: every man would think me an hypocrite indeed. And what accites your most worshipful thought to think so?

Poins. Why, because you have been so lewd, and so 60 much engraffed to Falstaff.

Prince. And to thee.

Poins. By this light, I am well spoke on, I can hear it with mine own ears. The worst that they can say of me is that I am a second brother, and that I am a proper fellow of my hands, and those two things I confess I cannot help...By the mass, here comes Bardolph.

'Enter BARDOLPH, and PAGE' in fantastic apparel

Prince. And the boy that I gave Falstaff. A' had him from me Christian, and look if the fat villain have not transformed him ape.   70

Bardolph. God save your grace!

Prince. And yours, most noble Bardolph!

Poins. Come, you virtuous ass, you bashful fool, must you be blushing? wherefore blush you now? What a maidenly man-at-arms are you become? Is't such a matter to get a pottle-pot's maidenhead?

Page. A' calls me e'en now, my lord, through a red lattice, and I could discern no part of his face from the window. At last I spied his eyes, and methought he had 80 made two holes in the ale-wife's new petticoat and so peeped through.

Prince. Has not the boy profited?

Bardolph. Away, you whoreson upright rabbit, away!

Page. Away, you rascally Althæa's dream, away!

Prince. Instruct us, boy. What dream, boy?

Page. Marry, my lord, Althæa dreamt she was delivered of a fire-brand, and therefore I call him her dream.

90 *Prince.* A crown's worth of good interpretation. There 'tis, boy.   [*gives him money*

Poins. O, that this blossom could be kept from cankers! Well, there is sixpence to preserve thee.

Bardolph. An you do not make him be hanged among you, the gallows shall have wrong.

Prince. And how doth thy master, Bardolph?

Bardolph. Well, my lord. He heard of your grace's coming to town. There's a letter for you.

[*the Prince opens and reads*

Poins. Delivered with good respect. And how doth 100 the martlemas, your master?

Bardolph. In bodily health, sir.

Poins. Marry, the immortal part needs a physician, but that moves not him—though that be sick, it dies not.

Prince. I do allow this wen to be as familiar with me as my dog, and he holds his place, for look you how he writes.   [*he shows the superscription*

Poins. 'John Falstaff, knight'—

Every man must know that as oft as he has occasion to name himself: even like those that are kin to the king, for they never prick their finger but they say, 'There's 110 some of the king's blood spilt.' 'How comes that?' says he, that takes upon him not to conceive. The answer is as ready as a borrower's cap, 'I am the king's poor cousin, sir.'

Prince. Nay, they will be kin to us, or they will fetch it from Japhet. But the letter—

[*reads*] 'Sir John Falstaff, knight, to the son of the king, nearest his father, Harry Prince of Wales, greeting.'

Poins. Why, this is a certificate.

Prince. Peace!   120

[*reads*] 'I will imitate the honourable Romans in brevity.'

Poins. He sure means brevity in breath, short-winded.

Prince [*reads*]. 'I commend me to thee, I commend thee, and I leave thee. Be not too familiar with Poins; for he misuses thy favours so much that he swears thou art to marry his sister Nell. Repent at idle times as thou may'st, and so farewell.

    'Thine, by yea and no, which is as much as to say as thou usest him, JACK FALSTAFF with my familiars, 130 JOHN with my brothers and sisters, and SIR JOHN with all Europe.'

Poins. My lord, I'll steep this letter in sack, and make him eat it.

Prince. That's to make him eat twenty of his words. But do you use me thus, Ned? must I marry your sister?

Poins. God send the wench no worse fortune! but I never said so.

140 *Prince.* Well, thus we play the fools with the time, and the spirits of the wise sit in the clouds and mock us. Is your master here in London?

Bardolph. Yea, my lord.

Prince. Where sups he? doth the old boar feed in the old frank?

Bardolph. At the old place, my lord, in Eastcheap.

Prince. What company?

Page. Ephesians, my lord, of the old church.

Prince. Sup any women with him?

150 *Page.* None, my lord, but old Mistress Quickly and Mistress Doll Tearsheet.

Prince. What pagan may that be?

Page. A proper gentlewoman, sir, and a kinswoman of my master's.

Prince. Even such kin as the parish heifers are to the town bull. Shall we steal upon them, Ned, at supper?

Poins. I am your shadow, my lord, I'll follow you.

Prince. Sirrah, you boy, and Bardolph, no word to 160 your master that I am yet come to town... [*he gives them money*] There's for your silence.

Bardolph. I have no tongue, sir.

Page. And for mine, sir, I will govern it.

Prince. Fare you well; go. [*Bardolph and the Page go* This Doll Tearsheet should be some road.

Poins. I warrant you, as common as the way between Saint Albans and London.

Prince. How might we see Falstaff bestow himself to-night in his true colours, and not ourselves be seen?

170 *Poins.* Put on two leathern jerkins and aprons, and wait upon him at his table as drawers.

Prince. From a god to a bull? a heavy descension! it
was Jove's case. From a prince to a prentice? a low
transformation! that shall be mine. For in every thing
the purpose must weigh with the folly. Follow me, Ned.

[*they go*

[2 3.]   *Warkworth. Before the Castle*

Enter NORTHUMBERLAND, LADY NORTHUMBERLAND,
and LADY PERCY

Northumberland. I pray thee, loving wife, and
  gentle daughter,
Give even way unto my rough affairs.
Put not you on the visage of the times,
And be like them to Percy troublesome.
  Lady Northumberland. I have given over, I will speak
  no more.
Do what you will, your wisdom be your guide.
  Northumberland. Alas, sweet wife, my honour is
  at pawn,
And, but my going, nothing can redeem it.
  Lady Percy. O, yet, for God's sake, go not to
  these wars!
The time was, father, that you broke your word,   10
When you were more endeared to it than now,
When your own Percy, when my heart's dear Harry,
Threw many a northward look to see his father
Bring up his powers—but he did long in vain.
Who then persuaded you to stay at home?
There were two honours lost, yours and your son's.
For yours, the God of heaven brighten it!
For his, it stuck upon him, as the sun
In the grey vault of heaven, and by his light
Did all the chivalry of England move   20

To do brave acts. He was indeed the glass
Wherein the noble youth did dress themselves.
He had no legs that practised not his gait;
And speaking thick, which nature made his blemish,
Became the accents of the valiant,
For those that could speak low and tardily
Would turn their own perfection to abuse,
To seem like him: so that in speech, in gait,
In diet, in affections of delight,
30 In military rules, humours of blood,
He was the mark and glass, copy and book,
That fashioned others. And him, O wondrous him!
O miracle of men! him did you leave,
Second to none, unseconded by you,
To look upon the hideous god of war
In disadvantage, to abide a field
Where nothing but the sound of Hotspur's name
Did seem defensible: so you left him.
Never, O never, do his ghost the wrong
40 To hold your honour more precise and nice
With others than with him! let them alone:
The marshal and the archbishop are strong:
Had my sweet Harry had but half their numbers,
To-day might I, hanging on Hotspur's neck,
Have talked of Monmouth's grave.

   Northumberland.   Beshrew your heart,
Fair daughter, you do draw my spirits from me
With new lamenting ancient oversights.
But I must go and meet with danger there,
Or it will seek me in another place,
50 And find me worse provided.

   Lady Northumberland.   O, fly to Scotland,
Till that the nobles and the arméd commons
Have of their puissance made a little taste.

Lady Percy. If they get ground and vantage of the king,
Then join you with them, like a rib of steel,
To make strength stronger; but, for all our loves,
First let them try themselves. So did your son,
He was so suffered, so came I a widow,
And never shall have length of life enough
To rain upon remembrance with mine eyes,
That it may grow and sprout as high as heaven,   60
For recordation to my noble husband.
   Northumberland. Come, come, go in with me. 'Tis
      with my mind
As with the tide swelled up unto his height,
That makes a still-stand, running neither way.
Fain would I go to meet the archbishop,
But many thousand reasons hold me back.
I will resolve for Scotland! there am I,
Till time and vantage crave my company.   [*they go*

[2.4.] *London. A private room at the Boar's Head
Tavern in Eastcheap; a table and chairs; doors at back
and to left and right*

   FRANCIS *laying the table with wine and fruit: enter
      another Drawer with a dish of apples*

   Francis. What the devil hast thou brought there?
apple-johns? thou knowest Sir John cannot endure an
apple-john.
   2 *Drawer.* Mass, thou say'st true. The prince once
set a dish of apple-johns before him, and told him there
were five more Sir Johns, and putting off his hat, said,
'I will now take my leave of these six dry, round, old,
withered knights.' It angered him to the heart. But he
hath forgot that.

10 *Francis.* Why then, cover and set them down, and see if thou canst find out Sneak's noise. Mistress Tearsheet would fain hear some music.

2 Drawer. Dispatch. The room where they supped is too hot, they'll come in straight.

Francis. Sirrah, here will be the prince and Master Poins anon, and they will put on two of our jerkins and aprons, and Sir John must not know of it. Bardolph hath brought word.

FALSTAFF enters singing from the left, and goes out right

2 Drawer [*looking after him*]. By the mass, here will 20 be old utis. It will be an excellent stratagem.

Francis. I'll see if I can find out Sneak.   [*he goes*

The HOSTESS and DOLL TEARSHEET enter from the room on the left

Hostess. I'faith, sweetheart, methinks now you are in an excellent good temperality: your pulsidge beats as extraordinarily as heart would desire, and your colour, I warrant you, is as red as any rose, in good truth, la! But, i'faith, you have drunk too much canaries, and that's a marvellous searching wine, and it perfumes the blood ere one can say 'What's this?' How do you now?

Doll [*faintly*]. Better than I was: hem!   [*they sit*
30 *Hostess.* Why, that's well said—a good heart's worth gold...Lo, here comes Sir John.

FALSTAFF returns, singing

Falstaff. 'When Arthur first in court'—[*to the drawer, aside*] Empty the jordan—'and was a worthy king'...
[*2 Drawer goes out, right*] How now, Mistress Doll?

Hostess. Sick of a calm, yea, good faith.

Falstaff. So is all her sect. An they be once in a calm, they are sick.

Doll. A pox damn you, you muddy rascal, is that all the comfort you give me?

Falstaff. You make fat rascals, Mistress Doll.   40

Doll. I make them! gluttony and diseases make them, I make them not.

Falstaff. If the cook help to make the gluttony, you help to make the diseases, Doll. We catch of you, Doll, we catch of you. Grant that, my poor virtue, grant that.

Doll. Yea, joy, our chains and our jewels.

Falstaff. 'Your brooches, pearls, and ouches.' For to serve bravely is to come halting off, you know—to come off the breach with his pike bent bravely, and to surgery bravely, to venture upon the charged chambers bravely— 50

Doll. Hang yourself, you muddy conger, hang yourself!

Hostess. By my troth, this is the old fashion! you two never meet but you fall to some discord. You are both, i' good troth, as rheumatic as two dry toasts, you cannot one bear with another's confirmities. [*to Doll*] What the good-year! one must bear, and that must be you— you are the weaker vessel, as they say, the emptier vessel.

Doll. Can a weak empty vessel bear such a huge full hogshead? there's a whole merchant's venture of 60 Bourdeaux stuff in him, you have not seen a hulk better stuffed in the hold....Come, I'll be friends with thee, Jack. Thou art going to the wars, and whether I shall ever see thee again or no, there is nobody cares.

FRANCIS returns

Francis. Sir, Ancient Pistol's below, and would speak with you.

Doll. Hang him, swaggering rascal! let him not come hither. It is the foul-mouth'dst rogue in England.

Hostess. If he swagger, let him not come here. No, by
70 my faith, I must live among my neighbours. I'll no
swaggerers, I am in good name and fame with the very
best: shut the door, there comes no swaggerers here,
I have not lived all this while to have swaggering now—
shut the door, I pray you.

Falstaff. Dost thou hear, hostess?

Hostess. Pray ye, pacify yourself, Sir John. There
comes no swaggerers here.

Falstaff. Dost thou hear? it is mine ancient.

Hostess. Tilly-fally, Sir John, ne'er tell me: an your
80 ancient swagger, a' comes not in my doors. I was before
Master Tisick, the debuty, t'other day, and (as he said
to me)—'twas no longer ago than Wednesday last—
'I' good faith, neighbour Quickly,' says he—Master
Dumb, our minister, was by then—'Neighbour Quickly
(says he) receive those that are civil, for (said he) you
are in an ill name'; now a' said so, I can tell whereupon:
'for (says he) you are an honest woman, and well
thought on, therefore take heed what guests you receive:
receive (says he) no swaggering companions'...There
90 comes none here: you would bless you to hear what he
said: no, I'll no swaggerers.

Falstaff. He's no swaggerer, hostess—a tame cheater,
i'faith. You may stroke him as gently as a puppy
greyhound. He'll not swagger with a Barbary hen, if
her feathers turn back in any show of resistance. Call
him up, drawer.   [*Francis goes out*

Hostess. Cheater, call you him? I will bar no honest
man my house, nor no cheater, but I do not love
swaggering, by my troth. I am the worse, when one
100 says swagger: feel, masters, how I shake, look you,
I warrant you.

Doll. So you do, hostess.

Hostess. Do I? yea, in very truth, do I, an 'twere an aspen leaf. I cannot abide swaggerers.

PISTOL, BARDOLPH, and PAGE enter

Pistol. God save you, Sir John!

Falstaff. Welcome, Ancient Pistol. Here, Pistol, I charge you with a cup of sack [*he drinks*]. Do you discharge upon mine hostess.

                [*filling and reaching out to him*

Pistol. I will discharge upon her, Sir John, with two bullets.   110

Falstaff. She is pistol-proof, sir; you shall not hardly offend her.

Hostess. Come, I'll drink no proofs, nor no bullets. I'll drink no more than will do me good, for no man's pleasure, I.

Pistol. Then to you, Mistress Dorothy, I will charge you.   [*he raises the cup*

Doll. Charge me! I scorn you, scurvy companion. What! you poor, base, rascally, cheating, lack-linen mate! Away, you mouldy rogue, away! I am meat for 120 your master.

Pistol. I know you, Mistress Dorothy.

Doll. Away, you cut-purse rascal! you filthy bung, away! by this wine, I'll thrust my knife in your mouldy chaps, an you play the saucy cuttle with me. Away, you bottle-ale rascal! you basket-hilt stale juggler, you!.... Since when, I pray you, sir? God's light, with two points on your shoulder? much!

Pistol. God let me not live, but I will murder your ruff for this.   130

Falstaff. No more, Pistol. I would not have you go off here. Discharge yourself of our company, Pistol.

Hostess. No, good Captain Pistol, not here, sweet captain.

Doll. Captain! thou abominable damned cheater, art thou not ashamed to be called captain? An captains were of my mind, they would truncheon you out, for taking their names upon you before you have earned them... You a captain! you slave, for what? for tearing a poor
140 whore's ruff in a bawdy-house...He a captain! hang him, rogue! he lives upon mouldy stewed prunes and dried cakes...A captain! God's light, these villains will make the word as odious as the word 'occupy', which was an excellent good word before it was ill sorted: therefore captains had need look to't.

· *Bardolph.* Pray thee, go down, good ancient.

Falstaff. Hark thee hither, Mistress Doll.

[they go aside

Pistol. Not I. I tell thee what, Corporal Bardolph, I could tear her. I'll be revenged of her.
150 *Page.* Pray thee, go down.

Pistol. I'll see her damned first,—to Pluto's damnéd lake, by this hand, to th'infernal deep, with Erebus and tortures vile also: hold hook and line, say I: down! down, dogs! down faitors! have we not Hiren here?

[he draws his sword

Hostess [trembling]. Good Captain Peesel, be quiet—'tis very late, i'faith—I beseek you now, aggravate your choler.

Pistol. These be good humours, indeed!
Shall pack-horses
160 And hollow pampered jades of Asia,
Which cannot go but thirty mile a day,
Compare with Cæsars and with Cannibals
And Trojant Greeks? nay, rather damn them with
King Cerberus, and let the welkin roar.
Shall we fall foul for toys?

Hostess. By my troth, captain, these are very bitter words.

Bardolph. Be gone, good ancient: this will grow to a brawl anon.

Pistol [shouts]. Die men, like dogs! give crowns like 170 pins! Have we not Hiren here?

Hostess. O' my word, captain, there's none such here. What the good-year! do you think, I would deny her? For God's sake, be quiet.

Pistol. Then, feed, and be fat, my fair Calipolis. Come, give's some sack.
'Si fortune me tormente, sperato me contento.'
Fear we broadsides? no, let the fiend give fire.
Give me some sack—and, sweetheart, lie thou there.
                              [*laying down his sword*
Come we to full points here? and are etceteras nothings? 180

Falstaff. Pistol, I would be quiet.

Pistol. Sweet knight, I kiss thy neaf. What! we have seen the seven stars.

Doll. For God's sake, thrust him down stairs. I cannot endure such a fustian rascal.

Pistol. Thrust him down stairs! know we not Galloway nags?

Falstaff. Quoit him down, Bardolph, like a shove-groat shilling. Nay, an a' do nothing but speak nothing, a' 190 shall be nothing here.

Bardolph. Come, get you down stairs.

Pistol. What! shall we have incision? shall we imbrue?
                              [*he snatches up his sword*
Then death rock me asleep, abridge my doleful days!
Why then, let grievous, ghastly, gaping wounds
Untwind the Sisters Three! Come, Atropos, I say!
                              [*he offers to fight*

Hostess. Here's goodly stuff toward!

Falstaff. Give me my rapier, boy.

Doll. I pray thee, Jack, I pray thee, do not draw.

Falstaff [*draws*]. Get you down stairs.

[*Bardolph seizes Pistol and forces him back towards
        the door on the right; Falstaff follows behind*

200 *Hostess.* Here's a goodly tumult! I'll forswear keeping
house, afore I'll be in these tirrits and frights. [*Falstaff
thrusts at Pistol*] So! murder, I warrant now. Alas,
alas! put up your naked weapons, put up your naked
weapons.

[*Bardolph pushes Pistol through the door, and
        goes after. Falstaff sheathes his sword and
        returns, panting and blowing, to his seat*

Doll. I pray thee, Jack, be quiet, the rascal's gone.
Ah, you whoreson little valiant villain, you.

Hostess. Are you not hurt i'the groin? methought a'
made a shrewd thrust at your belly.

BARDOLPH *returns*

Falstaff. Have you turned him out-a-doors?

210 *Bardolph.* Yea, sir. The rascal's drunk, you have hurt
him, sir, i'th shoulder.

Falstaff. A rascal! to brave me!

Doll. Ah, you sweet little rogue, you! Alas, poor ape,
how thou sweat'st! come, let me wipe thy face, come on,
you whoreson chops: ah, rogue! i'faith, I love thee.
Thou art as valorous as Hector of Troy, worth five of
Agamemnon, and ten times better than the Nine
Worthies. Ah, villain!   [*she fondles him*

Falstaff. A rascally slave! I will toss the rogue
220 in a blanket.

Doll. Do, an thou darest for thy heart. An thou dost,
I'll canvass thee between a pair of sheets.

Musicians enter

Page. The music is come, sir.

Falstaff. Let them play. Play, sirs. [*soft music*] Sit on my knee, Doll. A rascal bragging slave! the rogue fled from me like quicksilver.

Doll [*aside*]. I'faith, and thou follow'dst him like a church. [*sits on his knee*] Thou whoreson little tidy Bartholomew boar-pig, when wilt thou leave fighting a days and foining a nights, and begin to patch up thine 230 old body for heaven?

Enter behind, the PRINCE *and* POINS, *disguised like Drawers*

Falstaff. Peace, good Doll! do not speak like a death's-head, do not bid me remember mine end.

Doll. Sirrah, what humour's the prince of?

Falstaff. A good shallow young fellow, a' would have made a good pantler, a' would ha' chipped bread well.

Doll. They say, Poins has a good wit.

Falstaff. He a good wit? hang him, baboon! his wit's as thick as Tewkesbury mustard, there's no more conceit 240 in him than is in a mallet.

Doll. Why does the prince love him so, then?

Falstaff. Because their legs are both of a bigness, and a' plays at quoits well, and eats conger and fennel, and drinks off candles' ends for flap-dragons, and rides the wild-mare with the boys, and jumps upon joined-stools, and swears with a good grace, and wears his boots very smooth like unto the Sign of the Leg, and breeds no bate with telling of discreet stories—and such other gambol faculties a' has that show a weak mind and an able 250 body, for the which the prince admits him: for the prince himself is such another, the weight of a hair will turn the scales between their avoirdupois.

> [*she strokes his head*

(*Prince.* Would not this nave of a wheel have his ears cut off?

(*Poins.* Let's beat him before his whore.

(*Prince.* Look, whether the withered elder hath not his poll clawed like a parrot.

(*Poins.* Is it not strange that desire should so many 260 years outlive performance?

Falstaff. Kiss me, Doll.

> [*they kiss; the while Bardolph throws an arm about the Hostess's waist*

(*Prince.* Saturn and Venus this year in conjunction! what says th' almanac to that?

(*Poins.* And look whether the fiery Trigon, his man, be not lisping to his master's old tables, his note-book, his counsel-keeper.

Falstaff. Thou dost give me flattering busses.

Doll. By my troth, I kiss thee with a most constant heart.

270 *Falstaff.* I am old, I am old.

Doll. I love thee better than I love e'er a scurvy young boy of them all.

Falstaff. What stuff wilt have a kirtle of? I shall receive money o' Thursday—shalt have a cap to-morrow. A merry song, come! a' grows late, we'll to bed. Thou't forget me when I am gone.

Doll. By my troth, thou't set me a-weeping, an thou say'st so. Prove that ever I dress myself handsome till thy return. Well, hearken a'th' end.

280 *Falstaff.* Some sack, Francis.

Prince.
Poins. } Anon, anon, sir.   [*they hurry forward*

Falstaff [*starts up*]. Ha! a bastard son of the king's?
And art not thou Poins his brother?

Prince. Why, thou globe of sinful continents, what a
life dost thou lead?

Falstaff. A better than thou—I am a gentleman, thou
art a drawer.

Prince. Very true, sir, and I come to draw you out by
the ears.

Hostess. O, the Lord preserve thy good grace! by my 290
troth, welcome to London. Now the Lord bless that
sweet face of thine! O Jesu, are you come from Wales?

Falstaff. Thou whoreson mad compound of majesty,
by this light flesh and corrupt blood, [*he points to Doll*]
thou art welcome.

Doll. How! you fat fool, I scorn you.

(*Poins.* My lord, he will drive you out of your revenge,
and turn all to a merriment, if you take not the heat.

Prince. You whoreson candle-mine, you, how vilely
did you speak of me even now, before this honest, 300
virtuous, civil gentlewoman!

Hostess. God's blessing of your good heart! and so she
is, by my troth.

Falstaff. Didst thou hear me?

Prince. Yea, and you knew me, as you did when you
ran away by Gad's Hill. You knew I was at your back,
and spoke it on purpose to try my patience.

Falstaff. No, no, no, not so, I did not think thou wast
within hearing.

Prince. I shall drive you then to confess the wilful 310
abuse, and then I know how to handle you.

Falstaff. No abuse, Hal, o' mine honour, no abuse.

Prince. Not! to dispraise me, and call me pantler and
bread-chipper and I know not what?

Falstaff. No abuse, Hal.

Poins. No abuse?

Falstaff. No abuse, Ned, i'th' world, honest Ned, none. I dispraised him before the wicked, that the wicked might not fall in love with thee: in which doing, 320 I have done the part of a careful friend and a true subject, and thy father is to give me thanks for it. No abuse, Hal —none, Ned, none—no, faith, boys, none.

Prince. See now, whether pure fear and entire cowardice doth not make thee wrong this virtuous gentlewoman, to close with us...Is she of the wicked? is thine hostess here of the wicked? or is thy boy of the wicked? or honest Bardolph, whose zeal burns in his nose, of the wicked?

Poins. Answer, thou dead elm, answer.

330 *Falstaff.* The fiend hath pricked down Bardolph irre-coverable, and his face is Lucifer's privy-kitchen, where he doth nothing but roast malt-worms. For the boy, there is a good angel about him, but the devil† blinds him too.

Prince. For the women?

Falstaff. For one of them, she's in hell already, and burns poor souls. For th' other, I owe her money, and whether she be damned for that I know not.

Hostess. No, I warrant you.

Falstaff. No, I think thou art not. I think thou art 340 quit for that. Marry, there is another indictment upon thee, for suffering flesh to be eaten in thy house, contrary to the law, for the which I think thou wilt howl.

Hostess. All victuallers do so. What's a joint of mutton or two in a whole Lent?

Prince. You, gentlewoman—

Doll. What says your grace?

Falstaff. His grace says that which his flesh rebels against.   [*a knocking heard without*

Hostess. Who knocks so loud at door? look to th' door 350 there, Francis,

PETO enters

Prince. Peto, how now? what news?

Peto. The king your father is at Westminster,
And there are twenty weak and wearied posts
Come from the north, and as I came along
I met and overtook a dozen captains,
Bare-headed, sweating, knocking at the taverns,
And asking every one for Sir John Falstaff.

Prince. By heaven, Poins, I feel me much to blame,
So idly to profane the precious time,
When tempest of commotion, like the south   360
Borne with black vapour, doth begin to melt,
And drop upon our bare unarméd heads.
Give me my sword and cloak...Falstaff, good night.

[*Prince Henry, Poins, Peto, and Bardolph hasten away*

Falstaff. Now comes in the sweetest morsel of the
night, and we must hence and leave it unpicked...
[*more knocking heard*] More knocking at the door.

BARDOLPH returns

How now? what's the matter?

Bardolph. You must away to court, sir, presently;
A dozen captains stay at door for you.

Falstaff [*to the Page*]. Pay the musicians, sirrah. 370
Farewell hostess, farewell Doll. You see, my good
wenches, how men of merit are sought after. The un-
deserver may sleep, when the man of action is called on.
Farewell, good wenches: if I be not sent away post, I
will see you again ere I go.

Doll. I cannot speak. If my heart be not ready to
burst...[*sobs*] Well, sweet Jack, have a care of thyself.

Falstaff. Farewell, farewell.

[*he goes out with Bardolph*

Hostess. Well, fare thee well. I have known thee these
380 twenty-nine years, come peascod-time, but an honester
and truer-hearted man...[*sobs*] Well, fare thee well.

Bardolph [*at the door*]. Mistress Tearsheet!

Hostess. What's the matter?

Bardolph. Bid Mistress Tearsheet come to my master.

Hostess. O run, Doll, run, run, good Doll.

Bardolph. Come!

Hostess. She comes blubbered.   [*dries Doll's face*

Bardolph [*enters*]. Yea, will you come, Doll?
    [*he leads her forth; the Hostess goes out left*

[3. 1.]   *The palace at Westminster; past midnight*

'*Enter the* KING *in his nightgown*', *with a Page*

King. Go, call the Earls of Surrey and of Warwick:
But, ere they come, bid them o'er-read these letters,
And well consider of them—make good speed.
                    [*the Page goes*
How many thousand of my poorest subjects
Are at this hour asleep! O sleep, O gentle sleep,
Nature's soft nurse, how have I frighted thee,
That thou no more wilt weigh my eyelids down,
And steep my senses in forgetfulness?
Why rather, sleep, liest thou in smoky cribs,
10 Upon uneasy pallets stretching thee,
And hushed with buzzing night-flies to thy slumber,
Than in the perfumed chambers of the great,
Under the canopies of costly state,
And lulled with sound of sweetest melody?
O thou dull god, why li'st thou with the vile
In loathsome beds, and leav'st the kingly couch
A watch-case or a common 'larum-bell?
Wilt thou upon the high and giddy mast

Seal up the ship-boy's eyes and rock his brains
In cradle of the rude imperious surge,   20
And in the visitation of the winds,
Who take the ruffian billows by the top,
Curling their monstrous heads, and hanging them
With deafing clamour in the slippery clouds,
That, with the hurly, death itself awakes?
Canst thou, O partial sleep! give thy repose
To the wet sea-boy in an hour so rude,
And in the calmest and most stillest night,
With all appliances and means to boot,
Deny it to a king? Then, happy low, lie down!   30
Uneasy lies the head that wears a crown.

    '*Enter* WARWICK, SURREY *and* SIR JOHN BLUNT'

Warwick. Many good morrows to your majesty!
King. Is it good morrow, lords?
Warwick. 'Tis one o'clock, and past.
King. Why then, good morrow to you all, my lords.
Have you read o'er the letters that I sent you?
Warwick. We have, my liege.
King. Then you perceive the body of our kingdom,
How foul it is—what rank diseases grow,
And with what danger, near the heart of it.   40
Warwick. It is but as a body yet distempered,
Which to his former strength may be restored
With good advice and little medicine.
My Lord Northumberland will soon be cooled.
King. O God! that one might read the book of fate,
And see the revolution of the times
Make mountains level, and the continent,
Weary of solid firmness, melt itself
Into the sea! and, other times, to see
The beachy girdle of the ocean   50

Too wide for Neptune's hips; how chances mock
And changes fill the cup of alteration
With divers liquors! O, if this were seen,
The happiest youth, viewing his progress through,
What perils passed, what crosses to ensue,
Would shut the book, and sit him down and die.
'Tis not ten years gone
Since Richard and Northumberland, great friends,
Did feast together, and in two years after
60 Were they at wars: it is but eight years since
This Percy was the man nearest my soul;
Who like a brother toiled in my affairs,
And laid his love and life under my foot;
Yea, for my sake, even to the eyes of Richard
Gave him defiance...But which of you was by—
You, cousin Nevil, as I may remember— [to Warwick
When Richard, with his eye brimful of tears,
Then checked and rated by Northumberland,
Did speak these words, now proved a prophecy?
70 'Northumberland, thou ladder by the which
My cousin Bolingbroke ascends my throne'
(Though then, God knows, I had no such intent,
But that necessity so bowed the state,
That I and greatness were compelled to kiss)
'The time shall come,' thus did he follow it,
'The time will come, that foul sin, gathering head,
Shall break into corruption': so went on,
Foretelling this same time's condition,
And the division of our amity.
80 *Warwick.* There is a history in all men's lives,
Figuring the natures or the times deceased:
The which observed, a man may prophesy,
With a near aim, of the main chance of things
As yet not come to life, who in their seeds
And weak beginnings lie intreasuréd:

Such things become the hatch and brood of time;
And by the necessary form of this
King Richard might create a perfect guess
That great Northumberland, then false to him,
Would of that seed grow to a greater falseness, 　　90
Which should not find a ground to root upon,
Unless on you.
　　King.　　　　Are these things then necessities?
Then let us meet them like necessities—
And that same word even now cries out on us:
They say the bishop and Northumberland
Are fifty thousand strong.
　　Warwick.　　　　　　It cannot be, my lord.
Rumour doth double, like the voice and echo,
The numbers of the feared. Please it your grace
To go to bed: upon my soul, my lord,
The powers that you already have sent forth 　　100
Shall bring this prize in very easily:
To comfort you the more, I have received
A certain instance that Glendower is dead...
Your majesty hath been this fortnight ill,
And these unseasoned hours perforce must add
Unto your sickness.
　　King.　　　　I will take your counsel.
And were these inward wars once out of hand,
We would, dear lords, unto the Holy Land.　　*[they go*

[3. 2.]　　*Before Justice Shallow's house in*
Gloucestershire

*Enter SHALLOW and SILENCE, meeting; MOULDY,
SHADOW, WART, FEEBLE, BULLCALF and servants,
behind*

　　Shallow. Come on, come on, come on, give me your
hand, sir, give me your hand, sir! an early stirrer, by

the rood...[*they shake hands*] And how doth my good
cousin Silence?

Silence. Good morrow, good cousin Shallow.

Shallow. And how doth my cousin, your bedfellow?
and your fairest daughter and mine, my god-daughter
Ellen?

Silence. Alas, a black ousel, cousin Shallow.

10 *Shallow.* By yea and no, sir, I dare say my cousin
William is become a good scholar. He is at Oxford still,
is he not?

Silence. Indeed, sir, to my cost.

Shallow. A' must then to the inns o' court shortly:
I was once of Clement's Inn, where I think they will
talk of mad Shallow yet.

Silence. You were called 'lusty Shallow' then, cousin.

Shallow. By the mass, I was called any thing; and I
would have done any thing indeed too, and roundly
20 too...There was I, and little John Doit of Staffordshire,
and black George Barnes, and Francis Pickbone, and
Will Squele a Cots'ole man—you had not four such
swinge-bucklers in all the inns o' court again: and I
may say to you, we knew where the bona-robas were,
and had the best of them all at commandment...Then
was Jack Falstaff (now Sir John) a boy, and page to
Thomas Mowbray, Duke of Norfolk.

Silence. This Sir John, cousin, that comes hither anon
about soldiers?

30 *Shallow.* The same Sir John, the very same. I see
him break Scoggin's head at the court-gate, when a'
was a crack, not thus high: and the very same day did
I fight with one Sampson Stockfish, a fruiterer, behind
Gray's Inn...Jesu, Jesu, the mad days that I have
spent! and to see how many of my old acquaintance are
dead!

Silence. We shall all follow, cousin.

Shallow. Certain, 'tis certain, very sure, very sure.
Death, as the Psalmist saith, is certain to all, all shall die.
How a good yoke of bullocks at Stamford fair?   40

Silence. By my troth, I was not there.

Shallow. Death is certain. Is old Double of your town
living yet?

Silence. Dead, sir.

Shallow. Jesu, Jesu, dead! a' drew a good bow—and
dead! a' shot a fine shoot: John a Gaunt loved him well,
and betted much money on his head. Dead! a' would
have clapped i'th' clout at twelve score, and carried you
a forehand shaft a fourteen and fourteen and a half, that
it would have done a man's heart good to see. How 50
a score of ewes now?

Silence. Thereafter as they be, a score of good ewes
may be worth ten pounds.

Shallow. And is old Double dead!

'*Enter BARDOLPH, and one with him*'

Silence. Here come two of Sir John Falstaff's men, as
I think.

Shallow. Good morrow, honest gentlemen.

Bardolph. I beseech you, which is Justice Shallow?

Shallow. I am Robert Shallow, sir, a poor esquire of
this county, and one of the king's justices of the peace: 60
what is your good pleasure with me?

Bardolph. My captain, sir, commends him to you, my
captain, Sir John Falstaff, a tall gentleman, by heaven,
and a most gallant leader.

Shallow. He greets me well, sir. I knew him a good
backsword man. How doth the good knight? may I ask
how my lady his wife doth?

Bardolph. Sir, pardon! a soldier is better accommodated than with a wife.

70 *Shallow.* It is well said in faith, sir, and it is well said
indeed too. Better accommodated! it is good, yea,
indeed, is it. Good phrases are surely, and ever were,
very commendable. Accommodated: it comes of
'accommodo,' very good, a good phrase.

Bardolph. Pardon sir, I have heard the word. Phrase
call you it? By this day, I know not the phrase, but I will
maintain the word with my sword to be a soldier-like
word, and a word of exceeding good command, by
heaven...Accommodated, that is, when a man is, as they
80 say, accommodated, or when a man is being whereby
a' may be thought to be accommodated —which is an
excellent thing.

Enter FALSTAFF

Shallow. It is very just...Look, here comes good Sir
John. [*hurries forward*] Give me your good hand, give
me your worship's good hand. By my troth, you like
well, and bear your years very well. Welcome, good
Sir John.   [*they shake hands*

Falstaff. I am glad to see you well, good Master
Robert Shallow. Master Surecard, as I think?

90 *Shallow.* No, Sir John, it is my cousin Silence, in
commission with me.

Falstaff. Good Master Silence, it well befits you
should be of the Peace.

Silence. Your good worship is welcome.

Falstaff [*wipes his brow*]. Fie! this is hot weather,
gentlemen. Have you provided me here half a dozen
sufficient men?

Shallow. Marry, have we, sir. Will you sit?

Falstaff [*sits*]. Let me see them, I beseech you.

Shallow [*agitated*]. Where's the roll? where's the roll? 100
where's the roll?—Let me see, let me see, let me see.
So, so, so, so, so, so, so. Yea, marry, sir—Rafe Mouldy!
Let them appear as I call, let them do so, let them do so.
Let me see, where is Mouldy?

Mouldy. Here, an't please you.

Shallow. What think you, Sir John? a good-limbed
fellow, young, strong, and of good friends.

Falstaff. Is thy name Mouldy?

Mouldy. Yea, an't please you.

Falstaff. 'Tis the more time thou wert used.   110

Shallow. Ha, ha, ha! most excellent, i'faith! things
that are mouldy lack use: very singular good! in faith,
well said, Sir John, very well said.

Falstaff. Prick him.

Mouldy. I was pricked well enough before, and you
could have let me alone. My old dame will be undone
now, for one to do her husbandry and her drudgery.
You need not to have pricked me, there are other men
fitter to go out than I.

Falstaff. Go to. Peace, Mouldy, you shall go. 120
Mouldy, it is time you were spent.

Mouldy. Spent!

Shallow. Peace, fellow, peace—stand aside. Know
you where you are? For th' other, Sir John: let me see—
Simon Shadow!

Falstaff. Yea, marry, let me have him to sit under.
He's like to be a cold soldier.

Shallow. Where's Shadow?

Shadow [*a gaunt man*]. Here, sir.

Falstaff. Shadow, whose son art thou?   130

Shadow. My mother's son, sir.

Falstaff. Thy mother's son! like enough, and thy
father's shadow—so the son of the female is the shadow

of the male: it is often so, indeed, but much of the father's substance!

Shallow. Do you like him, Sir John?

Falstaff. Shadow will serve for summer. Prick him, [*aside*] for we have a number of shadows to fill up the muster-book.

140 *Shallow.* Thomas Wart!

Falstaff. Where's he?

Wart [*a tattered man*]. Here, sir.

Falstaff. Is thy name Wart?

Wart. Yea, sir.

Falstaff. Thou art a very ragged wart.

Shallow. Shall I prick him, Sir John?

Falstaff. It were superfluous, for his apparel is built up on his back, and the whole frame stands upon pins: prick him no more.

150 *Shallow.* Ha, ha, ha! you can do it, sir, you can do it, I commend you well...Francis Feeble!

Feeble [*a timid little man*]. Here, sir.

Shallow. What trade art thou, Feeble?

Feeble. A woman's tailor, sir.

Shallow. Shall I prick him, sir?

Falstaff. You may—but if he had been a man's tailor, he'd ha' pricked you. Wilt thou make as many holes in an enemy's battle as thou hast done in a woman's petticoat?

160 *Feeble.* I will do my good will, sir, you can have no more.

Falstaff. Well said, good woman's tailor! well said, courageous Feeble! thou wilt be as valiant as the wrathful dove or most magnanimous mouse. Prick the woman's tailor: well, Master Shallow; deep, Master Shallow.

Feeble. I would Wart might have gone, sir.

Falstaff. I would thou wert a man's tailor, that thou

mightst mend him and make him fit to go. I cannot put him to a private soldier, that is the leader of so many thousands. Let that suffice, most forcible Feeble.   170

Feeble. It shall suffice, sir.

Falstaff. I am bound to thee, reverend Feeble. Who is next?

Shallow. Peter Bullcalf o' th' green!

Falstaff. Yea, marry, let's see Bullcalf.

Bullcalf [*a stout young man*]. Here, sir.

Falstaff. 'Fore God, a likely fellow! Come, prick me Bullcalf, till he roar again.

Bullcalf. O Lord! good my lord captain—

Falstaff. What, dost thou roar before thou art pricked? 180

Bullcalf. O Lord, sir! I am a diseased man.

Falstaff. What disease hast thou?

Bullcalf. A whoreson cold, sir, a cough, sir, which I caught with ringing in the king's affairs upon his coronation-day, sir.

Falstaff. Come, thou shalt go to the wars in a gown, we will have away thy cold, and I will take such order that thy friends shall ring for thee....Is here all?

Shallow. Here is two more called than your number, you must have but four here, sir. And so, I pray you, 190 go in with me to dinner.

Falstaff. Come, I will go drink with you, but I cannot tarry dinner. I am glad to see you, by my troth, Master Shallow.

Shallow. O, Sir John, do you remember since we lay all night in the windmill in Saint George's field?

Falstaff. No more of that, good Master Shallow, no more of that.

Shallow. Ha, 'twas a merry night. And is Jane Nightwork alive?   200

Falstaff. She lives, Master Shallow.

Shallow. She never could away with me.

Falstaff. Never, never, she would always say she could not abide Master Shallow.

Shallow. By the mass, I could anger her to th' heart. She was then a bona-roba. Doth she hold her own well?

Falstaff. Old, old, Master Shallow.

Shallow. Nay, she must be old, she cannot choose but be old, certain she's old, and had Robin Nightwork by
210 old Nightwork before I came to Clement's Inn.

Silence. That's fifty five year ago.

Shallow. Ha, cousin Silence, that thou hadst seen that that this knight and I have seen! Ha, Sir John, said I well?

Falstaff. We have heard the chimes at midnight, Master Shallow.

Shallow. That we have, that we have, that we have, in faith, Sir John, we have—our watch-word was 'Hem, boys!' Come, let's to dinner, come, let's to dinner.
220 Jesus, the days that we have seen! Come, come.

[he leads Falstaff in; Silence follows

Bullcalf. Good Master Corporate Bardolph, stand my friend, and here's four Harry ten shillings in French crowns for you. In very truth, sir, I had as lief be hanged, sir, as go. And yet for mine own part, sir, I do not care, but rather because I am unwilling, and for mine own part have a desire to stay with my friends; else, sir, I did not care for mine own part so much.

Bardolph. Go to, stand aside.

Mouldy. And, good master corporal captain, for my old
230 dame's sake, stand my friend. She has nobody to do any thing about her when I am gone, and she is old and cannot help herself. You shall have forty, sir.

[he shows him a shilling

Bardolph. Go to, stand aside.

Feeble. By my troth I care not, a man can die but once, we owe God a death, I'll ne'er bear a base mind. An't be my dest'ny, so—an't be not, so. No man's too good to serve's prince, and let it go which way it will, he that dies this year is quit for the next.

Bardolph. Well said! th'art a good fellow.

Feeble. Faith, I'll bear no base mind.　　240

FALSTAFF and the JUSTICES return

Falstaff. Come, sir, which men shall I have?

Shallow. Four of which you please.

(*Bardolph.* Sir, a word with you. I have three pound to free Mouldy and Bullcalf.

(*Falstaff.* Go to, well.

Shallow. Come, Sir John, which four will you have?

Falstaff. Do you choose for me.

Shallow. Marry then, Mouldy, Bullcalf, Feeble, and Shadow.

Falstaff. Mouldy and Bullcalf! for you, Mouldy, stay 250 at home till you are past service: and for your part, Bullcalf, grow till you come unto it: I will none of you.

Shallow. Sir John, Sir John, do not yourself wrong, they are your likeliest men, and I would have you served with the best.

Falstaff. Will you tell me, Master Shallow, how to choose a man? Care I for the limb, the thews, the stature, bulk, and big assemblance of a man? give me the spirit, Master Shallow...Here's Wart, you see what a ragged appearance it is, a' shall charge you and dis- 260 charge you with the motion of a pewterer's hammer, come off and on swifter than he that gibbets on the brewer's bucket. And this same half-faced fellow, Shadow—give me this man. He presents no mark to the enemy, the foeman may with as great aim level at the

edge of a penknife. And for a retreat, how swiftly will
this Feeble, the woman's tailor, run off! O, give me the
spare men, and spare me the great ones. Put me a
caliver into Wart's hand, Bardolph.   [*he does so*
270 *Bardolph.* Hold, Wart, traverse! thus, thus, thus.

Falstaff. Come, manage me your caliver. So, very
well, go to, very good, exceeding good. [*Wart handles
his weapon with ridiculous and awkward action*] O, give
me always a little, lean, old, chopt, bald shot....Well said,
i'faith, Wart, th'art a good scab. Hold, there's a tester
for thee.

Shallow [*takes the caliver*]. He is not his craft's master,
he doth not do it right. I remember at Mile-end Green,
when I lay at Clement's Inn—I was then Sir Dagonet in
280 Arthur's show—there was a little quiver fellow, and a'
would manage you his piece thus, and a' would about
and about, and come you in, and come you in: 'rah-
tah-tah,' would a' say; 'bounce,' would a' say; and
away again would a' go, and again would a' come:
I shall ne'er see such a fellow.

Falstaff. These fellows will do well, Master Shallow.
God keep you, Master Silence, I will not use many
words with you. Fare you well, gentlemen both. I
thank you. I must a dozen mile to-night...Bardolph,
290 give the soldiers coats.

Shallow. Sir John, the Lord bless you! God prosper
your affairs! God send us peace! At your return,
visit our house, let our old acquaintance be renewed.
Peradventure I will with ye to the court.

Falstaff. 'Fore God, would you would, Master
Shallow.

Shallow. Go to, I have spoke at a word. God keep
you.

Falstaff. Fare you well, gentle gentlemen. [*Shallow*

and Silence go in] On, Bardolph; lead the men away. 300
[*Bardolph marches them off*] As I return, I will fetch
off these justices. I do see the bottom of Justice Shallow.
Lord, Lord, how subject we old men are to this vice of
lying! This same starved justice hath done nothing but
prate to me of the wildness of his youth, and the feats he
hath done about Turnbull Street—and every third word
a lie, duer paid to the hearer than the Turk's tribute.
I do remember him at Clement's Inn, like a man
made after supper of a cheese-paring. When a' was
naked, he was for all the world like a forked radish, 310
with a head fantastically carved upon it with a knife.
A' was so forlorn, that his dimensions to any thick sight
were invisible. A' was the very genius of famine, yet
lecherous as a monkey, and the whores called him
mandrake. A' came ever in the rearward of the fashion,
and sung those tunes to the overscutched huswives that
he heard the carmen whistle, and sware they were his
fancies or his good-nights. And now is this Vice's dagger
become a squire, and talks as familiarly of John a
Gaunt as if he had been sworn brother to him, and I'll 320
be sworn a' ne'er saw him but once in the Tilt-yard,
and then he burst his head for crowding among the
marshal's men. I saw it, and told John a Gaunt he
beat his own name, for you might have trussed him and
all his apparel into an eel-skin—the case of a treble
hautboy was a mansion for him, a court. And now has
he land and beefs! Well, I'll be acquainted with him
if I return, and 't shall go hard but I'll make him a
philosopher's two stones to me. If the young dace be
a bait for the old pike, I see no reason in the law of 330
nature but I may snap at him...Let time shape, and there
an end.   [*he goes off*

[4. 1.]   *Gaultree Forest, Yorkshire*

The ARCHBISHOP *of* YORK (*clad in armour*), MOWBRAY,
    HASTINGS, LORD BARDOLPH *and others*

Archbishop. What is this forest called?
Hastings. 'Tis Gaultree Forest, an't shall please
    your grace.
Archbishop. Here stand, my lords, and send
    discoverers forth
To know the numbers of our enemies.
Hastings. We have sent forth already.
Archbishop.   'Tis well done.
My friends and brethren in these great affairs,
I must acquaint you that I have received
New-dated letters from Northumberland,
Their cold intent, tenour and substance, thus:
10 Here doth he wish his person, with such powers
As might hold sortance with his quality,
The which he could not levy; whereupon
He is retired, to ripe his growing fortunes,
To Scotland, and concludes in hearty prayers
That your attempts may overlive the hazard
And fearful meeting of their opposite.
Mowbray. Thus do the hopes we have in him
    touch ground
And dash themselves to pieces.

A Messenger comes up

Hastings.   Now, what news?
Messenger. West of this forest, scarcely off a mile,
20 In goodly form comes on the enemy,
And by the ground they hide I judge their number
Upon or near the rate of thirty thousand.
Mowbray. The just proportion that we gave them out
Let us sway on and face them in the field.

*WESTMORELAND, with attendant officers, is
seen approaching*

Archbishop. What well-appointed leader fronts us here?
Mowbray. I think it is my Lord of Westmoreland.
Westmoreland. Health and fair greeting from
    our general,
The prince, Lord John and Duke of Lancaster.
  Archbishop. Say on, my Lord of Westmoreland,
    in peace.
What doth concern your coming?
  Westmoreland.   Then, my lord,   30
Unto your grace do I in chief address
The substance of my speech...If that rebellion
Came like itself, in base and abject routs,
Led on by bloody youth, guarded with rags,
And countenanced by boys and beggary;
I say, if damned commotion so appeared
In his true, native and most proper shape,
You, reverend father, and these noble lords
Had not been here, to dress the ugly form
Of base and bloody insurrection   40
With your fair honours. You, lord Archbishop,
Whose see is by a civil peace maintained,
Whose beard the silver hand of peace hath touched,
Whose learning and good letters peace hath tutored,
Whose white investments figure innocence,
The dove and very blessed spirit of peace,
Wherefore do you so ill translate yourself
Out of the speech of peace that bears such grace,
Into the harsh and boist'rous tongue of war?
Turning your books to graves, your ink to blood,   50
Your pens to lances, and your tongue divine
To a loud trumpet and a point of war?

Archbishop. Wherefore do I this? so the
    question stands.
Briefly to this end: we are all diseased,
And with our surfeiting and wanton hours
Have brought ourselves into a burning fever,
And we must bleed for it: of which disease
Our late king, Richard, being infected, died.
But, my most noble Lord of Westmoreland,
60 I take not on me here as a physician,
Nor do I as an enemy to peace
Troop in the throngs of military men;
But rather show awhile like fearful war,
To diet rank minds, sick of happiness,
And purge the obstructions, which begin to stop
Our very veins of life...Hear me more plainly.
I have in equal balance justly weighed
What wrongs our arms may do, what wrongs we suffer,
And find our griefs heavier than our offences.
70 We see which way the stream of time doth run,
†And are enforced from our most quiet shore
By the rough torrent of occasion,
And have the summary of all our griefs,
When time shall serve, to show in articles;
Which long ere this we offered to the king,
And might by no suit gain our audience:
When we are wronged and would unfold our griefs,
We are denied access unto his person
Even by those men that most have done us wrong.
80 The dangers of the days but newly gone,
Whose memory is written on the earth
With yet appearing blood, and the examples
Of every minute's instance (present now)
Hath put us in these ill-beseeming arms—
Not to break peace or any branch of it,

But to establish here a peace indeed,
Concurring both in name and quality.

Westmoreland. When ever yet was your appeal denied?
Wherein have you been galléd by the king?
What peer hath been suborned to grate on you,   90
That you should seal this lawless bloody book
Of forged rebellion with a seal divine,
And consecrate commotion's bitter edge?

 Archbishop. My brother general, the commonwealth,
To brother born an household cruelty
I make my quarrel in particular.

Westmoreland. There is no need of any such redress,
Or if there were, it not belongs to you.

Mowbray. Why not to him in part, and to us all
That feel the bruises of the days before,   100
And suffer the condition of these times
To lay a heavy and unequal hand
Upon our honours?

Westmoreland.   O my good Lord Mowbray,
Construe the times to their necessities,
And you shall say, indeed, it is the time,
And not the king, that doth you injuries.
Yet for your part, it not appears to me,
Either from the king, or in the present time,
That you should have an inch of any ground
To build a grief on: were you not restored   110
To all the Duke of Norfolk's signories,
Your noble and right well remembered father's?

Mowbray. What thing, in honour, had my father lost,
That need to be revived and breathed in me?
The king that loved him, as the state stood then,
Was force perforce compelled to banish him:
And then that Henry Bolingbroke and he,
Being mounted and both rouséd in their seats,

Their neighing coursers daring of the spur,
120 Their arméd staves in charge, their beavers down,
Their eyes of fire sparkling through sights of steel,
And the loud trumpet blowing them together;
Then, then, when there was nothing could have stayed
My father from the breast of Bolingbroke...
O, when the king did throw his warder down,
(His own life hung upon the staff he threw!)
Then threw he down himself and all their lives
That by indictment and by dint of sword
Have since miscarried under Bolingbroke.

130 *Westmoreland*. You speak, Lord Mowbray, now you
        know not what.
The Earl of Hereford was reputed then
In England the most valiant gentleman.
Who knows on whom fortune would then have smiled?
But if your father had been victor there,
He ne'er had borne it out of Coventry:
For all the country in a general voice
Cried hate upon him; and all their prayers and love
Were set on Hereford, whom they doted on,
And blessed and graced indeed more than the king....

140 But this is mere digression from my purpose.
Here come I from our princely general
To know your griefs, to tell you from his grace
That he will give you audience, and wherein
It shall appear that your demands are just
You shall enjoy them, every thing set off
That might so much as think you enemies.

    Mowbray. But he hath forced us to compel this
        offer,
And it proceeds from policy, not love.

    Westmoreland. Mowbray, you overwéen to take
        it so:

This offer comes from mercy, not from fear: 150
For, lo! within a ken our army lies,
Upon mine honour, all too confident
To give admittance to a thought of fear:
Our battle is more full of names than yours,
Our men more perfect in the use of arms,
Our armour all as strong, our cause the best;
Then reason will our hearts should be as good:
Say you not then our offer is compelled.
   Mowbray. Well, by my will, we shall admit no
        parley.
   Westmoreland. That argues but the shame of   160
        your offence.
A rotten case abides no handling.
   Hastings. Hath the Prince John a full commission,
In very ample virtue of his father,
To hear and absolutely to determine
Of what conditions we shall stand upon?
   Westmoreland. That is intended in the general's name.
I muse you make so slight a question.
   Archbishop. Then take, my Lord of Westmoreland,
        this schedule,
For this contains our general grievances.
Each several article herein redressed,   170
All members of our cause, both here and hence,
That are insinewed to this action,
Acquitted by a true substantial form,
And present execution of our wills
To us and to our purposes confined,
We come within our awful banks again,
And knit our powers to the arm of peace.
   Westmoreland. This will I show the general. Please
        you, lords,
In sight of both our battles we may meet;

180 And either end in peace, which God so frame!
    Or to the place of diff'rence call the swords
    Which must decide it.
        Archbishop.   My lord, we will do so.
                        [*Westmoreland departs with his men*
        Mowbray. There is a thing within my bosom tells me
    That no conditions of our peace can stand.
        Hastings. Fear you not that: if we can make our peace
    Upon such large terms and so absolute
    As our conditions shall consist upon,
    Our peace shall stand as firm as rocky mountains.
        Mowbray. Yea, but our valuation shall be such,
190 That every slight and false-derivéd cause,
    Yea, every idle, nice and wanton reason,
    Shall to the king taste of this action;
    That were our royal faiths martyrs in love,
    We shall be winnowed with so rough a wind
    That even our corn shall seem as light as chaff,
    And good from bad find no partition.
        Archbishop. No, no, my lord. Note this—the king
            is weary
    †Of dainty and such picking grievances,
    For he hath found to end one doubt by death
200 Revives two greater in the heirs of life:
    And therefore will he wipe his tables clean,
    And keep no tell-tale to his memory
    That may repeat and history his loss
    To new remembrance; for full well he knows
    He cannot so precisely weed this land
    As his misdoubts present occasion:
    His foes are so enrooted with his friends,
    That plucking to unfix an enemy,
    He doth unfasten so and shake a friend.
210 So that this land, like an offensive wife
        That hath enraged him on to offer strokes,

As he is striking, holds his infant up,
And hangs resolved correction in the arm
That was upreared to execution.

Hastings. Besides, the king hath wasted all his rods
On late offenders, that he now doth lack
The very instruments of chastisement,
So that his power, like to a fangless lion,
May offer, but not hold.

Archbishop.   'Tis very true,
And therefore be assured, my good lord marshal,   220
If we do now make our atonement well,
Our peace will, like a broken limb united,
Grow stronger for the breaking.

Mowbray.   Be it so.
Here is returned my Lord of Westmoreland.

*WESTMORELAND comes back; Prince JOHN and
his army being seen in the distance*

Westmoreland. The prince is here at hand. Pleaseth
your lordship
To meet his grace just distance 'tween our armies?

Mowbray. Your grace of York, in God's name then
set forward.

Archbishop. Before! and greet his grace. My lord,
we come.

[4. 2.]   *They go forward*

Prince John [*meeting them*]. You are well en-
countered here, my cousin Mowbray.
Good day to you, gentle lord archbishop,
And so to you, Lord Hastings, and to all.
My Lord of York, it better showed with you
When that your flock, assembled by the bell,
Encircled you to hear with reverence
Your exposition on the holy text,

Than now to see you here an iron man talking,
Cheering a rout of rebels with your drum,
10 Turning the word to sword, and life to death.
That man that sits within a monarch's heart,
And ripens in the sunshine of his favour,
Would he abuse the countenance of the king,
Alack, what mischiefs might he set abroach
In shadow of such greatness! With you, lord bishop,
It is even so. Who hath not heard it spoken
How deep you were within the books of God?
To us the speaker in his parliament,
To us th'imagined voice of God himself,
20 The very opener and intelligencer
Between the grace, the sanctities of heaven
And our dull workings? O, who shall believe
But you misuse the reverence of your place,
Employ the countenance and grace of heaven,
As a false favourite doth his prince's name,
In deeds dishonourable? You have ta'en up,
Under the counterfeited zeal of God,
The subjects of His substitute, my father,
And both against the peace of heaven and him,
30 Have here up-swarmed them.

Archbishop.   Good my Lord of Lancaster,
I am not here against your father's peace,
But as I told my Lord of Westmoreland,
The time misordered doth, in common sense,
Crowd us and crush us to this monstrous form,
To hold our safety up...I sent your grace
The parcels and particulars of our grief,
The which hath been with scorn shoved from the court,
Whereon this Hydra son of war is born,
Whose dangerous eyes may well be charmed asleep
40 With grant of our most just and right desires;
And true obedience, of this madness cured,

Stoop tamely to the foot of majesty.

  Mowbray. If not, we ready are to try our fortunes
To the last man.

  Hastings.   And though we here fall down,
We have supplies to second our attempt:
If they miscarry, theirs shall second them,
And so success of mischief shall be born,
And heir from heir shall hold this quarrel up,
Whiles England shall have generation.

  Prince John. You are too shallow, Hastings, much   50
    too shallow,
To sound the bottom of the after-times.

  Westmoreland. Pleaseth your grace to answer
    them directly
How far forth you do like their articles?

  Prince John. I like them all, and do allow them
    well,
And swear here, by the honour of my blood,
My father's purposes have been mistook,
And some about him have too lavishly
Wrested his meaning and authority.
My lord, these griefs shall be with speed redressed—
Upon my soul, they shall. If this may please you,   60
Discharge your powers unto their several counties,
As we will ours, and here between the armies
Let's drink together friendly and embrace,
That all their eyes may bear those tokens home
Of our restoréd love and amity.

                [*as he speaks attendants bring up a table*
                    with flagons of wine and cups thereon

  Archbishop. I take your princely word for these
    redresses.

  Prince John. I give it you, and will maintain my word.
And thereupon I drink unto your grace.

                        [*they drink together*

Hastings. Go, captain, and deliver to the army
70 This news of peace. Let them have pay, and part.
I know it will well please them. Hie thee, captain!

                                [an officer obeys

Archbishop. To you, my noble Lord of Westmoreland.
Westmoreland. I pledge your grace, and if you knew
    what pains
I have bestowed to breed this present peace,
You would drink freely: but my love to ye
Shall show itself more openly hereafter.
Archbishop. I do not doubt you.
Westmoreland.   I am glad of it.

                                  [they drink

Health to my lord and gentle cousin, Mowbray.
Mowbray. You wish me health in very happy season,
80 For I am on the sudden something ill.
Archbishop. Against ill chances men are ever merry,
But heaviness foreruns the good event.
Westmoreland. Therefore be merry, coz, since
    sudden sorrow
Serves to say thus, 'some good thing comes to-morrow.'
Archbishop. Believe me, I am passing light in spirit.
Mowbray. So much the worse, if your own rule be true.

                                [shouts heard

Prince John. The word of peace is rendered. Hark,
    how they shout!
Mowbray. This had been cheerful after victory.
Archbishop. A peace is of the nature of a conquest,
90 For then both parties nobly are subdued,
And neither party loser.
Prince John.   Go, my lord,
And let our army be dischargéd too.

                          [Westmoreland goes

And, good my lord, so please you, let our trains

March by us, that we may peruse the men
We should have coped withal.

   Archbishop.   Go, good Lord Hastings,
And, ere they be dismissed, let them march by.

                       [Hastings goes

   Prince John. I trust, lords, we shall lie to-night
    together.

WESTMORELAND *returns*

Now, cousin, wherefore stands our army still?
   Westmoreland. The leaders, having charge from you
    to stand,
Will not go off until they hear you speak.   100
   Prince John. They know their duties.

HASTINGS *returns*

   Hastings. My lord, our army is dispersed already:
Like youthful steers unyoked, they take their courses
East, west, north, south, or like a school broke up,
Each hurries toward his home and sporting-place.
   Westmoreland. Good tidings, my Lord Hastings! for
    the which
I do arrest thee, traitor, of high treason,
And you, lord archbishop, and you, Lord Mowbray,
Of capital treason I attach you both.

              [they are placed under guard

   Mowbray. Is this proceeding just and honourable?   110
   Westmoreland. Is your assembly so?
   Archbishop. Will you thus break your faith?
   Prince John.   I pawned thee none.
I promised you redress of these same grievances
Whereof you did complain, which by mine honour
I will perform with a most Christian care.
But, for you, rebels, look to taste the due

Meet for rebellion and such acts as yours.
Most shallowly did you these arms commence,
Fondly brought here and foolishly sent hence.
120 Strike up our drums, pursue the scattered stray;
God, and not we, hath safely fought to-day.
Some guard these traitors to the block of death,
Treason's true bed and yielder up of breath.

[the drums strike up and they march away

[4. 3.] '*Alarum. Excursions.*' *Skirmishes between* PRINCE JOHN'*s soldiers and parties of rebels in flight.* FALSTAFF *comes up and encounters one* COLEVILE; *they make ready to fight*

Falstaff. What's your name, sir? of what condition are you, and of what place?

Colevile. I am a knight, sir, and my name is Colevile of the Dale.

Falstaff. Well then, Colevile is your name, a knight is your degree, and your place the dale: Colevile shall be still your name, a traitor your degree, and the dungeon your place—a dale deep enough, so shall you be still Colevile of the Dale.

10 *Colevile.* Are not you Sir John Falstaff?

Falstaff. As good a man as he, sir, whoe'er I am... Do ye yield, sir? or shall I sweat for you? If I do sweat, they are the drops of thy lovers, and they weep for thy death. Therefore rouse up fear and trembling, and do observance to my mercy.

Colevile. [*kneels*] I think you are Sir John Falstaff, and in that thought yield me.

Falstaff. I have a whole school of tongues in this belly of mine, and not a tongue of them all speaks any other
20 word but my name. An I had but a belly of any indifferency, I were simply the most active fellow in

Europe: my womb, my womb, my womb undoes me.
Here comes our general.

Prince JOHN of LANCASTER, WESTMORELAND,
BLUNT and others return

Prince John. The heat is past, follow no further now,
Call in the powers, good cousin Westmoreland.
                              [*Westmoreland hurries away*
Now, Falstaff, where have you been all this while?
When every thing is ended, then you come:
These tardy tricks of yours will, on my life,
One time or other break some gallows' back.

Falstaff. I would be sorry, my lord, but it should be 30
thus: I never knew yet but rebuke and check was the
reward of valour: do you think me a swallow, an arrow,
or a bullet? have I, in my poor and old motion, the
expedition of thought? I have speeded hither with the
very extremest inch of possibility. I have foundered
nine score and odd posts, and here, travel-tainted as I
am, have, in my pure and immaculate valour, taken
Sir John Colevile of the Dale, a most furious knight and
valorous enemy...But what of that? he saw me and
yielded, that I may justly say, with the hook-nosed fellow 40
†of Rome, 'I came, saw and overcame.'

Prince John. It was more of his courtesy than your
deserving.

Falstaff. I know not. Here he is, and here I yield him.
And I beseech your grace, let it be booked with the rest
of this day's deeds, or by the Lord, I will have it in a
particular ballad else, with mine own picture on the top
on't, Colevile kissing my foot: to the which course if
I be enforced, if you do not all show like gilt two-pences
to me, and I in the clear sky of fame o'ershine you as 50
much as the full moon doth the cinders of the element,

which show like pins' heads to her, believe not the word
of the noble: therefore let me have right, and let desert
mount.

Prince John. Thine's too heavy to mount.

Falstaff. Let it shine then.

Prince John. Thine's too thick to shine.

Falstaff. Let it do something, my good lord, that may
do me good, and call it what you will.

60 *Prince John.* Is thy name Colevile?

Colevile. It is, my lord.

Prince John. A famous rebel art thou, Colevile.

Falstaff. And a famous true subject took him.

Colevile. I am, my lord, but as my betters are
That led me hither. Had they been ruled by me,
You should have won them dearer than you have.

Falstaff. I know not how they sold themselves, but
thou like a kind fellow gavest thyself away gratis, and I
thank thee for thee.

*Trumpets afar off sound retreat; WESTMORELAND
returns*

Prince John. Now, have you left pursuit?

70 *Westmoreland.* Retreat is made and execution stayed.

Prince John. Send Colevile with his confederates
To York, to present execution.
Blunt, lead him hence, and see you guard him sure.

[*they lead Colevile away*
And now dispatch we toward the court, my lords,
I hear the king my father is sore sick.
Our news shall go before us to his majesty,
Which, cousin, you shall bear to comfort him,
And we with sober speed will follow you.

Falstaff. My lord, I beseech you, give me leave to go
80 through Gloucestershire: and, when you come to court,
stand my good lord, pray, in your good report.

Prince John. Fare you well, Falstaff. I, in my
    condition,
Shall better speak of you than you deserve.   [*he goes*
    Falstaff. I would you had but the wit, 'twere better
than your dukedom. Good faith, this same young
sober-blooded boy doth not love me, nor a man cannot
make him laugh—but that's no marvel, he drinks no
wine. There's never none of these demure boys come
to any proof, for thin drink doth so over-cool their blood,
and making many fish-meals, that they fall into a kind of 90
male green-sickness, and then when they marry they get
wenches. They are generally fools and cowards, which
some of us should be too, but for inflammation...A good
sherris-sack hath a two-fold operation in it. It ascends
me into the brain, dries me there all the foolish and dull
and crudy vapours which environ it, makes it apprehensive, quick, forgetive, full of nimble, fiery, and
delectable shapes, which delivered o'er to the voice, the
tongue, which is the birth, becomes excellent wit. The
second property of your excellent sherris is the warming 100
of the blood, which before (cold and settled) left the liver
white and pale, which is the badge of pusillanimity and
cowardice; but the sherris warms it and makes it course
from the inwards to the parts extremes. It illumineth the
face, which as a beacon gives warning to all the rest of
this little kingdom, man, to arm. And then the vital
commoners, and inland petty spirits, muster me all to
their captain, the heart; who, great and puffed up with
this retinue, doth any deed of courage; and this valour
comes of sherris. So that skill in the weapon is nothing 110
without sack (for that sets it a-work), and learning a mere
hoard of gold kept by a devil, till sack commences it
and sets it in act and use....Hereof comes it that Prince
Harry is valiant, for the cold blood he did naturally

inherit of his father he hath, like lean, sterile and bare land, manured, husbanded and tilled with excellent endeavour of drinking good and good store of fertile sherris, that he is become very hot and valiant....If I had a thousand sons, the first humane principle I would teach
120 them should be, to forswear thin potations, and to addict themselves to sack.

*BARDOLPH comes up behind and touches
him on the shoulder*

How now, Bardolph?

Bardolph [*chuckles*]. The army is dischargéd all and gone.

Falstaff. Let them go. I'll through Gloucestershire, and there will I visit Master Robert Shallow, esquire. I have him already tempering between my finger and my thumb, and shortly will I seal with him. Come away.   [*they go*

[4. 4.]   *Westminster. The Jerusalem chamber*

*The KING in a chair of state; PRINCE THOMAS of
CLARENCE, PRINCE HUMPHREY of GLOUCESTER, the
EARLS of WARWICK, KENT and others, standing about
him*

King. Now, lords, if God doth give successful end
To this debate that bleedeth at our doors,
We will our youth lead on to higher fields,
And draw no swords but what are sanctified:
Our navy is addressed, our power collected,
Our substitutes in absence well invested,
And every thing lies level to our wish—
Only we want a little personal strength;

And pause us till these rebels now afoot
Come underneath the yoke of government.   10
   Warwick. Both which we doubt not but your majesty
Shall soon enjoy.
   King.   Humphrey, my son of Gloucester,
Where is the prince your brother?
   Gloucester. I think he's gone to hunt, my lord,
      at Windsor.
   King. And how accompanied?
   Gloucester.   I do not know, my lord.
   King. Is not his brother, Thomas of Clarence,
      with him?
   Gloucester. No, my good lord, he is in presence here.
   Clarence [*comes forward*]. What would my lord
      and father?
   King. Nothing but well to thee, Thomas of Clarence.
How chance thou art not with the prince thy brother? 20
He loves thee, and thou dost neglect him, Thomas.
Thou hast a better place in his affection
Than all thy brothers: cherish it, my boy,
And noble offices thou mayst effect
Of mediation after I am dead,
Between his greatness and thy other brethren:
Therefore, omit him not, blunt not his love,
Nor lose the good advantage of his grace
By seeming cold or careless of his will.
For he is gracious, if he be observed: 30
He hath a tear for pity, and a hand
Open as day for melting charity:
Yet notwithstanding, being incensed, he's flint,
As humorous as winter, and as sudden
As flaws congealéd in the spring of day:
His temper, therefore, must be well observed.
Chide him for faults, and do it reverently,

When you perceive his blood inclined to mirth:
But, being moody, give him line and scope,
40 Till that his passions, like a whale on ground,
Confound themselves with working. Learn this, Thomas,
And thou shalt prove a shelter to thy friends,
A hoop of gold to bind thy brothers in,
That the united vessel of their blood,
Mingled with venom of suggestion,
(As, force perforce, the age will pour it in)
Shall never leak, though it do work as strong
As aconitum or rash gunpowder.
   Clarence. I shall observe him with all care and love.
50   *King.* Why art thou not at Windsor with him, Thomas?
   Clarence. He is not there to-day, he dines in London.
   King. And how accompanied? canst thou tell that?
   Clarence. With Poins, and other his continual followers.
   King. Most subject is the fattest soil to weeds,
And he, the noble image of my youth,
Is overspread with them! therefore my grief
Stretches itself beyond the hour of death:
The blood weeps from my heart when I do shape,
In forms imaginary, th'unguided days
60 And rotten times that you shall look upon,
When I am sleeping with my ancestors:
For when his headstrong riot hath no curb,
When rage and hot blood are his counsellors,
When means and lavish manners meet together,
O, with what wings shall his affections fly
Towards fronting peril and opposed decay!
   Warwick. My gracious lord, you look beyond
     him quite:
The prince but studies his companions
Like a strange tongue, wherein, to gain the language,
70 'Tis needful that the most immodest word

Be looked upon and learned—which once attained,
Your highness knows, comes to no further use
But to be known and hated...So, like gross terms,
The prince will in the perfectness of time
Cast off his followers, and their memory
Shall as a pattern or a measure live,
By which his grace must mete the lives of other,
Turning past evils to advantages.

    King. 'Tis seldom when the bee doth leave her comb
In the dead carrion...   80

WESTMORELAND enters

             Who's here? Westmoreland?
Westmoreland. Health to my sovereign, and
    new happiness
Added to that that I am to deliver!
Prince John your son doth kiss your grace's hand:
Mowbray, the Bishop Scroop, Hastings and all
Are brought to the correction of your law;
There is not now a rebel's sword unsheathed,
But Peace puts forth her olive every where.
The manner how this action hath been borne
Here at more leisure may your highness read,
With every course in his particular.   90

    King. O Westmoreland, thou art a summer bird,
Which ever in the haunch of winter sings
The lifting up of day. Look! here's more news.

HARCOURT enters

    Harcourt. From enemies heaven keep your majesty,
And when they stand against you, may they fall
As those that I am come to tell you of!
The Earl Northumberland and the Lord Bardolph,
With a great power of English and of Scots,

Are by the shrieve of Yorkshire overthrown.
100 The manner and true order of the fight,
This packet, please it you, contains at large.

   King. And wherefore should these good news make
     me sick?
Will Fortune never come with both hands full,
†But mete her fair words still in foulest terms?
She either gives a stomach and no food—
Such are the poor, in health; or else a feast
And takes away the stomach—such are the rich,
That have abundance and enjoy it not...
I should rejoice now at this happy news,
110 And now my sight fails, and my brain is giddy.
O me! come near me, now I am much ill.

   He swoons, falling to the floor; the princes run to him

   Gloucester. Comfort, your majesty!
   Clarence.   O my royal father!
   Westmoreland. My sovereign lord, cheer up yourself,
     look up!
   Warwick. Be patient, princes. You do know these fits
Are with his highness very ordinary.
Stand from him, give him air, he'll straight be well.
   Clarence. No, no, he cannot long hold out these pangs.
Th'incessant care and labour of his mind
Hath wrought the mure, that should confine it in,
120 So thin that life looks through and will break out.
   Gloucester. The people fear me, for they do observe
Unfathered heirs and loathly births of nature.
The seasons change their manners, as the year
Had found some months asleep and leaped them over.
   Clarence. The river hath thrice flowed, no ebb
     between,
And the old folk (time's doting chronicles)

Say it did so a little time before
That our great-grandsire, Edward, sicked and died.
Warwick. Speak lower, princes, for the king recovers.
Gloucester. This apoplexy will certain be his end.   130
King. I pray you, take me up, and bear me hence
Into some other chamber: softly, pray.

> [*Warwick and Westmoreland carry him out,*
> *the princes following*

[4. 5.]   *Another chamber*

The KING *on a bed;* CLARENCE, GLOUCESTER,
WARWICK *and others in attendance*

King. Let there be no noise made, my gentle friends,
Unless some dull and favourable hand
Will whisper music to my weary spirit.
Warwick. Call for the music in the other room.
King. Set me the crown upon my pillow here.
Clarence. His eye is hollow, and he changes much.

Prince HENRY *enters in haste*

Warwick. Less noise, less noise! [*he places the crown*
Prince.   Who saw the Duke of Clarence?
Clarence. I am here, brother, full of heaviness.
Prince. How now! rain within doors, and none abroad!
How doth the king?   10
Gloucester. Exceeding ill.
Prince.   Heard he the good news yet?
Tell it him.
Gloucester. He altered much upon the hearing it.
Prince. If he be sick with joy, he'll recover without
physic.
Warwick. Not so much noise, my lords. [*sees Prince
Henry*] Sweet prince, speak low;
The king your father is disposed to sleep.

Clarence. Let us withdraw into the other room.

Warwick. Will't please your grace to go along with
us?

20 *Prince.* No, I will sit and watch here by the king.

                         [they go out by the left door

Why doth the crown lie there upon his pillow,

Being so troublesome a bedfellow?

O polished perturbation! golden care!

That keep'st the ports of slumber open wide

To many a watchful night! sleep with it now?

Yet not so sound and half so deeply sweet

As he whose brow with homely biggen bound

Snores out the watch of night. O majesty!

When thou dost pinch thy bearer, thou dost sit

30 Like a rich armour worn in heat of day,

That scald'st with safety...[*he draws near*] By his gates
of breath

There lies a downy feather which stirs not:

Did he suspire, that light and weightless down

Perforce must move. [*he cries out*] My gracious lord!
my father!

This sleep is sound indeed, this is a sleep

That from this golden rigol hath divorced

So many English kings. Thy due from me

Is tears and heavy sorrows of the blood,

Which nature, love, and filial tenderness,

40 Shall (O dear father!) pay thee plenteously:

My due from thee is this imperial crown,

Which, as immediate from thy place and blood,

Derives itself to me...[*he sets it on his head*] Lo, where
it sits,

Which God shall guard! and put the world's
whole strength

Into one giant arm, it shall not force

This lineal honour from me: this from thee
Will I to mine leave, as 'tis left to me.
   [*he kneels a moment in prayer, and then stricken with*
   grief slowly departs by the door on the right. A pause
King. [*stirs*] Warwick! Gloucester! Clarence!

   WARWICK and the young princes return in haste

Clarence.   Doth the king call?
Warwick. What would your majesty? How fares
   your grace?
King. Why did you leave me here alone, my lords? 50
Clarence. We left the prince my brother here, my liege,
Who undertook to sit and watch by you.
   King. The Prince of Wales! Where is he? let me
   see him:
He is not here.
   Warwick [*points to the door on the right*]. This door is
   open, he is gone this way.
   Gloucester. He came not through the chamber where
   we stayed.
   King. Where is the crown? who took it from
   my pillow?
   Warwick. When we withdrew, my liege, we left
   it here.
   King. The prince hath ta'en it hence: go, seek him out:
Is he so hasty that he doth suppose   60
My sleep my death?
Find him, my Lord of Warwick. Chide him hither.
                      [*Warwick departs*
This part of his conjoins with my disease,
And helps to end me...See, sons, what things you are!
How quickly nature falls into revolt
When gold becomes her object!
For this the foolish over-careful fathers

Have broke their sleep with thoughts,
Their brains with care, their bones with industry;
70 For this they have engrosséd and piled up
The cank'red heaps of strange-achievéd gold;
For this they have been thoughtful to invest
Their sons with arts and martial exercises.
When, like the bee, culling from every flower
The virtuous sweets,
Our thighs with wax, our mouths with honey, packed,
We bring it to the hive; and, like the bees,
Are murdered for our pains. This bitter taste
Yields his engrossments to the ending father.

WARWICK returns

80 Now, where is he that will not stay so long
Till his friend sickness have determined me?
Warwick. My lord, I found the prince in the
next room,
Washing with kindly tears his gentle cheeks,
With such a deep demeanour in great sorrow,
That tyranny, which never quaffed but blood,
Would, by beholding him, have washed his knife
With gentle eye-drops. He is coming hither.
King. But wherefore did he take away the crown?

The Prince enters with the crown

Lo, where he comes. Come hither to me, Harry.
90 Depart the chamber, leave us here alone.
[*exeunt Warwick and the rest*
Prince. I never thought to hear you speak again.
King. Thy wish was father, Harry, to that thought.
I stay too long by thee, I weary thee.
Dost thou so hunger for mine empty chair
That thou wilt needs invest thee with my honours

Before thy hour be ripe? O foolish youth!
Thou seek'st the greatness that will overwhelm thee.
Stay but a little, for my cloud of dignity
Is held from falling with so weak a wind
That it will quickly drop: my day is dim.   100
Thou hast stol'n that which after some few hours
Were thine without offence—and at my death
Thou hast sealed up my expectation!
Thy life did manifest thou lov'dst me not,
And thou wilt have me die assured of it.
Thou hid'st a thousand daggers in thy thoughts,
Whom thou hast whetted on thy stony heart,
To stab at half an hour of my life.
What! canst thou not forbear me half an hour?
Then get thee gone and dig my grave thyself,   110
And bid the merry bells ring to thine ear
That thou art crownéd, not that I am dead:
Let all the tears that should bedew my hearse
Be drops of balm to sanctify thy head.
Only compound me with forgotten dust,
Give that which gave thee life unto the worms,
Pluck down my officers, break my decrees,
For now a time is come to mock at form:
Harry the Fifth is crowned! up, vanity!
Down, royal state! all you sage counsellors, hence!   120
And to the English court assemble now
From every region apes of idleness!
Now, neighbour confines, purge you of your scum:
Have you a ruffian that will swear, drink, dance,
Revel the night, rob, murder and commit
The oldest sins the newest kind of ways?
Be happy, he will trouble you no more:
England shall double gild his treble guilt,
England shall give him office, honour, might:

130 For the fifth Harry from curbed licence plucks
   The muzzle of restraint, and the wild dog
   Shall flesh his tooth on every innocent.
   O my poor kingdom! sick with civil blows
   When that my care could not withhold thy riots,
   What wilt thou do when riot is thy care?
   O, thou wilt be a wilderness again,
   Peopled with wolves, thy old inhabitants!
      Prince [*kneeling*]. O, pardon me, my liege! but for
         my tears,
   The moist impediments unto my speech,
140 I had forestalled this dear and deep rebuke,
   Ere you with grief had spoke and I had heard
   The course of it so far...There is your crown;
                    [*he sets it on the pillow once more*
   And He that wears the crown immortally
   Long guard it yours! If I affect it more
   Than as your honour and as your renown,
   Let me no more from this obedience rise,
   Which my most inward true and duteous spirit
   Teacheth this prostrate and exterior bending!
   God witness with me, when I here came in,
150 And found no course of breath within your majesty,
   How cold it struck my heart! if I do feign,
   O, let me in my present wildness die,
   And never live to show th'incredulous world
   The noble change that I have purposéd.
   Coming to look on you, thinking you dead—
   And dead almost, my liege, to think you were—
   I spake unto this crown as having sense,
   And thus upbraided it: 'The care on thee depending
   Hath fed upon the body of my father,
160 Therefore, thou best of gold art worst of gold.
   Other, less fine in carat, is more precious,

Preserving life in med'cine potable:
But thou, most fine, most honoured, most renowned,
Hast eat thy bearer up'...Thus, my most royal liege,
Accusing it, I put it on my head,
To try with it, as with an enemy
That had before my face murdered my father,
The quarrel of a true inheritor.
But if it did infect my blood with joy,
Or swell my thoughts to any strain of pride,   170
If any rebel or vain spirit of mine
Did with the least affection of a welcome
Give entertainment to the might of it,
Let God for ever keep it from my head,
And make me as the poorest vassal is,
That doth with awe and terror kneel to it!
 King. O my son!
God put it in thy mind to take it hence,
That thou mightst win the more thy father's love,
Pleading so wisely in excuse of it...   180
Come hither, Harry, sit thou by my bed,
And hear, I think, the very latest counsel
That ever I shall breathe. God knows, my son,
By what by-paths and indirect crookt ways
I met this crown, and I myself know well
How troublesome it sate upon my head:
To thee it shall descend with better quiet,
Better opinion, better confirmation;
For all the soil of the achievement goes
With me into the earth. It seemed in me   190
But as an honour snatched with boist'rous hand,
And I had many living to upbraid
My gain of it by their assistances,
Which daily grew to quarrel and to bloodshed,
Wounding supposéd peace: all these bold fears

Thou see'st with peril I have answeréd:
For all my reign hath been but as a scene
Acting that argument; and now my death
Changes the mood: for what in me was purchased,
200 Falls upon thee in a more fairer sort;
So thou the garland wear'st successively.
Yet, though thou stand'st more sure than I could do,
Thou art not firm enough, since griefs are green,
And all my friends, which thou must make thy
    friends,
Have but their stings and teeth newly ta'en out;
By whose fell working I was first advanced,
And by whose power I well might lodge a fear
To be again displaced: which to avoid,
I cut them off—and had a purpose now
210 To lead out many to the Holy Land,
Lest rest and lying still might make them look
Too near unto my state…Therefore, my Harry,
Be it thy course to busy giddy minds
With foreign quarrels; that action hence borne out
May waste the memory of the former days….
More would I, but my lungs are wasted so
That strength of speech is utterly denied me.
How I came by the crown, O God, forgive!
And grant it may with thee in true peace live!
220 *Prince.* My gracious liege,
You won it, wore it, kept it, gave it me,
Then plain and right must my possession be,
Which I with more than with a common pain
'Gainst all the world will rightfully maintain.

Enter PRINCE JOHN *of Lancaster,* WARWICK,
and others

King. Look, look, here comes my John of Lancaster.

Prince John. Health, peace, and happiness to my
    royal father!

King. Thou bring'st me happiness and peace, son John,
But health, alack, with youthful wings is flown
From this bare withered trunk: upon thy sight
My worldly business makes a period....   230
Where is my Lord of Warwick?

Prince.   My Lord of Warwick!

            [*Warwick comes forward*

King. Doth any name particular belong
Unto the lodging where I first did swoon?

Warwick. 'Tis called Jerusalem, my noble lord.

King. Laud be to God! even there my life must end.
It hath been prophesied to me many years,
I should not die but in Jerusalem;
Which vainly I supposed the Holy Land:
But bear me to that chamber, there I'll lie,
In that Jerusalem shall Harry die.   240

            [*they carry him forth*

[5.1.] *Gloucestershire. The hall of Shallow's house; in
the centre a large door leading out; doors to inner rooms
right and left*

SHALLOW *enters, bringing in* FALSTAFF;
    BARDOLPH *and page follow*

Shallow. By cock and pie, sir, you shall not away
to-night. What, Davy, I say!

Falstaff. You must excuse me, Master Robert Shallow.

Shallow. I will not excuse you, you shall not be
excused, excuses shall not be admitted, there is no excuse
shall serve, you shall not be excused .... Why, Davy!

*DAVY comes from within; FALSTAFF sits and
talks with Bardolph*

Davy. Here, sir.

Shallow. Davy, Davy, Davy, Davy, let me see, Davy,
let me see, Davy, let me see—yea, marry, William cook,
10 bid him come hither. Sir John, you shall not be excused.

Davy. Marry, sir, thus: those precepts cannot be
served. And, again, sir, shall we sow the hade land with
wheat?

Shallow. With red wheat, Davy. But for William
cook, are there no young pigeons?

Davy. Yes, sir. Here is now the smith's note for
shoeing and plough-irons.

Shallow. Let it be cast and paid...Sir John, you shall
not be excused.

20 *Davy.* Now, sir, a new link to the bucket must needs
be had: and, sir, do you mean to stop any of William's
wages, about the sack he lost the other day at Hinckley
fair?

Shallow. A' shall answer it...Some pigeons, Davy,
a couple of short-legged hens, a joint of mutton, and any
pretty little tine kickshaws, tell William cook.

(*Davy.* Doth the man of war stay all night, sir?

(*Shallow.* Yes, Davy. I will use him well. A friend
i' th' court is better than a penny in purse. Use his men
30 well, Davy, for they are arrant knaves, and will backbite.

(*Davy.* No worse than they are backbitten, sir, for
they have marvellous foul linen.

Shallow. Well conceited, Davy. About thy business,
Davy.

Davy. I beseech you, sir, to countenance William
Visor of Woncot against Clement Perkes o'th' hill.

Shallow. There is many complaints, Davy, against

that Visor. That Visor is an arrant knave, on my
knowledge.

Davy. I grant your worship, that he is a knave, sir: 40
but yet, God forbid, sir, but a knave should have some
countenance at his friend's request. An honest man, sir,
is able to speak for himself, when a knave is not. I have
served your worship truly, sir, this eight years, and if I
cannot once or twice in a quarter bear out a knave
against an honest man, I have but a very little credit
with your worship. The knave is mine honest friend,
sir—therefore, I beseech your worship, let him be
countenanced.

Shallow. Go to, I say he shall have no wrong. Look 50
about, Davy...[*Davy goes*]. Where are you, Sir John?
Come, come, come, off with your boots. Give me your
hand, Master Bardolph.

Bardolph. I am glad to see your worship.

Shallow. I thank thee with all my heart, kind Master
Bardolph—and [*to the Page*] welcome, my tall fellow.
Come, Sir John.   [*he goes in*

Falstaff [*rising slowly*]. I'll follow you, good Master
Robert Shallow. Bardolph, look to our horses. [*Bardolph
goes out, with the Page*] If I were sawed into quantities, 60
I should make four dozen of such bearded hermits'
staves as Master Shallow...It is a wonderful thing to see
the semblable coherence of his men's spirits and his.
They, by observing of him, do bear themselves like
foolish justices; he, by conversing with them, is turned
into a justice-like serving-man. Their spirits are so
married in conjunction, with the participation of society,
that they flock together in consent, like so many wild-
geese. If I had a suit to Master Shallow, I would
humour his men with the imputation of being near 70
their master: if to his men, I would curry with Master

Shallow that no man could better command his servants.
It is certain that either wise bearing or ignorant carriage
is caught, as men take diseases, one of another: therefore,
let men take heed of their company. I will devise matter
enough out of this Shallow to keep Prince Harry in
continual laughter the wearing out of six fashions—
which is four terms, or two actions—and a' shall laugh
without intervallums. O, it is much that a lie with a
80 slight oath, and a jest with a sad brow, will do with a
fellow that never had the ache in his shoulders! O, you
shall see him laugh till his face be like a wet cloak ill
laid up!

Shallow [*within*]. Sir John!

Falstaff. I come, Master Shallow. I come, Master
Shallow.   [*he goes in*

[5.2.]   *Westminster. A Room in the Palace.*

WARWICK and the LORD CHIEF JUSTICE meeting

Warwick. How now, my lord chief justice?
    whither away?

L. Chief Justice. How doth the king?

Warwick. Exceeding well, his cares are now all
    ended.

L. Chief Justice. I hope, not dead.

Warwick.   He's walked the way of nature,
And to our purposes he lives no more.

L. Chief Justice. I would his majesty had called me
    with him:
The service that I truly did his life
Hath left me open to all injuries.

Warwick. Indeed I think the young king loves
    you not.

L. Chief Justice. I know he doth not, and do   10
    arm myself
To welcome the condition of the time,
Which cannot look more hideously upon me
Than I have drawn it in my fantasy.

Enter PRINCE JOHN, CLARENCE, GLOUCESTER,
    WESTMORELAND, and others

Warwick. Here come the heavy issue of dead Harry.
O, that the living Harry had the temper
Of he, the worst of these three gentlemen!
How many nobles then should hold their places,
That must strike sail to spirits of vile sort!
    L. Chief Justice. O God, I fear all will be over-
       turned!
    Prince John. Good morrow, cousin Warwick,   20
       good morrow.
    Gloucester.⎫
    Clarence. ⎬ Good morrow, cousin.   [*a pause*
    Prince John. We meet like men that had forgot
       to speak.
    Warwick. We do remember, but our argument
Is all too heavy to admit much talk.
    Prince John. Well, peace be with him that hath made
       us heavy!
    L. Chief Justice. Peace be with us, lest we be heavier!
    Gloucester. O, good my lord, you have lost a
       friend, indeed,
And I dare swear you borrow not that face
Of seeming sorrow, it is sure your own.
    Prince John. Though no man be assured what grace 30
       to find,
You stand in coldest expectation.
I am the sorrier, would 'twere otherwise.

Clarence. Well, you must now speak Sir John
    Falstaff fair,
Which swims against your stream of quality.
    L. Chief Justice. Sweet princes, what I did, I did
        in honour,
Led by th'impartial conduct of my soul;
And never shall you see that I will beg
A ragged and forestaled remission.
If truth and upright innocency fail me,
40 I'll to the king my master that is dead,
And tell him who hath sent me after him.
    Warwick. Here comes the prince.

'*Enter the* PRINCE *and* BLUNT'

    L. Chief Justice. Good morrow, and God save
        your majesty!
    Prince. This new and gorgeous garment, majesty,
Sits not so easy on me as you think...
Brothers, you mix your sadness with some fear:
This is the English, not the Turkish court,
Not Amurath an Amurath succeeds,
But Harry Harry! Yet be sad, good brothers,
50 For by my faith, it very well becomes you;
Sorrow so royally in you appears
That I will deeply put the fashion on,
And wear it in my heart: why then, be sad,
But entertain no more of it, good brothers,
Than a joint burden laid upon us all.
For me, by heaven, I bid you be assured,
I'll be your father and your brother too.
·Let me but bear your love, I'll bear your cares:
Yet weep that Harry's dead, and so will I.
60 But Harry lives that shall convert those tears
By number into hours of happiness.

Prince John, &c. We hope no otherwise from
    your majesty.

Prince. You all look strangely on me—[*to the Lord
    Chief Justice*] and you most.

You are, I think, assured I love you not.

L. Chief Justice. I am assured, if I be measured
    rightly,

Your majesty hath no just cause to hate me.

Prince. No!

How might a prince of my great hopes forget
So great indignities you laid upon me?
What! rate, rebuke, and roughly send to prison   70
Th'immediate heir of England! Was this easy?
May this be washed in Lethe, and forgotten?

L. Chief Justice. I then did use the person of
    your father,

The image of his power lay then in me,
And, in th'administration of his law,
Whiles I was busy for the commonwealth,
Your highness pleaséd to forget my place,
The majesty and power of law and justice,
The image of the king whom I presented,
And struck me in my very seat of judgement;   80
Whereon, as an offender to your father,
I gave bold way to my authority,
And did commit you: if the deed were ill,
Be you contented, wearing now the garland,
To have a son set your decrees at nought?
To pluck down Justice from your awful bench?
To trip the course of law and blunt the sword ·
That guards the peace and safety of your person?
Nay more, to spurn at your most royal image,
And mock your workings in a second body?   90
Question your royal thoughts, make the case yours;

Be now the father and propose a son,
Hear your own dignity so much profaned,
See your most dreadful laws so loosely slighted,
Behold yourself so by a son disdained;
And then imagine me taking your part,
And in your power soft silencing your son:
After this cold considerance sentence me,
And as you are a king speak in your state
100 What I have done that misbecame my place,
My person, or my liege's sovereignty.
  Prince. You are right Justice, and you weigh this well.
Therefore still bear the balance and the sword.
And I do wish your honours may increase,
Till you do live to see a son of mine
Offend you, and obey you, as I did:
So shall I live to speak my father's words:
'Happy am I, that have a man so bold,
That dares do justice on my proper son;
110 And not less happy, having such a son,
That would deliver up his greatness so
Into the hands of Justice.'—You did commit me:
For which, I do commit into your hand
Th'unstainéd sword that you have used to bear;
With this remembrance, that you use the same
With the like bold, just, and impartial spirit
As you have done 'gainst me...There is my hand.
You shall be as a father to my youth,
My voice shall sound as you do prompt mine ear,
120 And I will stoop and humble my intents
To your well-practised wise directions....
And, princes all, believe me, I beseech you—
My father is gone wild into his grave!
For in his tomb lie my affections,
And with his spirits sadly I survive,

To mock the expectation of the world,
To frustrate prophecies, and to raze out
Rotten opinion, who hath writ me down
After my seeming. The tide of blood in me
Hath proudly flowed in vanity till now: 130
Now doth it turn and ebb back to the sea,
Where it shall mingle with the state of floods,
And flow henceforth in formal majesty.
Now call we our high court of parliament,
And let us choose such limbs of noble counsel,
That the great body of our state may go
In equal rank with the best governed nation,
That war, or peace, or both at once, may be
As things acquainted and familiar to us—
In which you, father, shall have foremost hand....   140
                    [*to the Lord Chief Justice*
Our coronation done, we will accite,
As I before remembered, all our state.
And (God consigning to my good intents)
No prince nor peer shall have just cause to say,
God shorten Harry's happy life one day.   [*they go*

[5. 3.] *Gloucestershire. The orchard behind Justice*
SHALLOW's house; tables and benches under an arbour;
a fine summer's evening

SHALLOW and FALSTAFF, followed by SILENCE,
BARDOLPH, PAGE and DAVY, come from within; their
gait is unsteady

  Shallow. Nay, you shall see my orchard, where, in an
arbour, we will eat a last year's pippin of my own
graffing, with a dish of caraways, and so forth—come,
cousin Silence [*he stays him from falling*]—and then to
bed.

Falstaff. 'Fore God, you have here a goodly dwelling and a rich.

Shallow. Barren, barren, barren—beggars all, beggars all, Sir John—marry, good air. Spread, Davy, spread,
10 Davy, well said, Davy.

> [*Davy sets dishes of fruit and wine
> upon the tables*

Falstaff. This Davy serves you for good uses, he is your serving-man and your husband.

Shallow. A good varlet, a good varlet, a very good varlet, Sir John: [*he hiccoughs*] by the mass, I have drunk too much sack at supper: a good varlet. Now sit down, now sit down—come, cousin.

> [*Shallow, Falstaff and Silence sit at a table*

Silence [*drunkenly*]. Ah, sirrah! quoth-a,
we shall—

Do nothing but eat, and make good cheer,   [*singing*
And praise God for the merry year,
20   When flesh is cheap and females dear,
And lusty lads roam here and there
         So merrily,
And ever among so merrily.

Falstaff. There's a merry heart! Good Master Silence, I'll give you a health for that anon.

Shallow. Give Master Bardolph some wine, Davy.

Davy. Sweet sir, sit [*seating Bardolph and the Page at another table*]—I'll be with you anon—Most sweet sir, sit; master page, good master page, sit. Proface! what
30 you want in meat, we'll have in drink: but you must bear; the heart's all.   [*he goes in*

Shallow. Be merry, Master Bardolph, and my little soldier there, be merry.

Silence [*sings*]. Be merry, be merry, my wife has all,
For women are shrews, both short and tall,

'Tis merry in hall when beards wag all,
    And welcome merry Shrove-tide.
Be merry, be merry.
Falstaff. I did not think Master Silence had been a
man of this mettle.   40
Silence. Who, I? I have been merry twice and once
ere now.

    DAVY *returns with russet apples*

Davy. There's a dish of leather-coats for you.
                        [*sets them before Bardolph*
Shallow. Davy!
Davy. Your worship! I'll be with you straight.
[*to Bardolph*] A cup of wine, sir?   [*he pours it out*
Silence [*sings*]. A cup of wine, that's brisk and fine,
    And drink unto thee, leman mine,
        And a merry heart lives long-a.
Falstaff. Well said! Master Silence.   50
Silence. An we shall be merry, now comes in the
sweet o' th' night.
Falstaff [*toasts him*]. Health and long life to you,
Master Silence.
Silence [*sings*]. Fill the cup and let it come,
    I'll pledge you a mile to the bottom.
Shallow. Honest Bardolph, welcome [*toasts him*]. If
thou want'st any thing, and wilt not call, beshrew thy
heart. Welcome, my little tine thief [*to the Page*], and
welcome indeed too. I'll drink to Master Bardolph, 60
and to all the caballeros about London.
Davy. I hope to see London once ere I die.
Bardolph. An I might see you there, Davy,—
Shallow. By the mass, you'll crack a quart together,
ha? will you not, Master Bardolph?
Bardolph. Yea, sir, in a pottle-pot.

Shallow. By God's liggens, I thank thee. The knave
will stick by thee, I can assure thee that. A' will not out,
a'. 'Tis true bred!   [*one knocks at door*
70 *Bardolph.* And I'll stick by him, sir.

Shallow. Why, there spoke a king. Lack nothing, be
merry. [*knocking again*] Look who's at door there.
Ho! who knocks?   [*Davy goes within*

Silence drinks a bumper to Falstaff

Falstaff. Why, now you have done me right.
Silence [*sings*]. Do me right,
            And dub me knight,
                Samingo.
Is't not so?
Falstaff. 'Tis so.
80 *Silence.* Is't so? Why then, say an old man can do
somewhat.

Davy returns, with Pistol following

Davy. An't please your worship, there's one Pistol
come from the court with news.

Falstaff. From the court? let him come in. How now,
Pistol?

Pistol. Sir John, God save you.

Falstaff. What wind blew you hither, Pistol?

Pistol. Not the ill wind which blows no man to good...
Sweet knight, thou art now one of the greatest men in
90 this realm.

Silence. By'r lady, I think a' be—but goodman Puff of
Barson.

Pistol. Puff!
Puff i'thy teeth, most recreant coward base!
Sir John, I am thy Pistol and thy friend,
And helter-skelter have I rode to thee,

And tidings do I bring and lucky joys
And golden times and happy news of price.

Falstaff. I pray thee now, deliver them like a man of
this world.   100

Pistol. A foutre for the world and worldlings base!
I speak of Africa and golden joys.

Falstaff. O base Assyrian knight, what is thy news?
Let King Cophetua know the truth thereof.

Silence [*sings*]. And Robin Hood, Scarlet and John.

Pistol. Shall dunghill curs confront the Helicons?
And shall good news be baffled?
Then, Pistol, lay thy head in Furies' lap.

Shallow. Honest gentleman, I know not your breeding.   110

Pistol. Why then, lament therefore.

Shallow. Give me pardon, sir. If, sir, you come with
news from the court, I take it there's but two ways,
either to utter them or conceal them. I am, sir, under
the king, in some authority.

Pistol. Under which king, Besonian? speak, or die.

Shallow. Under King Harry.

Pistol.   Harry the fourth? or fifth?

Shallow. Harry the fourth.

Pistol.   A foutre for thine office!
Sir John, thy tender lambkin now is king;
Harry the fifth's the man: I speak the truth: 120
When Pistol lies, do this; and fig me, like
The bragging Spaniard.

Falstaff. What! is the old king dead?

Pistol. As nail in door! the things I speak are just.

Falstaff. Away, Bardolph, saddle my horse. Master
Robert Shallow, choose what office thou wilt in the
land, 'tis thine: Pistol, I will double-charge thee with
dignities.

Bardolph. O joyful day! I would not take a knight-
130 hood for my fortune.

Pistol. What! I do bring good news?

Falstaff [*to Davy*]. Carry Master Silence to bed...
Master Shallow, my Lord Shallow—be what thou wilt,
I am Fortune's steward—get on thy boots, we'll ride all
night: O, sweet Pistol [*they embrace*]. Away, Bardolph.
[*Bardolph goes*] Come, Pistol, utter more to me, and
withal devise something to do thyself good. Boot, boot,
Master Shallow! I know the young king is sick for me.
Let us take any man's horses—the laws of England are at
140 my commandment. Blessed are they that have been my
friends, and woe to my lord chief justice!

Pistol. Let vultures vile seize on his lungs also!
'Where is the life that late I led' say they?
Why, here it is; welcome these pleasant days.

> [*they hurry within, Davy and servants
> carrying Master Silence*

[5. 4.]   *A street in London*

Enter BEADLES, *dragging in Hostess* QUICKLY
and DOLL TEARSHEET

Hostess [*struggles*]. No, thou arrant knave! I would to
God that I might die, that I might have thee hanged.
Thou hast drawn my shoulder out of joint.

1 *Beadle*. The constables have delivered her over to
me, and she shall have whipping-cheer enough, I
warrant her. There hath been a man or two lately killed
about her.

Doll. Nut-hook, nut-hook, you lie. [*he strikes her*]
Come on, I'll tell thee what, thou damned tripe-visaged
10 rascal, an the child I go with do miscarry, thou wert

better thou hadst struck thy mother, thou paper-faced villain.

Hostess. O the Lord, that Sir John were come! he would make this a bloody day to somebody: but I pray God the fruit of her womb miscarry!

1 Beadle. If it do, you shall have a dozen of cushions again—you have but eleven now…Come, I charge you both go with me, for the man is dead that you and Pistol beat amongst you.

Doll. I'll tell you what, you thin man in a censer, I will 20 have you as soundly swinged for this—you blue-bottle rogue, you filthy famished correctioner, if you be not swinged, I'll forswear half-kirtles.

1 Beadle. Come, come, you she knight-errant, come.

Hostess. O God, that right should thus overcome might! Well, of sufferance comes ease.

Doll. Come, you rogue, come, bring me to a justice.

Hostess. Ay, come, you starved blood-hound.

Doll. Goodman death! goodman bones!   30

Hostess. Thou atomy thou!

Doll. Come, you thin thing; come, you rascal!

1 Beadle. Very well!   [*they hale them away to prison*

[5. 5.] *A public place near Westminster Abbey; a great concourse of people; guards line the way*

'*Enter strewers of rushes*'

1 Strewer. More rushes, more rushes.

2 Strewer. The trumpets have sounded twice.

3 Strewer. 'Twill be two o'clock ere they come from the coronation. Dispatch, dispatch.   [*they pass on*

*'Trumpets sound'; 'the King and his train' come up in
procession, and pass into the Abbey; after a while
FALSTAFF, SHALLOW, PISTOL, BARDOLPH, and the
Page approach and take their places in the throng*

Falstaff. Stand here by me, Master Robert Shallow,
I will make the king do you grace, I will leer upon him
as a' comes by, and do but mark the countenance that he
will give me.

Pistol. God bless thy lungs, good knight.

10 *Falstaff.* Come here, Pistol, stand behind me. [*to
Shallow*] O, if I had had time to have made new liveries,
I would have bestowed the thousand pound I borrowed
of you. But 'tis no matter, this poor show doth better,
this doth infer the zeal I had to see him.

Shallow. It doth so.

Falstaff. It shows my earnestness of affection—

Pistol. It doth so.

Falstaff. My devotion—

Pistol. It doth, it doth, it doth.

20 *Falstaff.* As it were, to ride day and night, and not to
deliberate, not to remember, not to have patience to
shift me—

Shallow. It is best, certain.

Falstaff. But to stand stained with travel, and sweating
with desire to see him, thinking of nothing else, putting
all affairs else in oblivion, as if there were nothing else
to be done but to see him.

Pistol. 'Tis 'semper idem', for 'obsque hoc nihil est.'
'Tis 'all in every part'.

30 *Shallow.* 'Tis so, indeed.

Pistol. My knight, I will inflame thy noble liver,
And make thee rage.
Thy Doll, and Helen of thy noble thoughts,

Is in base durance and contagious prison,
Haled thither
By most mechanical and dirty hand:
Rouse up revenge from ebon den with fell Alecto's
     snake,
For Doll is in: Pistol speaks nought but truth.
  Falstaff. I will deliver her.
                         [*trumpets heard, and a great shout*
  Pistol. There roared the sea, and trumpet-   40
     clangor sounds.

      '*The* KING *and his train,*' *with the* LORD CHIEF
            JUSTICE, *come from the Abbey*

  Falstaff. God save thy grace, King Hal! my royal Hal!
  Pistol. The heavens thee guard and keep, most royal
imp of fame!
  Falstaff. God save thee, my sweet boy!
  (*King.* My lord chief justice, speak to that vain man.
  L. Chief Justice. Have you your wits? know you what
     'tis you speak?
  Falstaff. [*thrusts past him*] My king! my Jove! I
     speak to thee, my heart!
  King. I know thee not, old man. Fall to thy prayers.
How ill white hairs become a fool and jester!
I have long dreamed of such a kind of man,   50
So surfeit-swelled, so old, and so profane;
But, being awaked, I do despise my dream.
Make less thy body hence, and more thy grace,
Leave gormandizing, know the grave doth gape
For thee thrice wider than for other men.
Reply not to me with a fool-born jest,
Presume not that I am the thing I was,
For God doth know, so shall the world perceive,
That I have turned away my former self;

60 So will I those that kept me company.
When thou dost hear I am as I have been,
Approach me, and thou shalt be as thou wast,
The tutor and the feeder of my riots:
Till then, I banish thee, on pain of death,
As I have done the rest of my misleaders,
Not to come near our person by ten mile...
For competence of life I will allow you,
That lack of means enforce you not to evils.
And as we hear you do reform yourselves,
70 We will, according to your strengths and qualities,
Give you advancement. .[*to the Lord Chief Justice*] Be
it your charge, my lord,
To see performed the tenour of my word....
Set on. .   [*the procession passes on*
    Falstaff. Master Shallow, I owe you a thousand pound.
    Shallow. Yea, marry, Sir John, which I beseech you
to let me have home with me.
    Falstaff. That can hardly be, Master Shallow...Do
not you grieve at this. I shall be sent for in private to
him; look you, he must seem thus to the world: fear not
80 your advancements—I will be the man yet that shall
make you great.
    Shallow. I cannot perceive how, unless you give me
your doublet, and stuff me out with straw. I beseech
you, good Sir John, let me have five hundred of my
thousand.
    Falstaff. Sir, I will be as good as my word. This that
you heard was but a colour.
    Shallow. A colour that I fear you will die in, Sir John.
    Falstaff. Fear no colours, go with me to dinner: come
90 Lieutenant Pistol, come, Bardolph—I shall be sent for
soon at night.

Prince JOHN returns with the LORD CHIEF
JUSTICE and officers

L. *Chief Justice* [*to the officers*]. Go, carry Sir John
    Falstaff to the Fleet,
Take all his company along with him.

                    [*they arrest Falstaff and his party*
Falstaff. My lord, my lord—
    L. *Chief Justice.* I cannot now speak, I will hear
        you soon.
Take them away.

    Pistol. 'Si fortuna me tormenta, spero me contenta.'
                            [*the officers lead them off*
    Prince John.. I like this fair proceeding of the king's.
He hath intent his wonted followers
Shall all be very well provided for;   100
But all are banished till their conversations
Appear more wise and modest to the world.
    L. *Chief Justice.* And so they are.
    Prince John. The king hath called his parliament,
        my lord.
    L. *Chief Justice.* He hath.
    Prince John. I will lay odds that, ere this year expire,
We bear our civil swords and native fire
As far as France. I heard a bird so sing,
Whose music, to my thinking, pleased the king...
Come, will you hence?   [*they go* 110

Epilogue

First my fear, then my curtsy, last my speech.

My fear is your displeasure, my curtsy my duty, and my speech to beg your pardons. If you look for a good speech now, you undo me, for what I have to say is of mine own making, and what indeed I should say will, I doubt, prove mine own marring: but to the purpose, and so to the venture. Be it known to you, as it is very well, I was lately here in the end of a displeasing play, to pray your patience for it and to promise you a better.
10 I meant indeed to pay you with this; which, if like an ill venture it come unluckily home, I break, and you, my gentle creditors, lose. Here I promised you I would be, and here I commit my body to your mercies: bate me some, and I will pay you some, and, as most debtors do, promise you infinitely: and so I kneel down before you; but, indeed, to pray for the Queen.

If my tongue cannot entreat you to acquit me, will you command me to use my legs? and yet that were but light payment, to dance out of your debt. But a good con-
20 science will make any possible satisfaction, and so would I...All the gentlewomen here have forgiven me; if the gentlemen will not, then the gentlemen do not agree with the gentlewomen, which was never seen before in such an assembly.

One word more, I beseech you. If you be not too much cloyed with fat meat, our humble author will continue the story, with Sir John in it, and make you merry with fair Katharine of France; where (for any thing I know) Falstaff shall die of a sweat, unless already a' be killed
30 with your hard opinions; for Oldcastle died martyr, and this is not the man...My tongue is weary, when my legs are too, I will bid you good night.

THE COPY FOR
2 *HENRY IV*, 1600 & 1623

The only quarto of *2 Henry IV* extant, and probably, for reasons to be presently examined, the only one ever printed, was entered by the publishers Andrew Wise and William Aspley in the Stationers' Register on 23 August 1600, and no doubt went to press immediately after. This text was, by the editors of *The Cambridge Shakespeare*, 1864, 'regarded as having' a 'higher critical value' than that in the Folio; and its latest students, Dr Greg (p. 115, *The Editorial Problem in Shakespeare*, 1942) and Professor Shaaber (pp. 488–94, *New Variorum* edition of *2 Henry IV*, 1940)[1], have independently concluded that it was actually printed from Shakespeare's original MS., i.e. the so-called 'foul papers' from which the book-holder prepared prompt-copy for use in performance. As for the F. text, here also the finding of the Cambridge editors, that it 'was probably printed from a transcript of the original MS.', still holds the field, though opinions differ on the nature of this transcript, i.e. whether it was the theatrical prompt-book or a copy therefrom; while authorities like the Arden editor of the play, Sir Edmund Chambers, and Dr Greg, are all inclined to suspect that what the printers actually used in 1622–3 was not such a transcript itself, but a copy of the quarto which had first been collated with a transcript. Professor Shaaber, however, appears to me to have come as near as the available evidence allows to proving (i) that there is no need to posit the use of a quarto in 1622 at all, and (ii) that

[1] Owing to the war Prof. Shaaber's edition did not reach this country until Dr Greg's book had been set up in type.

the MS. handled by Jaggard's compositors was not a prompt-book but a transcript therefrom, purged of profanity and to some extent of obscenity, and prepared for reading and not acting, in all likelihood 'by Crane or by some other professional scribe of similar working habits' (*op. cit.* p. 513). Whoever the scribe, he was clearly anxious to make the text as presentable to readers as he could, a solicitude conspicuous first in the 'thoroughgoing revision of the vulgar and colloquial language' of the dialogue, which revision even extended apparently to the removal of 'anti-patriotic criticism' at one place and of un-Christian pessimism at another (v. notes 1.2. 210–16; 3.1. 53–6), and second in the very careful, and on the whole excellent, punctuation. This last is of considerable service to an editor; for, though not of course Shakespeare's, it deserves respect as that of a contemporary who was probably closely associated with his company. Indeed, as far as the prose scenes are concerned it is indispensable, since, in Shaaber's words (p. 514), 'there can hardly be another quarto more defectively punctuated' in those scenes. That is to say the pointing of F. is practically our sole guide for a large proportion of the play.

Such being the general textual situation, the present text will, in accordance with the principles laid down in *The Manuscript of Shakespeare's 'Hamlet'*, pp. 178–9, follow Q. rather than F., when variant readings appear to be of equal or almost equal aesthetic quality, unless other readings of the same class suggest that what Q. prints is due to some idiosyncrasy of the compositor or press-corrector. Compositors, for instance, are apt both to omit and to insert letters or small insignificant words; but inasmuch as omission is commoner than addition, the longer variant will be preferred when the merits are otherwise fairly evenly balanced (cf. notes 2.4. 38; 3.2. 197–8). On the other hand, we need not hesitate to follow F. in some fifty-five instances where it presents

what seems the more Shakespearian reading of the two
(cf. notes 2. 1. 26; 2. 2. 130; 3. 2. 57, 324; 4. 4. 32,
39; 5. 1. 26, 64). When, however, an obvious or
suspected misprint in Q. suggests a word of different
graphical formation, neither variant is likely to be correct and emendation may have to be resorted to, even
though the F. reading makes sense (cf. notes 2. 4. 333;
4. 4. 104; 4. 5. 81). Finally, there are ten misprints,
all but two I think indubitable, which being common
to both texts must be set down to Shakespeare's own
pen[1] and which I here give together with the emenda-
tions accepted in this edition:

Ind. 35 worm-eaten hole	worm-eaten hold	(Theobald
2. 2. 113 borrowed	borrower's	(Warburton)
3. 2. 313 inuincible	invisible	(Rowe)
4. 1. 34 rage	rags	(Singer)
4. 1. 36 appeare	appeared	(Pope)
4. 1. 180 At either	And either	(Thirlby)
4. 1. 185 Feare you not, that if	Fear you not that: if	(Pope)
4. 2. 19 imagine	imagined	(Rowe)
4. 4. 104 write ... letters	mete ... terms	(A. Walker)
4. 5. 204 thy friends	my friends	(Tyrwhitt)

If this seem a long list, I may remark that in Q 2 and F.
Hamlet I found eleven identical errors of the same sort,
not to mention four variants in which both texts are
certainly wrong and another eight variants, in which
both are probably wrong, though editors have generally
accepted one of the two (cf. *Manuscript of Shakespeare's
'Hamlet'*, pp. 297–8). Finally, there is one reading
common to Q. and F. 2 *Henry IV* which I leave
uncorrected, viz. the designation of L. Bardolph as
Sir John Umfrevile at 1. 1. 34. For though, as Dr P.
Maas points out (*R.E.S.* Jan. 1944, p. 77, n. 4), it
'cannot have been Shakespeare's intention', it had cer-

---

[1] See, however, Miss Walker's article in *R.E.S.* July 1951,
for a better explanation [1952].

tainly once been, and must have been overlooked when
the name Umfrevile was changed to L. Bardolph in
the stage-directions and most of the speech-prefixes.
In other words, it is what Shakespeare allowed to stand,
even though he did so by inadvertence. Nor is there
anything surprising in the oversight passing muster 'on
the stage from 1598 to 1623', seeing that this 'Umfrevile' might well be taken by prompter and players as
just another horseman on the busy road from Shrewsbury, as indeed all editors seem to have assumed down
to the middle of the twentieth century.

I now turn and consider briefly certain special features
of Q. which have attracted the attention of editors.

(i) *Traces of Shakespeare's hand*. Apart from the
usual stigmata of 'foul papers', Q. displays three of
unusual interest. Take first the stage-directions for the
royal procession at the beginning of 5.5, which are
given as follows in the two texts:

Q.

5.5.1   Enter ſtrewers of ruſhes.
    5   Trumpets ſound, and the King, and his traine
      paſſe ouer the ſtage: after them enter Falſtaffe,
      Shallow, Piſtol, Bardolfe, and the Boy.
  41   Enter the King and his traine.

F.

5.5.1   Enter two Groomes.
    5   Enter Falſtaffe, Shallow, Piſtoll, Bardolfe, and Page.
  41   The Trumpets ſound. Enter King Henrie the Fift,
      Brothers, Lord Chiefe Iuſtice.

As both Greg and Shaaber note, the F. directions
provide a clear indication of the presence of a playhouse
prompt-book somewhere behind that text. And all
editors have followed F. without noticing that they not
merely depart, as Q. shows, from Shakespeare's clear
intention, which was to have two processions, one to
and the other from the Abbey, but by so doing have

reduced the dialogue between the 'strewers' to non-
sense (cf. head-note 5. 5). Secondly, there is the occur-
rence of the name of the small-part actor 'Sincklo' in
the stage-directions and prefixes of 5. 4. From similar
occurrences of the name in other dramatic texts of the
period, it has been plausibly inferred that Sincklo or
Sinckler possessed a figure of unusual thinness (cf. *John
Sincklo as one of Shakespeare's Actors*, by A. Gaw,
Anglia, 1926, xlix. pp. 289–303), and it would seem
to follow that by naming him in this scene Shakespeare
was in effect ordering that the player cast for the part
of 1 Beadle should be the member of the company who
displayed physical characteristics appropriate to the
abuse that Doll and Quickly heap upon him (cf. head-
note 5. 4). Lastly, this text, almost without doubt, as
we have seen, printed from Shakespeare's autograph, is
associated in a striking fashion with the Three Pages in
the MS. *Boke of Sir Thomas More*, which many cautious
critics now believe to be in Shakespeare's autograph
also, by the appearance within it, on no fewer than
eighteen occasions, of the spelling 'Scilens', in full or
shortened form, for the name of Master Justice Silence,
a spelling so far only found elsewhere in those Three
Pages (cf. Pollard, etc., *Shakespeare's Hand in 'Sir
Thomas More'*, pp. 128–9).

(ii) *The eight cuts and the Censor.* Absolute proof
that F. derives from some text independent of Q. is
furnished by the fact that the latter lacks eight passages,
running in all to 150 lines, to supply which an editor is
obliged to have recourse to F., viz. 1. 1. 166–79;
1. 1. 189–209; 1. 3. 21–4; 1. 3. 36–55; 1. 3. 85–108;
2. 3. 23–45; 4. 1. 55–79; 4. 1. 103–39. Chambers and
Greg describe these as 'cuts' without attempting to
explain them; and the hypothesis usually accepted and
first advanced by the Cambridge editors is that they
were 'omitted or erased in order to shorten the play
for the stage'. Yet the abridgement is not appreciable,

and the cuts, which often leave the sense defective, seem too crude for stage-abridgement and suggest rather the censor's than the prompter's hand. Indeed, L. L. Schücking (*Times Literary Supplement*, 25 Sept. 1930) and A. Hart (*Shakespeare and the Homilies*, 1934, pp. 154–218), have independently made out a case for action by the ecclesiastical censor which I find it difficult not to accept. Differing in certain details, the two writers agree in associating this action with the fall of the Earl of Essex from power in 1599–1601. They point out that whereas *2 Henry IV* was written and produced while Elizabeth's favourite was in the ascendant, it was entered in the Register after his fall and at a peculiarly unfortunate moment for any book dealing with Henry Bolingbroke. In January 1599, Dr John Hayward published a book on the fall of Richard II, disguised as *The First Part of the Raigne of Henrie IV*, with a dedication to Essex in such terms that the latter asked the Archbishop of Canterbury, the authority for the licensing of books, to step in; and the dedication, after a considerable number of copies had been sold, was withdrawn. These facts were inevitably raked up at Essex's trial in June 1600, at which time the author, printer, and reader of books for the archbishop, Samuel Harsnett, prebendary of St Paul's and later Archbishop of York were closely examined before the Star Chamber; a later edition of the book suppressed; and Hayward himself, though probably entirely guiltless of the intentions fastened upon him, committed to the Tower for six months. Behind these proceedings there lies the strange identification, by herself as well as by her courtiers, of the Queen with Richard II, while there was a growing sense during the years of crisis that Bolingbroke, who deposed Richard, prefigured Essex (cf. pp. xxx f. Introduction, *Richard II*; New Shakespeare).

Such was the atmosphere in which on 23 August 1600

Wise and Aspley entered on the Register a book entitled 'the second parte of the history of Kinge Henry
the iiijth'. And one has only to imagine the bishops'
reader, who may have been the man who got into
trouble over *The First Part,* perusing the manuscript
to find a satisfactory explanation of the mutilations it
sustained. As Schücking notes, no fewer than five of
the eight passages deleted 'mention King Richard II
and his tragic fate', while some might well appear to
reflect upon the recent trial, and others again, which
deal with the rebel archbishop, would naturally seem
most undesirable to a clerical reader. Hart, indeed,
may be correct in detecting here a suspected parallel
with Oviedo, bishop of Dublin, who was in arms
against Elizabeth in 1600. In one cut alone, the first,
is it difficult for a modern eye to see dangerous matter;
but, as Shaaber remarks, 'political allusions hidden
from us may have been scented' by a nervous contemporary (*op. cit.* p. 492). In the absence of a better
hypothesis, which seems unlikely to be found, the
eight cuts may thus be set down, with some confidence,
to the political circumstances of the time of Q.'s
publication.

(iii) *The omission of 3. 1, and the suppression of Q.*
Hart goes further than this and attributes also to the
censorship the interesting bibliographical fact that Q.
exists in two issues, from one of which the first scene
of act 3 is absent. Had the omission occurred in the
later issue, there might be something to say for his
theory. But in point of fact it is the earlier issue which
lacks the scene, while an examination of the later one
shows that the printers have gone to much trouble to
insert the missing scene into an already printed book;
being compelled both to cancel a couple of leaves in
Sig. E in order to work in the new scene and of course
to reset[1] what they had cancelled, while it was lucky

[1] The variants of this resetting, labelled Q b in my Notes,
have of course no authority. These should of course be

for them that the new matter could be made to fill approximately four pages. In short, the scene was not first printed and then cut out, but first omitted and then added. To circumvent this difficulty Hart offers a series of suppositions, some of them extremely hazardous, which need not be debated here. Yet the fact from which he sets out, viz. that 3. 1 contains the only references in Q. to Richard's fall and Bolingbroke's usurpation not excised by the censor, is certainly note-worthy. Indeed, if there is anything at all in the argument of the foregoing paragraph, it is very difficult to see how the bishops' reader could have passed them over, the more so that they deal not only with Richard and Bolingbroke, but, in particular, with the double-crossing of the Duke of Northumberland, whose descendant, the ninth duke, at once brother-in-law to Essex and friend of Raleigh, his bitterest foe, stood in a like ambiguous light in the eyes of many in 1600.

Now the inserted scene, as Pollard suggested, and Greg agrees (*op. cit.* p. 116), probably occupied two sides of a single leaf of foolscap in Shakespeare's foul papers, and was omitted because the leaf had been mislaid. Further, inasmuch as the first issue was printed off before the omission was discovered, it seems possible that the leaf had been accidentally left behind at the playhouse, when the manuscript was delivered to the publishers. If so, then it is also possible that the censor of books, who would receive the manuscript from the publishers, not from the players, may never have seen the missing leaf at all. In other words, I suggest that the authorities did not become aware of the dangerous matter in scene 3. 1 until it had got into print and the book was being sold on the stalls. But by this time it was late autumn, if not later still, when everyone in London had become aware that the Essex affair was

distinguished from variants in different copies of Q., due to press-correction; cf. notes 3. 2. 57, 210; 4. 1. 30, 93; 4. 5. 160.

moving towards catastrophe. The very title of the book
would draw to its pages the curious eyes of 'decipherers',
anxious to curry favour, and such eyes would not be
long in discovering offence in 3. 1. There were the
dangerous references already noted; and there were
also the following lines:

> Then you perceive the body of our kingdom
> How foul it is—what rank diseases grow,
> And with what danger, near the heart of it,

lines which, uttered by a careworn monarch oppressed
with anxiety and denied sleep, might seem expressly
penned to mirror the condition and sentiments of the
great Queen herself at the end of this year. There was
nothing half as dangerous in Hayward's book, suppressed six months earlier; and if, as I suggest, the
offending scene had never been submitted to the censor,
the misdemeanour would be greatly aggravated, and
absolute suppression inevitably follow. We cannot, of
course, be certain that this is what happened; but there is
nothing impossible about it, and if it did happen, it would
afford a simple and neat explanation of two otherwise
puzzling phenomena: the similarity of the matter in
3. 1 to that which is so carefully excised elsewhere, and
the surprising absence of any reprint of this Falstaff
play after 1600.

P.S. [1952] A few changes have been made on
pp. 120, 121–2 at the kind suggestion of Sir Walter
Greg, who is also inclined to attribute the absence of
a Q 2 to action rather by Shakespeare's company than
by the authorities. It is possibly relevant to note that
the title-page of the Crichton Stuart copy of Q., now at
the National Library of Scotland, bears the following
memorandum in a contemporary hand: "31 Decēber
1610. price v d". The revision of pp. 115–18 called for
by Miss Walker's article on the copy for F. (*R.E.S.*,
July 1951), must, I fear, be left to a second edition.
But see notes on 2. 4. 123; 4. 1. 93; 4. 3. 8–9.

NOTES

All significant departures from Q. are recorded: the name of critic or editor who first suggested or printed the accepted reading being placed in brackets. Line-numeration for references to plays not yet issued in this edition is that found in Bartlett's *Concordance* and the *Globe Shakespeare*.

Q., except where otherwise specified, stands for the Quarto of *2 Henry IV* (1600); F. stands for the First Folio (1623). For the Dering MS. v. *1 Henry IV*, p. 107.

Other abbreviations of a general character are: G. = Glossary; O.E.D. = *The Oxford Dictionary*; S.D. = stage-direction; Sh. = Shakespeare; other names, together with common words, are abbreviated where convenient.

The following is a list of the principal books and editions cited by short titles in the Notes, and not already listed at the beginning of the Notes to *1 Henry IV*: Aspects = *Aspects of Shakespeare* (British Academy Lectures), 1933; Child = *English and Scottish Popular Ballads*, 5 vols. by F. J. Child, 1882–94; Clemen = *Shakespeares Bilder* by Wolfgang Clemen, 1936; Creizenach = *The English Drama in the Age of Shakespeare* by W. Creizenach, 1916; Deighton = *King Henry IV (part 2)*, ed. by K. Deighton (Macmillan's English Classics), 1893; E.M.I. = *Everyman in his Humour* (v. Jonson); E.M.O. = *Everyman out of his Humour* (v. Jonson); Kellner = *Restoring Shakespeare* by Leon Kellner, 1925; Ridley = *2 Henry IV* (New Temple Shakespeare) ed. by M. R. Ridley, 1934; Shaaber = *2 Henry IV* (New Variorum Shakespeare) ed. by M. A. Shaaber, 1940; Tucker Brooke = *The Shakespeare Apocrypha* ed. by C. F. Tucker Brooke, 1908.

Names of the Characters. Based on 'The Actors Names' printed at the end of the F. text, which, however, omits three speaking parts (the Porter in 1. 1, the L.C.J.'s Servant in 1. 2, the Messenger in 4. 1). and two mutes (the Earl of Kent, Sir John Blunt, v. notes 3. 1. 32; 4. 3. 73; 5. 2. 42). For the historical characters v. G. R. French, *Shakespeareana Genealogica*, 1869 and F. G. Stokes, *Shakespeare Dictionary of Characters and Proper Names*, 1924. (i) *Gower, Harcourt, Travers, Morton* seem to be characters invented by. Sh., while Gower has no apparent connexion with the poet. (ii) For *Colevile* v. head-note 4. 3 and for *Falstaff* v. *1 Henry IV*, Introduction, pp. viii–ix, Stage-History, p. xxix. (iii) *Lord Bardolph*. Shakespeare's carelessness with character-names is notorious, and deserves special study. At once chief writer and a leading player in a repertory company, he evidently and naturally found names a burden on his memory; cf. the substitution of Kemp and Cowley for Dogberry and Verges in *Ado*, 4. 2, the confusion between Geffrey and Richard, the Dauphin and his father, in *K. John* (v. Introduction, pp. xlii, xlv), the two Jaqueses in *As You Like It*, etc. It is not surprising then that when he found it wise to change the name 'Harvey' in *1 Henry IV*, and chose an alternative in 'Bardoll' or 'Bardolf', probably drawing upon memories of Stratford (v. *1 Henry IV*, 'Names of the Characters'), he forgot that a Lord Bardolph figured among the adherents of Northumberland and would have to appear as a character in *2 Henry IV*. Yet the inadvertent duplication causes no confusion in the theatre; Lord Bardolph is a minor character who only speaks in two scenes, was, indeed, originally intended only to speak in one (cf. notes 1. 1. 34–6; 1. 3. 81), and is never on the stage simultaneously with Bardolph. (iv) *Lord Chief Justice*, i.e. Sir William Gascoigne, Chief Justice of the King's Bench. Neither Elyot nor Shakespeare

mention his name, but Stow, who transcribes Elyot
(cf. *Library*, June 1945, p. 9), does so in a marginal
note (v. 5. 2. 103 note). (v) *Doll Tearsheet*. Tearsheet
is modelled on 'tear-cat', and is thus appropriate to a
shrewish whore; cf. note 2. 4. 222. Doll was a regular
name for a prostitute at this time; cf. Doll Common
in *The Alchemist*.

Acts and Scenes. No divisions in Q. Both acts and
scenes found as usual in F., which is followed by mod.
edd. except in act 1, where it reckons the Induction
as Scena Prima, act 1, scene 1 as Scena Secunda,
and so on; and in act 4, in which it rightly treats the
whole episode at Gaultree Forest, later divided into
three by Pope, as a single scene, and the two bedroom
scenes, first distinguished by the Cambridge edd., as
one, which they are theatrically, though not strictly so
in respect of locality.

Punctuation. Cf. above Note on the Copy, p. 116.
For reasons there explained I have based my punctuation of the prose on that of F. for the most part.
Clearly that in the copy for Q. was most scanty, and
had often to be supplied by the light of nature, as may
be seen from the following handful of variants:

1. 2. 14	F.	iudgement. Thou	Q.	iudgement thou
15	F.	heeles. I	Q.	heels I
190	F.	at him. For	Q.	at him for
2. 1. 44	F.	I arreſt you, at the ſuit of Miſt. Quickly		
	Q.	I arreſt you at the ſute of miſtris, quickly.		

On the other hand, it is unsafe to ignore Q., since it
sometimes supplies a pointing which is more likely to
be Sh.'s than that of F.; cf. note 1. 2. 165–6. The
verse is more carefully punctuated by Q., which I have
generally followed here, though occasionally I have
found it convenient to adopt the rather heavier stops
of F.

Stage-directions. Only those of Q. and F. which call for special comment are quoted in the Notes; for the rest, and for interesting comments on the differences between F. and Q., *v.* the table in Greg's *Editorial Problem in Shakespeare*, pp. 174–6.

Verse-lining. There is nothing in the Q. *2 Henry IV* to correspond with the chaotic lineation of Q. *1 Henry IV*. This means, I take it, that Sh. departed much more widely in Part 2 from his original draft than in Part 1, which is what I should expect, though the notes at 4. 3. 66–7, 79–81, 82–3, 123 suggest that traces of the draft are to be seen in places, since they show Falstaff and Bardolph speaking verse.

Induction

'Induction' usually = prologue-scene (cf. Creizenach, p. 276).

S.D. Capell read 'Warkworth. Before the Castle'. Cf. ll. 35–7 below and *1 Hen. IV*, 2. 3 head-note. *Enter Rumour...tongues* (Q.), the usual costume of Fama; cf. *Aen.* iv. 180–95 and note *1 Hen. IV*, 5. 2. 8. In Campion's Masque at the Marriage of the Earl of Somerset (26 Dec. 1613) given in the Banqueting room at Whitehall, 'Rumour' appeared 'in a skin coate full of winged Tongues, and ouer it an antick robe; on his head a Cap like a tongue, with a large paire of wings to it' (S. P. Vivian, *Campion's Works*, 1909, p. 151).

1. *will* would wish to.   3. *drooping* v. G.

4. *Making...horse* Cf. *Macb.* 1. 7. 22–3, 'horsed Upon the sightless couriers of the air'.

still = continually.

5. *acts* in the theat. sense; Rumour is the Presenter.

9–15. *I speak...matter* Prob. topical, pointing to summer of 1598 as date for *2 Hen. IV*. Panicky musters and 'prepared defence' against invasion by Spain was the story of 1596–7 (Oct. to Oct.), and that of the first

half of 1599. But 1599 is too late for *2 Hen. IV*; and
the unexpected child of the big year 1597 was a peace—
the Peace of Vervins between France and Spain,
signed 22 April 1598 and published on 26 May; to
England a 'grief' indeed, made, she felt sure, by 'covert
enmity' to 'wound' the Protestant world (cf. Harrison,
Sec. Eliz. Journal, Oct. 28, 1596 to Sept. 29, 1597
for 'fearful musters').

17. *of so easy...stop* such an easy, simple instrument. Cf. *Ham.* 3. 2. 353–74.

20. *what* why.

21. *anatomize* Q. 'anothomize', prob. Sh.'s spelling.

33. *peasant towns* v. G. 'town'. 'Country people
are the peculiar prey of rumour' (Shaaber).

35. *this...stone* Castles and city-walls were falling
to pieces in Sh.'s day; cf. *K. John*, 2. 1. 259; *Ric. II*,
3. 3. 52; 5. 5. 21, etc., and G. 'ragged'.

hold (Theobald) Q., F. 'hole'; an *e: d* misprint
assisted by 'the unfortunate association of "worm-
hole"' (Greg in *Aspects*, p. 159).

36. *Where* (F.) Q. 'When'—poss. minim-mis-
print; cf. MSH. pp. 106–8.

37. *crafty-sick* Cf. *1 Hen. IV*, 4. 1. 13 ff. and Hol.
iii. 522/1/39 [1961] which make no reference to 'craft',
but Sh. did not invent it; cf. Hardyng's *Chronicle* (ed.
1812, pp. 361–2):

> His father came not out of Northumberland
> But failed hym foule without witte or rede.

The posts come tiring on The exhausted posts follow
in quick succession.

I. I.

1. S.D. Camb. and mod. edd: give 'The Porter
opens the gate'; but ll. 5–6 contradict this. I follow
Singer, which renders L. Bard.'s 'Here comes the
earl' (out of sight of the Porter above) natural.

6. S.D. For 'hobbling' etc. v. ll. 145–9.

8. *should be* is likely to be; cf. *Macb.* 5. 5. 17.
stratagem v. G.

11. *bears down all* Cf. 'Thus will they [rioters] bear down all things', l. 40 of the Sh. Addition to *Sir Thomas More*, and *M.V.* 4. 1. 211.

16. *both the Blunts* Hol. tells us that Douglas slew Sir Walter B. at Shrewsbury (cf. *1 Hen. IV*, 5. 3. 1–13); Daniel (*C.W.* iii. 112), speaking of this, mentions the death of 'another Blunt which was the king's standard-bearer' (margin). Cf. the entry of 'Sir John Blunt' (3. 1. 32) for yet a third.

19. *brawn* v. G., *1 Hen. IV*, 2. 4. 107, and below 2. 4. 229.   *hulk* Cf. 2. 4. 61.

21. *fought...followed...fairly won* The alliteration reminds one of 'veni, vidi, vici'.

28. *whom* (F.) Q. 'who'.

30. *over-rode* out-rode (not 'over-take' as O.E.D. glosses). Bardolph-Umfrevile met Travers, turned him back (l. 34), and out-rode him (l. 36).

34–6. *Sir John Umfrevile...out-rode me* This, the Q. sp.-heading 'Vmfr.' at l. 161, and L. Bard.'s ignorance in 1. 3 (v. note 1. 3. 81) of the facts communicated here, indicate that the speeches assigned to L. Bard. in this scene once belonged to a character named 'Umfrevile'. No Sir John U. is known to history or chronicle; and though Hol. and Stowe mention a Sir Robert U., he belonged to the K.'s party and was with P. John at Gaultree Forest. It would seem that Sh., by a double error, re-christened this man and made him a rebel, which error, P. A. Daniel suggests (*New Sh. Soc. Trans.* 1877–9, p. 352), being pointed out to him, 'the change of name was made (though imperfectly) in order to bring the play more into agreement with the Chronicles'. For Sir R. Umfrevile's connexion with Warkworth Castle v. head-note *1 Hen. IV*, 2. 3.

48. *Staying...question* Cf. *M.V.* 4. 1. 342, 'I'll stay no longer question'. *Ha?* v. G.

50. *Of Hotspur Coldspur?* Suggested perhaps by *C.W.* iii. 114.

63. *a...usurpation* evidence of its forcible occupation.

65. *ran* Emphatic. He had not 'come' (Deighton).

70–4. *Even such...tongue* Cf. *M.V.* 5. 1. 1–15.

71. *So dull, so dead* Cf. G. 'dead' and 'so dead, so grim', *M.N.D.* 3. 2. 57.

74. *found* (*a*) felt, cf. *Meas.* 3. 1. 78; (*b*) discovered.

79. *stop...indeed* make me deaf to all things else, v. G. 'stop'.

84. *suspicion* apprehension.

88. *Tell thou...lies* To give the lie to an earl would be outrageous.

92. *Your spirit...true* Referring to 'his divination lies'. Deighton cites *1 Kings* xxii. 21–2.

96. *say so* (F.) Q. omits, prob. by accident, though it is not essential to the sense.

102. *sullen bell* Cf. *K. John*, 1. 1. 28 and note.

109–10. *Harry...earth* Cf. *Library*, June 1945, pp. 5–6 for the orig. of this unhistorical account of Hot.'s death.

114. *Being bruited once* Once it was known.

116–25. *mettle...steeled...abated...lead... heavy...arrows...field* W. Clemen, *Sh.'s Bilder* p. 95, sees here 'a series of quite dissimilar images, which nevertheless are linked by association and give birth to each other'. The series actually begins with 'fire and heat...tempered' (ll. 114–15); cf. G. 'mettle', 'abated', 'turn on', 'dull', 'heavy', etc.

123. *arrows fled* i.e. the arrows in the battle.

126. *Too* (F.) Q. 'So'—perhaps a misreading of 'to', a common sp. of 'too'.

127. *bloody* Cf. Pyrrhus 'head to foot...total gules' (*Ham.* 2. 2. 460–1).

128. *three times...king* Cf. *1 Hen. IV*, 5.3 and 5.4.

137. *In poison...physic* Cf. *Lucr.* 530–2:

> The poisonous simple sometimes is compacted
> In a pure compound; being so applied,
> His venom in effect is purified.

138. *Having...that* i.e. that, had I been well.

143. *keeper* v. G.   144. *grief...grief* v. G.

145. *nice* v. G.   148. *guard...wanton* v. G.

150. *approach* Imperative mood.

151. *time and spite* Hendiadys; cf. *Troil.* 3.3. 174, 'envious and calumniating time'.

153–60. *Let heaven kiss...the dead* Sh. expands this in the speech on Degree or Order in *Troil.* 1.3. 109–24; and what does not Pope's famous conclusion to *The Dunciad* owe to it? Cf. esp. Sh.'s string of stage metaphors with *The Dunciad*, iv. 655–6.

154. *flood* ocean. Cf. 'the bounded waters', *Troil.* 1.3. 111.

156. *To feed...act* On which human warfare is kept going from scene to scene.

159. *rude* violent, terrible.

161–2. *This strained...honour* F. omits l. 161; Q. gives it to 'Vmfr.' (v. note 1.1. 34–6), l. 162 to 'Bard.' and ll. 163 ff. to 'Mour.' Most edd. follow Capell, who agrees with Q. as to ll. 162, 163 ff. but gives l. 161 to Travers; yet Bard. stands for the orig. Umfrevile elsewhere and (as Pope saw) evidently should here. 'Bard.' was, I suggest, written in the margin of the MS. to replace 'Vmfr' without the latter being deleted; thus the Q. compositor was presented with three prefixes, which he distributed as best he could, while the prompter (F.) solved the problem by cutting out 'Vmfr' and his speech. I follow P. A. Daniel (*op. cit.* note ll. 34–6) in my distribution.

161. *strainèd passion* hysterical outburst, v. G. 'strain'.

164. *Lean on your* (F.) Q. 'Leaue on you'.

166–79. Q. omits; v. pp. 119–21. P. Maas (*R.E.S.* Jan. 1944, p. 77) assigns these 14 ll. to Travers, who has been mute since l. 48.

166–7. *cast...summed the account* For the imagery cf. note ll. 116–25.

170–1. *he walked...o'er* Cf. *1 Hen. IV*, 1.3.191–4, and below 1. 3. 33.

174. *lift him* i.e. to perilous heights (cf. l. 170).
trade v. G.

180–6. *We all...body and goods* Cf. G. 'engagéd to', 'work out'. The extended metaphor of merchant-venturing reminds us of *M.V.*, esp. 1. 1. 8–45. It echoes *1 Hen. IV*, 4. 1. 45–52, but there the image is of a game of chance.

182. *That...to one* That it was ten to one against our survival.

183–4. *ventured for...proposed, Choked* Q., F. Capell and most edd. read 'ventured, for...proposed Choked'; but 'we' can 'serve as subj. of "choked" quite as well as 'gain'" (Shaaber).

184. *Choked the respect* stifled the thought.

186. *put forth* (*a*) i.e. to sea, (*b*) invest.

188. *dare speak* (Q.) F. 'do ſpeake' which most edd. follow. He 'dares' because he 'hears *for certain*'.

189–209. *The gentle...follow him* Q. omits; v. pp. 119–21. A palpable cut which creates an ugly repetition, i.e. 'dare speak the truth' (l. 188)...'but to speak truth' (l. 210) in consecutive lines.

191. *double surety* i.e. of souls as well as of bodies.

192. *corpse* (Q.) F. 'Corpes'. Cf. *1 Hen. IV*, I. I. 43 (note).

204–5. *enlarge...stones* i.e. enhance the merit of his insurrection by making Richard out to be a martyr, v. *Ric. II*, 5. 5.

207. *bestride a bleeding land* Cf. *1 Hen. IV*, 5. 1. 122 (note).

210–11. *I knew...mind* Thus Sh. makes Mort.'s necessary exposition seem natural.

214. *make friends* gather supporters together.

1. 2.

S.D. Q. 'Enter fir Iohn alone, with his page bearing his sword and buckler.' For 'alone' (with a page following) cf. head-note 3. 1, and for 'hobbling with a stick', v. note ll. 239–41. The stick and the 'halt' are the more ludicrous that the 'crafty-sick' North. has just made a similar entry in 1. 1. Cf. *Fortunes*, p. 91. On the eighteenth-century stage the Page mimicked his master as he walked behind him (Sprague, p. 92). Pope read 'A street in London'.

1. *you giant* Underlines the appearance of the diminutive boy, the same prob. who played Maria in *Tw.Nt.* (cf. *Tw.Nt.* 1. 5. 206, note), carrying the sword and an immense buckler, as Sir John's squire.

what says:...water? The occasion for this diagnosis appears in ll. 239–41; cf. *Fortunes*, pp. 91–2.

4. *owed* v. G.

6. *sorts* i.e. doctors, princes, etc., v. G.

7. *foolish-compounded* (Pope) Q., F. omit hyphen.

clay-man (Q., F.) Being formed of clay (*Gen.* ii. 7; *Job* xxxiii. 6), man was inevitably far removed from reason. Fal. ignores 'the breath of life', which gave man his other nature.

8. *intends* (Q.) F. 'tends'. The meaning is the same.

11–12. *like a sow...but one* Cf. note l. 1 and *Tw.Nt.* 3. 2. 64, 'youngest wren of nine'.

13. *set me off* shew me off to the best advantage.

14. *mandrake* cf. 3. 2. 315 and G.

15. *to be worn...cap* It was a late Eliz. and Jacob. male fashion to wear a brooch or jewel in the hat;

cf. Linthicum, p. 221; *Tim*. 3. 2. 122; *L.L.L.* 5. 2. 615–18.

16. *manned with an agate* attended by a cameo; cf. l. 52, *Rom*. 1. 4. 55, *1 Hen. IV*, 2. 4. 69, and G. 'agate'.

18. *jewel* v. G. I conj. the omission of a second 'for' before 'the juvenal'.

19. *juvenal* v. G.   20. *fledge* = fledged.

21. *off* (Q.) F. 'on'. In Sh.'s day 'beard' included what we call whiskers, 'whiskers' meaning moustaches until the nineteenth century (v. O.E.D. 'whiskers'). Cf. *Ado*, 2. 1. 30, 'He that hath no beard is less than a man'.

22. *a face-royal* a first-rate face; with the obvious quibble, v. G. 'royal'.

23. *not a hair amiss* i.e. perfect; v. G. 'hair'.

24. *at* at the value of (cf. *Ham*. 4. 2. 58).

face-royal Quibble on 'royal' = 10*s*. piece; v. G. and *1 Hen. IV*, 1. 2. 135–6. 'It will remain', says Fal., 'a ten-bob face, for it will never lose even a sixpenn'oth of hair.'

25. *crowing* Although 'not yet fledge'.

26. *writ man* v. G.

26–7. *He may...of mine* Cf. *1 Hen. IV*, 1. 2. 17–18 for the same jest, which has, however, a different flavour to the P.'s face than behind his back; and Johnson's comment: 'At once obsequious and malignant, he satirizes in their absence those whom he lives by flattering.'

28. *Dommelton* (Q.) F. 'Dombledon'. Steevens conj. 'Dumbleton' after a place in Gloucestershire, and mod. edd. read accordingly. But 'dommel', 'dummel', or 'dumble' = a stupid, dull person (v. O.E.D. 'dummel'), and it is safer to follow Q.

29. *slops* Fal. is evidently rigging himself out; cf. 2. 1. 27–9.

33–4. *the Glutton...hotter!* i.e. Dives; cf. *1 Hen. IV*, 4. 2. 25 and *Luke* xvi. 24:

Have mercy on me, and send Lazarus, that he may dip
the tip of his finger in water, and cool my tongue; for I
am tormented in this flame.

34. *Achitophel* v. *2 Sam*. xv, xvii. 'The O.T.
counterpart of Judas Iscariot.... It was to his predilec-
tion for security and his refusal to take further chances
with Absalom that Fal. alluded' (Noble, p. 261).

35. *rascally yea-forsooth knave* (F.) Q. 'rascall: yea
forsooth knaue'. Q. prob. shows the press-corrector at
work: not understanding 'yea-forsooth' (v. G. and
1 Hen. IV, 3. 1. 247–56), he takes 'knave' to be an
intensification of 'rascal' and the 'y' to be a misprint.

37. *smooth-pates* (F.) Q. 'ſmoothy-pates'. Perhaps
a misreading of 'smoothe' (cf. 'horry' < 'horre' = hoar,
Q2 *Ham*. 4. 7. 168, and MSH. p. 112). Sleek round-
heads.

wear nothing but high shoes i.e. 'stand upon pantofles',
a common expression indicating pride; cf. *Euphues*
(Bond, i. 196, l. 24) and Linthicum, p. 253. In mod.
slang, 'stand on sixpenn'oth of ha'pence'.

38. *bunches...girdles* Typifying wealth and close-
ness; cf. Shylock's keys, *M.V.* 2. 5. 12 ff.

38–9. *through with...taking-up* got to the point of
securing their goods on straightforward credit. 'Honest'
is a good touch.

41. *offer to stop it* propose to satisfy me.

42. *two and twenty yards* Cf. Linthicum, pp. 209–
10. Slops would, in any case, require a good length,
but Falstaff's!

44. *security* over-confidence.

44–5. *for he hath...through it* A frequent Eliz.
jest on the cuckold's horn; i.e. the wealthier a citizen,
the more likely his wife to be unfaithful. Cf. Jonson,
E.M.I. 3. 6. 23–5, 'When such flowing store, Plenty
itself, falls in my wife's lap, The cornucopiae will be
mine, I know'.

46. *cannot he see* i.e. her goings-on (despite the

'lanthorn' he carries on his forehead). Lanthorns were
made of horn.

47. *Where's Bardolph?* (F.) Q. prints this before 'and
yet' (l. 45). Poss. it was written in the margin by Sh.
and wrongly inserted by the compositor (Shaaber).

48. *into Smithfield* (F.) Q. 'in Smithfield', v. G.
References to 'jades' purchased at Smithfield are
generally unfavourable; cf. Madden, p. 245.

50. *Paul's* v. G.

51. *Smithfield;* Q. 'Smithfield,'.

52. *stews* v. G. Prov.; cf. Apperson, p. 676:

Who goes to Westminster [notorious for bad characters]
for a wife, to Paul's for a man, or to Smithfield for a horse,
may meet with a whore, a knave and a jade.

53-4. *the nobleman...Bardolph* Cf. ll. 190-2 below,
and *Library*, June 1945, p. 7. The allusion is slight;
Sh. seems to assume that his audience (with its Inns-
of-Court students) will be familiar with the legend.
F.V. names Gadshill, not Bard., as the P.'s man involved. It appears from ll. 58-9, 98-9, 102-3, 130-3
that the L.C.J. had taken up the case of the Gad's
Hill robbery, and summoned Fal. to the Court of
King's Bench.

62. *some charge...Lancaster* Cf. ll. 200-1 below.

75-6. *were it...make it* even if a worse name than
rebellion could be found for it; 'can tell' = knows.

79. *setting...aside* Because knights and soldiers
cannot lie.

86. *grows to* is part of.

88. *hunt counter* v. G. i.e. you are a cur on the
wrong tack.

95. *have* (Q.) F. and most edd. 'hath'. See *R. II,*
2. 2. 20-2 n. [1961.]
age (F.) Q. 'an ague'—which smacks of press-
correction; cf. note l. 35.

96. *saltness...time* As 'opposed to the freshness of
youth' (Schmidt); cf. l. 173 'the bitterness of your

galls'. Perhaps also an insulting quibble on 'saltness' =lust (cf. *Oth*. 2. 1. 244).

time (F.) Q. 'time in you'—repetition of 'in you', l. 95.

100–1. *An't please...Wales* Fal. passes adroitly from Shrewsbury to the Welsh expedition that followed: Shrewsbury is now ancient history; ergo, what preceded it is more ancient still, while if the old judge will not attend to talk of his own health, he can hardly refuse, as a loyal subject, to speak of the King's. N.B. The first mention in Pt. 2 of the K.'s failing health; cf. *1 Hen. IV* 1. 1. 1.

lordship (F.) Q. 'lorſhip'.

105. *apoplexy* Hol. iii. 541.

108–15. *This apoplexy...deafness* Acc. to Bucknill (*Medical Knowledge of Sh.* 1860, p. 149), this diagnosis is correct.   110. *tingling* v. G.

111–12. *What* why.   *as it is* what it will.

113–15. *It hath...deafness* Cf. *1 Hen. IV* Introd. p. xxiii.

it=the old gen. form.

grief...study...Galen...deafness v. G.

118. *Very well* etc. Q. heads this *Old*=Oldcastle. Generally taken as evidence that the MS. of *2 Hen. IV* was in being before Old. was changed to Fal.; but, as Hart[1] (pp. 184–5) points out, this prefix may be 'ascribed to the subconscious memory of the poet' in the act of creation just as easily as to negligence in going over the MS. to alter the names, while the prefixes in this scene are most variable in form.

Very well 'I hear perfectly what you say' (Vaughan).

121. *punish...by the heels* commit you to prison, with irons on your ankles.

124. *poor as Job* Prov.; cf. Apperson, p. 505 and *M.W.W.* 5. 5. 151.

125. *patient* Taking up 'physician' (l. 123).

---

[1] *op. cit.* on p. 120 above.

126. *in respect of poverty* i.e. since I can't afford to pay your fines (or bribes).

128. *make...scruple* hesitate to believe. Quibble on 'scruple' the apothecary's weight, linking up with 'potion' and 'prescriptions'.

131. *for your life* of a capital character.

133. *land service* v. G. Pointing to his sword and buckler. A jest for the lawyers in the audience.

136–7. *He that...in less* Perhaps some lost jest here; he speaks 'of infamy as if it were a material in which he clothed himself' (Delius).

141. *slenderer* (F.) Q. 'flender'.

143–4. *the fellow...dog* 'I do not understand this joke' (Johnson). Nor has anyone else. Is it a reference to some representation (perhaps on the stage) of blind Tobit, led by a dog and stumbling (v. *Tobit*, xi. 10)? *M.V.* 2. 2. 62–3 is an echo of *Tobit*, v. 18.

147. *gilded over* Cf. *1 Hen. IV*, 5. 4. 157. The P.'s promise to 'gild' Fal.'s lie has apparently been kept; cf. *Fortunes*, p. 89.

148. *o'er-posting* v. G.

151–2. *wake...wolf* Prov. A variant of 'let sleeping dogs lie', v. Apperson, p. 578.

153. *as smell* F. 'as to fmell' *a fox* i.e. the L.C.J.; cf. l. 202.

154. *What* Why, cf. l. 111.

as a candle Cf. *Ric. II*, 1. 3. 223; *Macb.* 5. 5. 23; *3 Hen. VI*, 2. 6. 1.

156. *wassail candle* v. G.

tallow v. G. and *1 Hen. IV*, 2. 4. 108. Fal. has enough fat in him to burn as long as there is sack in the world to drink.

157. *wax* Obvious pun. *approve* prove, establish.

158. *on your* (F.) Q. 'in your'.

159. *effect* accompaniment.

160. *gravy* v. G. and *Fortunes*, p. 29; i.e. every hair has its drop of sweat; cf. 4. 3. 12–13 and *1 Hen. IV*, 2. 2. 106, 'lards the lean earth'.

162. *ill angel* bad coin; v. G. 'angel'.

163. *light* Because false or clipped.

164–5. *take me without weighing* accept me as true gold without testing me on the scales.

165. *cannot go* (*a*) am not current, (*b*) am no walker; cf. 2. 4. 161 and 1 *Hen. IV*, 2. 2. 12–13.

165–6. *go...I cannot tell. Virtue* Q. 'go. I cannot tell, virtue', F. 'go: I cannot tell. Vertue'. Edd. follow F., but Q., which makes 'I cannot tell' the preface to Fal.'s moralizing, gives a much easier reading (cf. Shaaber). *Virtue*=manliness; cf. 1 *Hen. IV*, 2. 4. 115.

166–7. *costermongers' times* (Q, without apostrophe.) F. 'coftor-mongers'; Capell and mod. edd. read 'costermonger times'. This peddling period.

167. *berrord* Q. 'Berod', F. 'Beare-herd'. I use for consistency the sp. found in *Ado* (v. *Ado*, G.). To lead tame bears needed the kind of 'valour' which inspired respect in old women and poltroons like Slender; cf. *M.W.W* 1. 1. 277–81.

168. *pregnancy* readiness of wit, a quality desirable in statesmen, soldiers and—waiters.

170. *this age shapes them, are* (F.) Q. 'his age fhapes the one'. Prob. 'thē are' misread as 'the one' (Kellner); cf. MSH. p. 327 and notes 1. 3. 28 ('on' misp. 'and'), 58 ('one' misp. 'on'), 71 ('are' misp. 'and'). *shapes* v. G.

173. *livers...galls* v. G. Cf. *Euphues* (Bond, i. 192, ll. 36–7), 'Doe you measure the hotte assaultes of youth by the colde skirmishes of age?'

173–4. *in the vaward* Lit. in advance of; so, a little past. Falstaffian idiom for 'in early middle age'.

174. *wags too* i.e. not only boys but naughty boys.

176–7. *written down...characters* v. G., quibbling on 'scroll'.

177–80. *moist eye...wit single* Cf. *Ham.* 2. 2. 198–201; v. G. 'dry', 'single'.

181. *blasted with antiquity* blighted with age

183–5. *I was born...belly* i.e. I've looked old since birth.

184. *something a* For 'something' as an adv. cf. 4. 2. 80.

185–6. *hallooing...anthems* 'Fal. has lost his voice in putting it to two unexceptionable uses—hallooing to the hounds (or in battle?) and singing anthems' (Shaaber). For Fal. as chorister, v. *1 Hen. IV*, 2. 4. 129.

188–9. *caper...marks* Poss. allusion to the caperings of Kempe, who later (1600) danced from London to Norwich, and after that attempted to dance over the Alps. Cf. *Fortunes*, pp. 124–5, and note 2. 4. 18.

190 ff. *For the box of the ear* etc. Cf. ll. 53–4. A link with *F.V.*, v. *Library*, June 1945, p. 7. Fal. introduces the topic to 'approve' his 'judgement and understanding'.

190. *ear* Q. 'yeere'. Cf. Jespersen, *Mod. Eng. Gram.* i. 13.332, wh. quotes the sp. from Thackeray!

192. *checked* v. G.

193–4. *marry, not...sack* Craig (ap. Arden) suggests an 'aside'. For 'old sack' v. note *1 Hen. IV*, 1. 2. 3–4.

202. *Yea...wit for it* Perhaps an aside also. Fal.'s suspicions, not quite borne out by ll. 60–3 above, are to be taken seriously, since they furnish a dramatic explanation for the almost complete separation in Part 2 of Fal. from the P. Cf. *Fortunes*, p. 98.

203–4. *But look...hot day* i.e. 'If it is too hot for him to exert himself, there will be little hope of... peace' (Deighton).

205. *two shirts* The number which the clown in *F.V.* (sc. 10) takes to the wars.

206. *day, and* F. 'day, if'.

207. *any thing but a bottle* Cf. *1 Hen. IV*, 5. 3. 51–4.

208. *spit white* i.e. spit. Fal. spat white as an effect of toping. Cf. Lyly's *Mother Bombie*, 3. 2. 47–8 (Bond, iii. 198), 'They haue sod...[their livers] in sacke

these fortie yeeres. That makes them spit white broth as they doo'.

208–9. *There is...thrust upon it* i.e. at the slightest sign of danger to the country I am sent to deal with it.

210–16. *but it was...motion* Omitted by F., poss., as Chambers suggests (*Wm. Sh.* i. 380), because it appeared 'anti-patriotic', cf. p. 116.

scoured to nothing=worn to a frazzle.

217. *be honest* behave yourself.

219. *a thousand pound* For Fal.'s preoccupation with this sum, v. *Fortunes*, p. 126.

220. *to...me forth* to fit me out.

222. *impatient...crosses* 'impatient' reflects back to 'patient' (l. 125); for 'crosses' v. G. and note 2.2.93.

224. *fillip...beetle* v. G. 'beetle'. 'The humour lies in the suggested use of a three-man beetle to produce so insignificant an application of force' (Arden).

227. *pinches* v. G.

227–8. *both...curses* both stages of life have their own curses which anticipate mine; v. G. 'degree'.

230. *What money...purse?* Suggested by ll. 219–22.

231. *Seven groats and two pence*=2s. 6d., v. G. 'groat'.

233. *lingers it out* protracts the disease.

234–8. *Go bear this letter...chin* The letter to the P. is read at 2.2. 117 ff., those to Lancaster and Westmoreland no doubt concerned the 'charge' (l. 62 above), and Mrs Ursula's was, I suspect, a request for a loan.

238. *of my chin* (Q.) F. 'on my chin'.

239–41. *A pox...toe...halt* Here is the reason for Fal.'s inquiry of the doctor (ll. 1–5), and for the limp I give him in my S.D. Is the disease one of age or youth (cf. ll. 225–8)? He cannot tell.

242. *colour* v. G.

pension Apparently the 'reward' for his 'day's service at Shrewsbury' (cf. *Fortunes*, pp. 90–2; note *1 Hen. IV*, 5.4. 161).

1. 3.

S.D. Q. 'Enter th' Archbiſhop, Thomas Mowbray (Earle Marſall) the Lord Haſtings, Fauconbridge, and Bardolſe.' This S.D. is clearly copied from a list given by Hol. (iii. 529; Stone, p. 151) of Northumberland's fellow-conspirators in 1405; but it was not noticed that acc. to Hol. of those named only Mowbray was asso- ciated with the Archb. himself. L. Bardolph fled to Scotland with North. in 1405 and was slain with him in 1408 at Bramham Moor; while Hastings and Fauconbridge, who app. belonged to another force, were executed at Durham (with Sir John Colevile). Thus, though dramatically out of place in 1. 1 (cf. note 1. 1. 34–6), L. Bardolph belongs historically to that scene, not this (v. note l. 81 below). N.B. 'Faucon- bridge' was copied from the list, but not made use of in the text (cf. Chambers, *Wm. Sh.* i. 231). Pope read 'York'; to which Theobald added 'The Archbishop's Palace'. For the theme of this scene cf. the discussion of the rebels in *1 Hen. IV*, 4. 3.

12. *supplies* v. G.

14. *incensèd...of injuries* kindled by his wrongs.

15. *The question then* etc. L. Bard. makes no reference to his recent visit to North.; cf. notes l. 81 and 1. 1. 34–6.

21–4. *Till...admitted* Q. omits; cf. pp. 119 ff. Perhaps 'a theme so bloody-faced' attracted the censor's pen. The cut leaves ll. 25 ff. in the air.

26. *cause* (Q.) F. 'caſe'; v. G. 'cause'=case.

27. *lined* v. G.

28. *Eating...promise* Cf. *Ham.* 3. 2. 91–2, 'I eat the air, promise-crammed'.

on (F.) Q. 'and'. Cf. note 1. 2. 170.

30. *much smaller* As it turned out.

32. *proper to* v. G.

33. *winking...destruction* Cf. 1. 1. 170–1, and note.

36–55. *Yes, if...or else* Q. omits; v. pp. 119 ff.

Ll. 49–50 would seem dangerous matter in times of unrest.

36–7. *Yes if...instant action* F. prints "action: a" (l. 37) and "hope: As" (l. 38). The chief crux of the text and much emended, the latest solution being Mackail's (*T.L.S.* corr. 30. 9. 26) which explains "indeed" as a verb. I adopt Alexander's punctuation (*The Tudor Sh.*, 1951); and, accepting the explanation of Miss Dodds (*Mod. Lang. Rev.*, LXII, 378), I paraphrase: "Yes, I agree, if we could even hope as much from the present war, now afoot and just about to come to battle, as one can hope from the buds of spring which are as like to get frost bitten as to yield fruit" [1952].

40. *despair* Subj. of 'gives warrant' understood.

41–62. *When we...winter's tyranny* An elaboration of the parable, *Luke* xiv. 28–30. E. I. Fripp (*Richard Quyny*, pp. 111–12) sees an echo of the rebuilding of New Place, Stratford, wh. Sh. bought on 4 May 1597. Cf. 4. 1. 109–10.

43. *figure of the house* Prob. a quibble, v. G.

47. *at least* at worst.

55. *opposite* = (*a*) the resources of our opponents, (*b*) the arguments against building.

56. *in paper* only on paper.

58. *one* (F.) Q. 'on'. A Sh. sp.; cf. note 1. 2. 170.

59. *through* (F.) Q. 'thorough'.

60. *part-created cost* half-built property.

61. *naked subject* = (*a*) exposed object, (*b*) helpless victim.

66. *a body* (F.) Q. 'fo, body'—perhaps the 'correction' of a misspelling.

70. *as the times do brawl* so troublous is the age.

71. *Are* (F.) Q. 'And'. Cf. note 1. 2. 170.

against the French Acc. to Hol. (iii. 528; not in Stone), shortly before the outbreak of the Archb.'s rebellion, the K. 'hearing of the preparation made for warre by the Frenchmen, levied fore thousand men which he sent unto Calis' under the command of P. Thomas.

74–5. *coffers...emptiness* Prov.; cf. Apperson, p. 182 and *Hen. V*, 4. 4. 70.

78. *need* Common for 'needs' or 'needeth' in 16th c. (O.E.D. v²); cf. 4. 1. 114. *be* (F.) Q. 'to be'.

78–80. *If he should...fear that* (F.) Q. (as prose) 'If he...fo, French and Welch he leaues his backe vnarmde, they baying...feare that'. Johnson notes: 'These lines, which were evidently printed [in Q.] from an interlined copy not understood, are properly regulated in [F.]'; and Shaaber suggests that Sh. first wrote 'they baying', realized that 'they' was obscure, and substituted 'the French and Welch' for it above or beside the line.

81. *Who is...hither?* 'L. Bard. is ignorant...that the force...is led by P. John; yet in sc. i he was present when Morton informed North. of this fact' (P. A. Daniel, *op. cit.* p. 282; v. note 1. 1. 34–6).

82. *Duke of Lancaster* Though P. John was born at Lan. and was therefore P. John of Lan., P. Henry of Monmouth, his elder brother, was actually Duke of Lan. The error, which recurs at 4. 1. 28, was traced by Ritson to Stow's account of the coronation of Henry IV (*Annals*, ed. 1592, p. 513. The passage does not appear in Howe's ed. of 1614).

84. *is substituted* i.e. acts for the king.

'*gainst* (F.) Q. 'againſt'. 'Compositor's unconscious substitution of the uncontracted for the contracted form' (Shaaber).

85–108. *Let us on...worst* Q. omits; v. pp. 119–21.

95–9. *Thou...vomit up* Cf. *Prov.* xxvi. 11; *2 Peter* ii. 22; *Hen. V*, 3. 7. 68–9, and Spurgeon's *Sh.'s Imagery*, pp. 195–9.

provok'st...up alludes to the taking of emetics (Deighton). For 'common' v. G.

103–5. *threw'st dust...Bolingbroke* Cf. *Ric. II*, 5. 2. 1–40.

108. *Past...worst* F. prints in italics and with

inverted commas denoting a maxim or 'sentence', cf.
Simpson, *Sh. Punct.* pp. 101–3.

109. *Shall we...set on?* Q. assigns to 'Bish.'—a
relic of the previous speech (85–108) deleted in that
text.

110. *time's subjects* the slaves of circumstance; cf.
note *1 Hen. IV*, 5. 4. 81–3, and G. 'time'.

2. 1.

S.D. Q. 'Enter Hosteffe of the Tauerne, and an
Officer or two'. F. 'Enter Hosteffe, with two Officers,
Fang, and Snare'. For 'or two' cf. 2. 4 head-note, and
Q2 *Ham.* 2. 1. S.D. Capell gave Fang a 'Boy' un-
necessarily, and edd. follow. Pope read 'London'
and Theobald 'A street'.

1–6. *Master...Master* 'A title not warranted by
their rank' (Arden). For 'Fang' and 'Snare' v. G.
I suggest that these parts were 'doubled' with Bullcalf
and Feeble in 3. 2, and the Beadles in 5. 4.

1. *entered* Before arresting for debt notice of the
alleged cause had to be entered at the Counter, or
Sheriff's court, in the Poultry.

5. *Sirrah* etc. The delay in Snare's entry was perhaps designed to draw attention to an extraordinary
figure and get-up.

13–19. *stabbed...foin...thrust* Equivocal; cf. G.
'stab', 2. 4. 230, Jonson, *E.M.I.* 4. 4. 15, and ll. 114–
19 below.

21. *fist* 'grip' (Arden), not 'punch' (O.E.D.); cf.
Cor. 4. 5. 131.

22. *vice* (F.) Q. 'view'—'vice' misread 'vue';
cf. MSH. pp. 106–8.

23. *undone* ruined.

by his going i.e. to the wars. Cf. *Fortunes*, p. 101.

24. *infinitive* Quick.'s language, like Dogberry's, was
not mere invention on Sh.'s part; similar blunders were
constantly on the lips of ill-educated persons in his day.

Cf. Wilson, *Arte of Rhetorique*, 1560 (p. 164, ed. Tudor and Stuart Lib.) for examples.

26. *continuantly* (F.) Q. 'continually'. Blunder for 'incontinently'=at once; v. p. 117.

26–7. *saving your manhoods* v. G. An apology for mentioning something unsavoury. The jest is that Pie Corner, where the cooks' stalls stood, was a particularly savoury spot. Cf. Jonson, *Alchemist*, 1. 1. 25–6.

27. *a saddle* Being in Smithfield (v. G.), Pie-corner was also a centre for saddlers (v. Sugden).

indited=invited (blunder).

28. *Lubber's head* i.e. Libbard's (=leopard's) head. Another of Quickly's blunders. Since the 'libbard's head' was often shown upon the elbow or knee of garments (v. Cotgrave, *Masquine*, and *L.L.L.* 5. 2. 545 (note)), it made an apt sign for a silk-merchant's shop (cf. Arden).

Lumbert A common sp. of 'Lombard' (O.E.D.). Lombard St. was the centre of bankers and mercers, mostly foreign, as the name suggests.

Smooth v. G. Perhaps more accommodating than Master Dommelton (1. 2. 28).

30–1. *brought...answer* i.e. taken before the sheriff.

31. *A hundred mark*=£66. 13s. 4d.

a long one i.e. a long mark or score.

42. *whose mare's dead?* i.e. what's the fuss? Cf. Apperson, 'mare', 7.

44. *Sir John* (F.) Q. omits.

48. S.D. taken from Capell.

49. *bastardly* 'A portmanteau word, blending "bastard" and "dastardly"' (Arden).

50–2. *honey-suckle...honey-seed* i.e. 'homicidal' and 'homicide'.

55. *rescue* v. G. 'Rescues' of arrested persons were not uncommon in the London streets at this time; cf. *Err.* 4. 4. 109–10.

57–8. *wot...wot ta?* Cf. G. 'wot', 'ta' and *Ham.* 5. 1. 269 note. *do!*=come on! *hempseed* v. G.

59. *Away, you scullion* F 3 and many edd., including Globe, assign this to Fal.

65. *what* why. Cf. 1. 2. 111, 154.

68. *hang'st* (F.) Q. 'hang'ft thou'—which throws the metre out.

73-4. *for all, all* (F.) Q. 'for al'.

78-9. *I think...I...get up* Usually explained as referring to the gallows ('the two-legged mare', v. O.E.D. 'mare', 2a), but as Malone notes an equivocal allusion is more apt to the context; cf. G. 'Galloway nag', *Cymb.* 1. 4. 114-15, and Jonson, *Volpone*, 4. 6. 24.

80. *Fie!* (F.) Q. omits. Cf. p. 116.

81. *good temper* kindly disposition.

86-7. *swear...upon...goblet* 'The most fitting "book" for Fal. to kiss' (Lobban).

87. *Dolphin chamber* Cf. *1 Hen. IV*, 2. 4. 26, note.

88. *sea-coal fire* v. G. 'sea-coal' and *M.W.W.* 1. 4. 7-8.

89. *Wheeson* v. G. Poss. a Sh. spelling.

90. *a singing-man at Windsor* Earle's character of 'The Common Singing-men in Cathedral Churches' (*Microcosmographie*, 1628, no. 69) shows the low reputation they had in this age. Cf. *Fortunes*, p. 104.

93. *Keech* v. G. In *Hen. VIII*, 1. 1. 55 the name is given to Wolsey, the butcher's son.

95. *mess* v. G.   96. *whereby* whereupon.

100. *madam* i.e. 'my lady', instead of 'gossip'.

102. *book-oath* Cf. *1 Hen. IV*, 2. 4. 48-9, note.

103. *mad* (F.) Q. 'made'. Cf. *1 Hen. IV*, 2. 4. 482, note.

104. *says...like you* i.e. claims you as the father of her child. Cf. *Fortunes*, p. 102.

105. *in good case* well-to-do.

106. *distracted her* sent her mad.

110. *cause* v. G.

112-13. *level consideration* seeing straight.

113–15. *you have...person* (Q.) F. 'I know you ha' practis'd vpon the easie-yeelding spirit of this woman'—a bowdlerizing paraphrase; cf. note l. 118 and p. 116.

118. *done with* (Q.) F. 'done'. All edd. follow F. but the 'with' makes all the difference, and retorts Fal.'s slanders upon himself.

120. *current* genuine (quibble on 'sterling').

123. *curtsy* (Q., F.) v. G. Most edd. read 'courtesy'.

124–5. *my humble...suitor* with all due respect, I am asking no favours (but demanding rights).

128–9. *You speak...reputation* You talk as though the K.'s commission entitled you to do what is wrong. But make amends for the sake of your reputation.

131. S.D. Q. 'enter a messenger'. Cf. *Names of the Characters*, 'Gower', p. 125.

138. *By this...tread on* A portmanteau oath: 'by this heavenly light', 'by this ground I tread on'.

142. *Glasses...drinking* i.e. glass is the only fashionable thing to drink out of. For its taking the place of plate at this period, v. *Sh. Eng.* i. 14; ii. 139–40.

143–4. *drollery* v. G.

story of the Prodigal Cf. *Fortunes*, pp. 34–5.

144. *the German hunting* i.e. of the wild boar; cf. *Cym.* 2. 5. 16.

German (F.) Q. 'Iarman'. A Sh. sp.; cf. *More Sh. Add.* l. 128; *M.W.W.* 4. 5. 80 note.

waterwork cheap imitation tapestry, v. G. and *Sh. Eng.* ii. 129–30. Ph. Henslowe was giving 6*d.* a yd. for such painted cloth in 1592 (Greg, *Henslowe's Diary*, i. 6).

145. *bed-hangers* (Q.) F. 'bed-hangings'—wh. all edd. follow; v. G.

146. *tapestries* (F.) Q. 'tapestrie'.

ten pound (F.) Q. 'x.l.' A large advance on the 30*s.* of l. 101.

148. *wench* 'A familiar or endearing form of address; used chiefly in addressing a daughter, wife or sweetheart' (O.E.D. 1 c).

wash thy face 'The poor dame has been crying' (Rolfe).

148–9. *draw the action* i.e. withdraw it. How cleverly he slips that in!

151. *set on* v. G. I.e. 'One so generous as you are could not have thought of such a thing on your own account' (Deighton).

152–3. *twenty nobles* i.e. about £6. 10s.; v. G. 'noble'.

155–6. *you'll be a fool still* 'you'll lose the chance of having me as your husband for the sake of a few pounds' (Deighton).

161. *hook on* stick to her, i.e. to extract the loan.

162. *Doll Tearsheet* v. *Names of the Characters*, p. 126.

164. *No more...her* He agrees as if conferring a favour. S.D. Q. 'exit hosteſſe and ſergeant' (l. 161).

165–78. *I have heard* etc. For this episode cf. *Fortunes*, p. 103.

168. *to-night* (Q.) F. 'laſt night'—wh. most edd. follow; the meaning is the same, v. G.

169. *Basingstoke* (F.) Q. 'Billingſgate'. A remarkable misprint, not easy to explain; cf. Greg, *Aspects*, p. 132 (top).

186–8. *Sir John...you go*. Q. prints as verse. Cf. G. 'being', 'take up'. An Eliz. officer had to raise his own company by impressment, wh. his commission empowered him to do; cf. *Fortunes*, pp. 84–5.

193. *if they...not* if they are unseemly.

195. *grace* style.

195–6. *tap for tap...fair* blow for blow and so part on good terms (with a suggestion of 'tit for tat is fair play').

2. 2.

S.D. Q. 'Enter the Prince, Poynes, ſir Iohn Ruſſel, with other'. F. 'Enter Prince Henry, Pointz, Bardolfe, and Page'. Fleay (*Wm. Sh.* p. 199), A. E. Morgan

(pp. 5 f.), and Chambers (*Wm. Sh.* i. 382) link this
with the prefix 'Ross.' at *1 Hen. IV*, 2. 4. 171–7 (Q.)
and with the names 'Haruey' and 'Rossill' wh. stand
for Bardolf and Peto in Q. and F. at 1. 2. 156. The
F. S.D. in which 'Sir John Russell and other' becomes
'Bardolfe and Page' seems to support this. Shaaber will
have none of it and takes Sir John Russell as 'another
one of those supernumerary characters, a member of
the entourage of the prince, wh. Sh.'s imagination
created so readily and then forgot to write a part for',
while, since Bard. does not enter until l. 67, he regards
the F. S.D. as 'a massed entry' characteristic of the
scribe responsible for that text (v. his note on p. 132).
But we get 'massed entries' in Q. (v. head-note 5. 2),
and it is difficult not to believe that when Sh. named
'Sir John Russell' as 'a member of the entourage of the
prince' he had Bard. in mind. Bard.'s prototype in
F.V. was almost certainly a knight.

Pope heads the sc. 'The same [i.e. London]. Another
street'. But the privacy of the P.'s house seems more
suitable to the dialogue. For 'newly arrived from
Wales' cf. the references to weariness, thirst and hard
labour (l. 28), and 1. 2. 100–1; 2. 1. 133–4, 167–70;
2. 4. 292. For the significance of the sc. v. *Fortunes*,
pp. 76–7.

3–4. *had* should have.

weariness...blood i.e. that a prince was beyond the
jurisdiction of fatigue, v. G. 'attach'.

5. *discolours* brings a blush to.

7. *small beer* Cf. *1 Hen. IV*, 1. 3. 233 (note).

8. *loosely studied* v. G.

13–15. *What a disgrace...to-morrow!* Cf. *K. John*,
1. 1. 186–9. It was a common practice with ill-
mannered gentry, often referred to in contemporary
drama, to forget, or affect to forget, their humbler
acquaintances.

16. *viz.* (F.) Q. 'with'. Cf. MSH. p. 112.

17. *peach-coloured* 'a deep, fresh pink....Allusions

to it in the drama are in connexion with gallants and
would-be courtiers' (Linthicum, p. 40).

once (Q.) F. 'ones'—a common sp. of 'once' in
the sixteenth and seventeenth centuries (v. O.E.D.)

bear i.e. in mind.

18. *for superfluity* as an extra.

19–21. *for it is...racket there* 'Whenever you have
at least two shirts (one to play in, another to change
into) you're sure to be found at the tennis-court'
(Shaaber). For 'tennis' v. G. The quibble in 'racket'
is obvious.

22–5. *the rest...kingdom* i.e. the spare shirt has
gone to make baby-clothes for illegitimate children;
v. G. 'low countries', 'holland'. The relation between
Holland and the rest of the Low Countries was, of
course, one of the outstanding questions of the age.

22. *thy low* (F.) Q. 'the low'. *have made a shift
to* (F.) Q. omits; v. G. 'make'.

23–7. *and God knows...strengthened* F. omits, as
both blasphemous and indecent; cf. p. 116.

24. *bawl out* (Pope) Q. 'bal out', i.e. bawl out of;
cf. Franz, § 540.

inherit his kingdom i.e. by dying (and so save the
cost of their maintenance), alluding to *Matt.* xviii. 3.

25–6. *not in the fault* not to blame (and therefore
to be kept alive).

26–7. *kindreds...strengthened* i.e. the number of
your offspring mounts up; v. G. 'kindred'.

29–31. *Tell me...time is?* Poins turns the conversation to the inheriting of another kind of kingdom.

32. *one thing* something; cf. 4. 1. 183.

33–4. *an excellent good thing* e.g. that 'the old
man' is dead.

37–8. *I stand...tell* your piece of news won't
bowl me over; v. G. 'push' and *1 Hen. IV*, 3. 2. 66.

39–42. *Marry...indeed too* First telling him what
he expects to hear, Hal then tries the truth on him,
in a bantering tone. *indeed*=in very truth.

45. *book* v. G. The Devil's account-book; cf. 4. 2. 17.

46. *Let the end...man* Prov.; cf. Apperson, 'end' 3.

48–9. *hath in reason...sorrow* has made it impossible for me to display any decent feeling on the matter. 'Ostentation' (v. G.) is contrasted with 'inwardly' (l. 47); cf. also G. 'reason'.

53. *hypocrite* 'An allusion perhaps to the saying of Publius Syrus "Haeredis fletus sub persona risus est" (Aulus Gellius, *Noctes*, xvii, xiv)...quoted in Montaigne's *Essays*, i. 37, and in Jonson, *Volpone*, 1. 5. 22–3' (Arden).

55. *blessed* lucky.

58. *accites* A quibble, v. G. Poins's 'thought' is represented as a magistrate ('most worshipful') sitting in judgement on Hal's conduct.

60. *so lewd* so 'fast'. Cf. *1 Hen. IV*, 3. 2. 13.

62. *And to thee* The quiet bitterness of this escapes Poins. It is Hal's last word to him in private.

65. *second brother* Younger sons were proverbially hard-up.

65–6. *a proper...hands* a fine strapping fellow.

67. S.D. For 'in fantastic apparel' cf. 'transformed...Ape' (l. 70), and 1. 2. 17. From ll. 73 ff. it seems that Bard. is slightly 'lit up' at this entry.

73. *Come, you virtuous ass*, etc. Theobald and later edd. unwarrantably transfer this to Bard. and make him address the Page. But, as Shaaber notes, the blushing refers to Bard.'s face (cf. *1 Hen. IV*, 2. 4. 308–12), and the Page's speech seconds Poins's sally.

76. *to get...maidenhead* A common jest.

77. *e'en now* (Camb.) Q. 'enow' F. 'euen now'.

77–8. *through...lattice*, i.e. from the ale-house, where he had been drinking his pottle; v. G. 'red lattice'.

80. *new petticoat* (F.) Q. 'peticote'. Adams (*ap.* Shaaber) shows that 'red petticoat' is being used in 1604 for a woman of ill fame; cf. note *1 Hen. IV*, 1. 2. 11, 'flame-coloured taffeta'.

82. *profited* i.e. at Falstaff's school; v. G.

83. *upright rabbit* baby rabbit on two legs; cf. G. 'rabbit'.

rabbit F. 'Rabbet', Q. 'rabble'.

85. *Althaea's dream* Hecuba 'dreamt she was delivered of a firebrand' before the birth of Paris; Althaea at the birth of Meleager was told that he would live as long as the brand on the fire was not consumed. Whether or not Sh. is responsible for the confusion, it is a natural one and at least argues some knowledge on the part of the Page. The references to Hecuba's dream in *Troil.* 2. 2. 110, and to Althaea in *2 Hen. VI*, 1. 1. 234, are correct.

87. *Althaea* Q. 'Althear'.

93. *cankers* Cf. *Ham.* 1. 3. 39, 'The canker galls the infants of the spring'.

to preserve thee Alluding to the cross on Eliz. silver coinage; cf. G. 'cross' and 1. 2. 222.

94. *him be hanged* (F.) Q. omits 'be'. [1961.]

95. *shall have wrong* will be robbed of its due.

99. *with good respect* most politely. Ironical comment on Bard.'s offhand delivery.

100. *martlemas* i.e. flesh illimitable; v. G. and *Fortunes*, p. 30.

102–3. *the immortal...dies not* Alluding to *Matt.* ix. 12.

105. *holds his place* makes the most of his rank, v. G. 'place'.

106. S.D. Cf. note l. 117.

108. *must know that* has to be told he's a knight.

112. *takes...conceive* pretends not to understand.

113. *ready...cap* quick as politeness from a man who wants to borrow money.

borrower's (Warburton) Q., F. 'borrowed'. Cf. *Tim.* 2. 1. 18–19 and v. p. 117. Perhaps a pen-slip on Sh.'s part.

115–16. *or they...Japhet* even if they have to go back to the father of all Europeans: cf. *Gen.* x. 2–5.

116. *But the letter* (Q.) F. 'But to the letter'.

117–32. *Sir John...all Europe* Q. gives '*Prince*' the reading of the letter down to 'brevity' and, though omitting the prefix before l. 124, clearly intended the rest as his, since ll. 133–4 are given to '*Poynes*'. F. omits this last prefix and heads l. 107 '*Poin. Letter*' wh. led Hanmer and all later edd. to assign the whole to Poins; Arden, which I follow, alone reverting to Q.

The letter, dispatched at 1.2.235, is at once a greeting to Hal on returning from Wales (1.2.100–1) and a farewell as Fal. leaves for York; the encounter in 2.4 being unexpected. For the impudence of its style and tone, v. *Fortunes*, pp. 105–6 and cf. *1 Hen. VI*, 4.1.50 ff.

119. *certificate* licence or patent, issued by a sovereign or nobleman to one of inferior rank. For the style of address cf. the patents cited in Chambers, *Eliz. Stage*, ii. 56; iv. 265–6.

124–5. *I commend...leave thee* Reads like a parody of that 'honourable Roman' Caesar's 'veni, vidi, vici', which Fal. himself quotes at 4.3.41. Cf. note 1.1.21.

I commend me to thee=kind regards! A polite message to an equal (cf. 1.2.222–3; 3.2.62).

I commend thee=I think well of you. A piece of effrontery.

127. *Repent* etc. Pious wishes were common in letters of the age.

at idle times 'when you have nothing better to do' (Deighton).

129–30. *Thine...usest him* 'Thine to use' was a common epistolary formula, and 'by yea and no' (cf. *Matt*. v. 34–7) a puritan expletive much laughed at. Combining them, Fal. implies '"Yours" if you use me well, not yours if you use me badly' (Deighton).

130. *familiars* (F.) Q. 'family'.

135. *That's...his words* i.e. that is to illustrate

the proverbial 'eat one's words' many times over.
'Twenty' is indefinite (cf. 2. 4. 353).

140. *play...time* fool away our life; v. G. 'time'
(ii), cf. *Ant.* 3. 2. 60.

141. *the wise* i.e. like the angels; cf. *Ham.* 4. 3. 47,
'I see a cherub that sees them', and *Meas.* 2. 2. 122–3.

144–5. *the old boar...frank* The nearest Sh. comes
to speaking directly of the Boar's Head Tavern; v. G.
'frank' and *1 Hen. IV*, 2. 4. S.D. *F.V.* calls it 'the
olde Tauerne in Eastcheape'.

148. *Ephesians...of the old church* Cf. *M.W.W.*
4. 5. 16 and 'Corinthian', *1 Hen. IV*, 2. 4. 11 (G.).
'An irreverent allusion to "the prime church of
Ephesus" whose practice in matters of church government was regarded among Puritans as authoritative',
v. Middleton, *Family of Love*, 1. 3. 113; "I cannot
find that either plays or players were allowed in the
prime church of Ephesus by the elders"' (Arden). Cf.
Rev. ii. 1–5 and what St Paul hints of the Ephesians
before their conversion (*Eph.* v. 3–8); cf. also *Sir
John Oldcastle*, 4. 3. 138 (Tucker Brooke, p. 153),
'I am neither heretike nor puritane, but of the old
church: ile sweare, drinke ale, kisse a wench', etc.

152. *pagan* prostitute.   153. *proper* respectable.

155. *heifers* Q. 'Heicfors', cf. 'Heycfer', *Wint.* (F.)
1. 2. 124 < Mid. Eng. 'hekfere'.

158. *shadow* v. G.   165. *road* v. G. and note
l. 166–7.

166–7. *as common...London* i.e. as the Great North
Road. Skeat (*ap.* Shaaber) cites *Piers Plowman*, iii.
127, 'Heo (=she) is...As comuyn as the cart-wei to
knaves and to alle'.

172. *descension* (Q.) F. 'declension'. Cf. the theol.
'Descension into Hell'.

173. *Jove's case* Cf. *2 Hen. VI*, 4. 1. 48; *M.W.W.*
5. 5. 3 ff.   *prince* (F.) Q. 'pince'.

175. *the purpose...folly* 'a foolish purpose requires
as foolish a behaviour' (Schmidt).

2.3.

S.D. Capell read 'Warkworth. Before the Castle'.
Cf. *Ind*. S.D.

2. *give way* v. G.   3. *times* v. G.

4. *Percy* North. is 'the Percy'.

7. *at pawn* at stake.

11. *endeared* (F.) Q. 'endeere'. Cf. MSH. p. 109;
v. G.

18. *stuck upon him,* v. G. 'stick'.

20. *move* Like the planets.

21–2. *the glass...themselves* Cf. *Ham*. 3.1.156
and G. 'glass'.

23–45. *He had...Monmouth's grave* Q. omits; cf.
pp. 119 ff. Schücking suggests that the description
recalled the person of Essex.

23. *He had no legs...gait* A glimpse of the aping
of favourites at Eliz.'s court.

24. *speaking thick* v. G. 'thick'.

27. *turn...abuse* debase their own good speech.

29. *affections of delight* v. G.

31. *mark* v. G.

copy and book pattern and study. Cf. *Lucr*. 615–16:

> For princes are the glass, the school, the book,
> Where subjects' eyes do learn, do read, do look.

36. *In disadvantage* against odds; cf. *Cor*. 1.6.49.
abide a field give battle.

38. *defensible* able to make defence.

40. *precise and nice* punctiliously.

46. *draw...from me* Lit. drain the 'vital spirits'
(v. G.) from my blood by your melancholy. Cf.
M.N.D. 3.2.97, and *1 Hen. IV*, 2.4.327–8 (note).

52. *taste* trial, v. G.

53. *ground* v. G. and cf. 'vantage of ground',
2.1.79.

54. *a rib of steel* As in a barrel. Cf. note 4.4.43–8
and *Ham*. 1.3.63. 'A favourite image with Sh.',
Spurgeon, p. 127.

55. *for all our loves* for all our sakes.

56. *suffered* allowed (to 'try himself').

59. *remembrance* 'Alluding to...rosemary' (Warburton); cf. *Ham.* 4. 5. 174; *Wint.* 4. 4. 73–6.

64. *still-stand...way* Cf. *Tw.Nt.* 1. 5. 158–9; *Temp.* 2. 1. 218–19.

67. *I will resolve* At this point it becomes clear that he intended to do so all along, and that his women knew it.

2. 4.

S.D. Q. 'Enter a Drawer or two'. Cf. head-note 2. 1. Pope read 'London Tavern in Eastcheap'; and Camb. 'The Boar's-head' before 'Tavern'. See head-note *1 Hen. IV*, 2. 4. J. C. Adams (*Globe Playhouse,* p. 285) regards this as an upper-stage scene (cf. ll. 146, 150, 184–99); H. Granville-Barker disagrees (v. *M.L.R.* xxxix. 298).

1. *What the devil* etc. F. heads this and Francis's later speeches '1 Drawer'; Q. 'Francis'.

2. *apple-johns* v. G. and *1 Hen. IV*, 3. 3. 4 (G.). Here seems symbolical of impotence; cf. ll. 257–60, and note l. 256. Cf. also Jonson, *Barth. Fair,* 1. 3. 55.

10. *cover* i.e. for the 'banquet' (of wine and fruit), served in another room after supper. Cf. *Shrew,* 5. 2 and the dessert after 'hall' in combination rooms at Cambridge.

11. *noise* v. G. Cf. the 'noyse of Musitians at the 'olde Tauerne' (*F.V.* ii. 99).

18. S.D. Q. 'Enter Will'. Ignored by most edd. Arden (Introd. xvii–xviii) suggests that it may='Enter Will Kempe', a S.D. we find at *Rom.* 4. 5. 100 (Q2) and head of *Ado* 4. 2 (Q1). For Kempe as the poss. 'creator' of Falstaff v. *Fortunes,* pp. 124–5. In any case Fal. would have to leave the supper-room before the 'ladies' for the purpose revealed in l. 33. Ridley and Shaaber identify 'Will' with a '3 Drawer' to whom they assign ll. 13–14; but the entry is too late for this, and no such character is needed.

20. *old utis* i.e. rare fun, v. G.

23–4. *temperality...pulsidge...extraordinarily* i.e. temper (=condition)...pulse...ordinarily.

26. *canaries* i.e. Canary. Perhaps by confusion with 'canaries', the dance (Arden).

27. *perfumes* She means 'inflames', cf. 4. 3. 39.

29. *hem!* The cough (cf. 3. 2. 218) ill conceals the hiccough, which Quickly interprets as the topers' exclamation of encouragement; cf. *1 Hen. IV*, 2. 4. 16 (note).

30–1. *a good...gold* She misquotes the prov. 'A good name is worth gold', v. Apperson, p. 261.

32. '*When Arthur...court*' The opening words of the ballad 'The Noble Acts of Arthur' (v. p. 323, Deloney's *Works* ed. Mann).

33. *empty the jordan* Cf. Earle, *Microcosmographie*, 1628, 'A Tavern'.

35. *calm* i.e. qualm. Some assert that the two words were pron. alike; cf. the quibble at *L.L.L.* 5. 2. 279. But v. Jespersen, *Mod. Eng. Gram.* i. 2. 327; and if no blunder be intended Fal.'s reply loses its point.

36–7. *So is...are sick* 'All courtesans when their trade is at a stand are apt to be sick' (Douce), v. G. 'sect'. If Fal. means 'sex' and merely refers 'to the prov. shrewishness of all women' (Shaaber), why is Doll so indignant?

38. *A pox damn you* (Q.) F. and all edd. omit; cf. p. 116.

40. *You...fat rascals* 'Rascal'=a lean deer (v. G. *1 Hen. IV*); it is therefore absurd, Fal. implies, to call him a rascal; v. G. 'make'.

41. *diseases* 'To grow fat and bloated is one of the consequences of the venereal disease' (Monck Mason).
makes them (F.) Q. 'make'. [1961.]

46. *joy* pet.
our chains etc. Doll interprets 'catch' as 'snatch'.

47. *brooches...ouches* 'With brooches, rings and owches' is a line, perhaps deliberately misquoted, from

another ballad, *The Boy and the Mantle,* which runs 'With brooches and rings' in the only authentic version extant (Child, i, no. 29). Cf. l. 41 and G. 'ouch'. Poss. Fal. sings as before; he is in a gay humour.

47–50. *For to...chambers bravely* A series of mil. terms quibbling upon syphilis and its treatment. 'The passage deserves not a laborious research' (Johnson), and I have not laboured; but G. will explain the meaning in part to those interested in this corner of Sh.'s brain. Remarkably enough F. does not omit the passage; but v. next note.

51–2. *Hang...hang yourself* F. omits, perhaps accidentally instead of ll. 47–50. Cf. p. 116.

55. *rheumatic* She means 'choleric' (hot and dry, like 'toast'); the rheumatic 'humour' or 'complexion' is cold and wet.

two dry toasts 'which cannot meet but they grate one another' (Johnson).

56. *confirmities* i.e. infirmities. Cf. *Romans* xv. 1, 'We which are strong ought to bear the infirmities of the weak'.

57. *one must bear* Cf. *Shrew,* 2. 1. 199–202.

58. *the weaker vessel* Cf. *1 Peter* iii. 7—a source of much quibbling.

60. *merchant's venture* merchantman's cargo.

65. *Ancient* v. G.　　66. *swaggering* hectoring.

75. *Dost thou hear?* i.e. Listen!

76. *pacify yourself* She means 'satisfy yourself' (=rest assured).

79. *Tilly-fally* v. G. and cf. R. W. Chambers, *Thomas More,* pp. 25–6.

and (Q.) F. and mod. edd. omit.

79–80. *an...swagger, a' comes not* (J. C. Maxwell) Q. '& your ancient swaggerer comes not'. F. omits '&' and most edd. follow Q. *M.L.R.* (1947), p. 485, and W. W. Grey, *F.F.* p. 275 (1961). [1961.]

80–1. *I was...t'other day* 'She had evidently been

summoned...for keeping a noisy disreputable house'
(Latham, *Sh. Jahrb.* XXXII. 141).

81. *Tisick* v. G.

debuty v. G. and *1 Hen. IV*, 3. 3. 116.

83–4. *Master Dumb* Unpreaching parsons were
styled 'dumb dogs' by the Puritans of the time.

by then i.e. also on the bench.

86. *now a'...whereupon* 'I know now why he
said so, it was for admitting such riotous fellows as
your ancient' (Deighton).

89. *companions* v. G.

90. *you would bless you* you would be surprised;
v. G. 'bless'.

92. *tame cheater* gentle card-sharper. Cant for
decoy-duck; v. G. 'cheater'.

94. *Barbary hen* guinea-fowl, 'whose feathers are
naturally ruffled' (Rolfe). For quibble, v. G.

99. *I am the worse* I feel ill.

106–8. *I charge...hostess* Usually explained 'I
toast you' etc. O.E.D. gives no support for 'charge'=
toast, and (adopting Capell's S.D. in l. 108) I interpret,
'Here is a cup of sack for you; empty it in the Hostess's
name'. Fal. is anxious for Pist. to propitiate Quickly;
he quibbles of course on Pist.'s name, cf. 'charge and
discharge', 3. 2. 260.

109–10. *discharge...two bullets* Delius supposes an
indecent quibble; and Fal.'s reply seems to support
this; cf. the same word-play in Webster, *Duchess of
Malfy*, 2. 2. 37–47.

111. *pistol-proof* Implies, I suppose, that she is past
bearing.

not hardly (Q.) F. 'hardly'. The superfluous nega-
tive in vulgar use.

118. *Charge me!* Ll. 120–1 show the meaning she
attaches to 'charge'.

120–1. *I am...master* i.e. I'm not for the likes
of you. Prov. from Plautus, *Rud.* 425, 'non ego sum

pollucta pago' (v. Apperson, 'meat' 10). Fal. was lit. Pist.'s 'master'. For 'meat' cf. note ll. 341–4.

123. *filthy bung* (Q.F.) Innes conj. 'filch bung' (=purse stealer). Cf. *R.E.S.* July '51, p. 219. [1952.]

125. *cuttle* Meaning doubtful, v. G.

126. *basket-hilt stale juggler* 'a practiser of stale sword tricks' (Herford), 'pretending to pass as a soldier' (Deighton), v. G. 'basket-hilt' and Jonson, *Barth. Fair*, 2. 6. 60.

127. *Since when?* i.e. have you affected soldiering?

127–8. *with two points...much* i.e. and dressed for the part! the idea! v. G. 'point', 'much'. The soldier's cuirass was fastened by 'points' on the shoulder.

129–30. *murder your ruff* Cf. ll. 139–40. Freq. references in the drama to this practice, one not yet extinct among corner-boys of mod. cities; cf. L. A. G. Strong, *The Bay*, ch. ix.

131–2. *No more...Pistol* F. omits.

133–4. *sweet captain* Quick. hopes to pacify him by giving him a commission.

135–45. *Captain! thou...had need look to't* Clearly intended to involve Capt. Falstaff and so provoke a fight; cf. 5. 4. 18–19 (note) and *Fortunes*, p. 107.

137. *truncheon you out*, v. G. 'truncheon'. Capt. Fluellen performs this duty in *Hen. V*, 5. 1.

141–2. *mouldy...cakes* 'the refuse provisions of bawdy-houses and pastry-cooks' shops' (Steevens); v. G. 'stewed prunes'.

142–4. *God's light...sorted* F. omits, as blasphemous and obscene, and substitutes 'Thefe Villaines will make the word Captaine odious'. Cf. p. 116, and v. G. 'occupy'.

151–2. *damnèd lake* (Reed, 1803) Q., F. 'damnd lake'. Pist. suddenly remembers his part again.

151–3. *I'll see...vile* Malone detects in this a burlesque of ll. 1230–54 of Peele's *Battle of Alcazar*, 1594 (v. Malone Soc. Rep. 1907); but it also contains other echoes, e.g. Arden cites 'Plutoes loathsome lake'

(l. 946 of *Alphonsus*, Mal. Soc. Rep.). In fact, Pist.'s head is stuffed with play-ends from the old-fashioned ranting drama of the early nineties, mostly misunderstood. And when memory of these fails, he makes do with anything in mind, e.g. the angler's rhyming tag: 'Hold hook and line, then all is mine.'

153–4. *down...dogs* Arden sees an echo of a line in *The Play of Stucley* (v. Simpson, *School of Sh.* i. 255).

154. *faitors* (Capell) Q. 'faters', F. 'Fates', v. G. Q. may be an *e: o* misprint or just Sh.'s spelling.

have we not Hiren here? Prob. from a lost play by Peele, *The Turkish Mahomet and Hiren the Fair Greek*; v. G. 'Hiren'. Pist., like other heroes of romance, names his sword after a famous beauty (cf. note l. 179). There is, of course, a quibble on 'iron'.

155–7. *Good...choler.* Fright makes Quick.'s confusion worse confounded. As Arden notes 'Peesel' is a sp. of Pizzle, and perhaps should be so printed.

158. *good humours* a fine way to carry on.

159–65. *Shall pack-horses...toys* Arranged as verse by Pope. Ll. 159–60 are based on Marlowe, *2 Tamburlane*, 4. 3. 1–2:

> Holla, ye pampered jades of Asia!
> What! can ye draw but twenty miles a day?

N.B. 'Holla' becomes 'hollow', 'Hannibals' 'Cannibals', and 'Cerberus' 'a king', while 'Trojant Greeks' shows a fine impartiality in the secular dispute on the comparative merits of the two armies of the *Iliad*.

164. *roar* (?) resound with their cries.

165. *toys* trifles (like Doll).

170–1. *Die men...pins* Perhaps another half-remembered tag from *The Turkish Mahomet*: to judge from the slump in diadems, a world-conqueror is speaking. *Die men* (F.) Q. 'Men'.

175. *Then feed...Calipolis* Burlesques Peele's *Alcazar* again, in which at l. 596 (Mal. Soc. Rep.)

Muly Mahamet enters with a lump of lion's flesh upon his sword and, offering it to his wife, says:

> Hold thee, Calipolis, feed and faint no more...
> Feed and be fat that we may meet the foe
> With strength and terror to revenge our wrong.

Pist., I suggest, as he speaks offers Quick. in like manner an apple-john, picked up from the table on the point of his sword.

177. *Si fortune...contento* (Q.) If fortune torments me, hope contents me. It is idle to attempt to correct the language, which Dr Henry Thomas describes (privately) as 'corrupt Italian or Franco-Italian'. Douce first suggested that Pist. reads out the motto from his sword. Cf. 5. 5. 97.

178 *give fire* shoot.

179. *sweetheart* Proves Hiren to be a woman's name and not merely a quibble upon 'iron'. For the gesture Shaaber cites *Rom.* 3. 1. 5–8 and Arden parallels from other dramas.

180. *Come we...nothings?* (Q.) 'Shall we stop here? shall we have no further entertainment?' (Johnson). But Pistol quibbles, v. O.E.D. 'etcetera', 2 b, *Rom.* 2. 1. 38, and *Ham.* 3. 2. 114–19.

182. *I kiss thy neaf* i.e. I take respectful leave. The language and action of chivalry (cf. O.E.D. 'kiss', vb. 6e). The 'tame cheater' is ready to go quietly; but Doll will have him thrown out.

182–3. *we have...stars* i.e. it won't be the first night I have spent out of doors. He has used the royal 'we' throughout, and does not here include Fal. as some imagine.

186–7. *Galloway nags* 'common hacknies' (Johnson), v. G. and 2. 2. 163. Pist., I take it, refers to the stature of Doll, played by a boy.

188–9. *Quoit...shilling* Cf. Jonson, *E.M.I.* (1616), 3. 5. 16, 'make it run as smooth off the tongue as a shove-groat shilling'; v. G. *Quoit* (F.) Q. 'Quaite'.

192. *incision...imbrue* v. G.; the first word surgical, the other high falutin'.

193. *death...asleep* From a song, attrib. to George Boleyn, br. of Anne B., as he awaited execution in 1536 (v. Padelford, *Early Sixt. Cent. Lyrics*, pp. 102, 148).

abridge...days Cf. 1 *Tamburlane*, 5.2.223, 'abridge thy baneful days' (Arden).

194. *let grievous...wounds* Cf. the alliteration of *Pyramus and Thisbe* in *M.N.D.*

195. *Untwind* (Q., F.) v. G. The Fates were three old spinsters; Clotho held the distaff, Lachesis drew the thread, and the shears of Atropos cut it short.

198. *I pray...draw* Cf. this apparent solicitude with ll. 124, 136–45, 227–8.

201. *tirrits* Poss. a portmanteau word, composed of 'terror' and 'fits'. For S.D. cf. 'murder...now' (l. 202) and ll. 210–11. Bard., the chucker-out, does not draw.

205. *I pray...gone* Refers 'to some superfluous thrashing about by Fal. after Pist. has gone' (Shaaber), cf. *Fortunes*, p. 141, n. 59.

213–18. *Ah...ah...Ah* (F.) Q. 'A...a...a'. A Sh. spelling.   216. *Hector* v. G.

219. *A rascally* (F.) Q. 'Ah rascally'—which Q. again misinterprets. [1961.]

219–20. *toss...blanket* v. G.

222. *canvass* toss. Equivocal; cf. Massinger, *City Madam*, 2.1 (ed. Gifford, p. 385):

> In all these places [suburbs]
> I have had my several pagans billeted
> For my own tooth, and after ten-pound suppers,
> The curtains drawn, my fiddlers playing all night
> *The shaking of the sheets*, which I have danced
> Again and again with my cockatrice....

227–8. *like a church* Contrasted with 'quicksilver'. The aside (as I take it) exhibits the part Fal. had played in the late action; cf. *Fortunes*, p. 107.

228–9. *tidy...boar-pig* v. G. and Jonson, *Barth. Fair*.

230. *foining* Cf. G. and note 2. 1. 13–19.

234. *what...prince of?* what sort of person is the P.? The question suggests to Lloyd collusion on Doll's part; but it is a natural one (Fal. as the P.'s friend being a big catch), and she has been asked to change the subject.

236–40. *pantler...Tewkesbury mustard* v. G.

243. *their legs* Cf. 2. 3. 23 and l. 248 below. Legs were important to men of fashion until the trouser eclipsed them. Cf. G. Meredith, *The Egoist*, ch. 11.

244. *conger and fennel* Conger was thought to induce stupidity; and fennel, used in fish-sauce, was (a) a digestive, and (b) symbolical of flattery, and thus appropriate to the P.'s 'shadow'.

245. *flap-dragons* v. G.

246. *wild-mare* see-saw.

jumps...stools Cf. G. 'joined-stool' and Jonson, *Silent Woman*, 4. 1. 97 ff., 'If shee loue wit, giue verses ...if activity, be seene o' your barbary often, or leaping ouer stooles for the credit of your back', and *ibid.* 5. 1. 45.

248. *smooth...Leg* well-fitting like a fashion-plate, v. G. 'smooth', 'Sign of the Leg', and cf. Linthicum, p. 246, for fashions in boots.

249. *with...stories* by underhand tale-bearing; cf. *V.A.* 655–7, 'This bate-breeding spy....This carry-tale', and *L.L.L.* 5. 2. 463–6.

gambol=horse-play.

253. *the scales* (F.) Q. 'ſcales'.

avoirdupois Q. 'haber de poiz'.

254. *Would not* i.e. isn't he asking to.

nave of a wheel Combining knavery with rotundity (Clarke). Cf. note *1 Hen. IV*, 1. 2. 24.

254–5. *ears cut off* i.e. in the pillory; the punishment for perjury.

256. *beat him* The punishment for incontinence; cf. *Lear*, 4. 6. 164–5.

257. *whether* (Collier) Q. 'where'⇒contraction of 'whether'. Cf. 'look whether' (l. 264).

withered elder (*a*) impotent old man, (*b*) 'elder', driest and most sapless of trees when withered. Cf. 'apple-johns', l. 2.

262. *Saturn...conjunction* 'Indeed a prodigy!... Saturn and Venus are never conjoined' (Johnson). Saturn, patriarch of the gods, was a 'withered elder'.

264. *Trigon* The fieriest conjunction known to astrologers (v. G.); referring to the exhalations in Bard.'s face.

265. *lisping* v. *L.L.L.* 5. 2. 323–4. *master's* (F.) Q. 'maſter,'.

265–6. *his master's...keeper* the old confidante (i.e. bawd) of his master; lit. one who made his engagements and kept his secrets; v. G. 'tables', and *Oth.* 4. 2. 94.

279. *hearken a'th' end* wait and see; cf. 2. 2. 46 note.

281. *Anon, anon, sir* Cf. *1 Hen. IV*, 2. 4. 25–95.

283. *And art...brother?* Addressed to Poins; 'his brother'=another bastard.

284. *continents* (*a*) parts of the world, (*b*) contents. Cf. *Ham.* 5. 2. 115, and G. 'globe'.

290. *thy good grace* (F.) Q. 'thy grace', v. p. 116.

294. *by this...blood* An extension of the oath 'by this light'. 'Fal. insults Doll in order to divert attention from his slanders' (Shaaber).

298. *take...heat* Cf. *3 Hen. VI*, 5. 1. 49, 'Strike now, or else the iron cools', and *Lear*, 1. 1. 312, 'We must do something and i' the heat'.

300. *even now* (F.) Q. 'now'.

305–6. *you knew...Gad's Hill* Throws an interesting light, which has been too little regarded, on the problem of this incident.   311. *abuse* slander.

313. *Not!* (Malone) Q., F. and most mod. edd. 'Not'.

319. *with thee* (Q.) F. 'with him'. Fal. turns from one to the other (Ridley).

325. *close with* make it up with.

329. *dead elm* rotten support. Cf. *Err.* 2. 2. 174;
Vergil, *Georgics*, i. 2–3. Fal. is letting his vine (Doll)
down badly; cf. 'withered elder' (l. 256).

333. *the devil blinds* (Q.) F. 'the Deuill outbids'
wh. all edd. follow. I propose 'the devil's behind'.
The 'too' fits neither text, and persuades me that
'blinds' is a misprint, not of 'outbids' (wh. would
be graphically impossible) but of 'behind', or rather
that 'behind', carelessly written in Sh.'s MS. (as the
makeshift 'outbids' shows), was first misread 'blynd'
(an *e: l+h: y* error, v. MSH. p. 112), and that 'devils
blind' was then corrected to 'devil blinds'.

336. *burns* infects, v. G.

337. *damned* ruined, v. G.

338. *No I warrant you* Sig. E 3 begins here in Q.
For the variant readings that follow, v. p. 121 note.

340. *quit* (*a*) absolved (for that good deed), (*b*) well
paid (by my favour in return).

341–4. *flesh...mutton* Many detect quibbling on
'flesh' (cf. 'fleshmonger', *Meas.* 5. 1. 329) and 'mutton'
=prostitute (cf. 'laced mutton', *Two Gent.* 1. 1. 96).
Shaaber demurs; but 'The duke...would eat mutton
on Fridays' (*Meas.* 3. 2. 174) offers a close parallel.

342. *the law* i.e. the statutes of 1549 and 1563,
forbidding victuallers to sell flesh in Lent, etc., in order
to encourage the fisheries and so strengthen the navy;
v. *Sh. Eng.* i. 319.

347–8. *His grace...against* i.e. His 'grace' (politeness) calls her a lady, but his manhood knows her to
be something very different. Vaughan cites *Gal.* v. 17,
'For the flesh lusteth against the spirit, and the spirit
against the flesh'. For 'rebel' v. *All's Well*, G.
'rebellion', and Jonson, *Volpone*, 3. 7. 254.

353. *twenty* cf. 2. 2. 135, note.
posts v. G.

355–7. *a dozen captains...Falstaff* A summons
for neglect of duty; cf. ll. 368–9, 2. 1. 66–8, 185,

4. 3. 26–9, *Fortunes*, p. 139, n. 28, and Stoll, *Sh. Studies*, p. 432.

356. *Bare-headed* A sign of extreme haste and urgency; cf. *Sh. Eng.* ii. 109.

360. *commotion* v. G.

the south the S.W. wind; cf. *1 Hen. IV*, 5. 1. 3–6.

368. *court* For this purpose, and in mod. terms, the 'War Office'. *presently* at once.

370. *Pay...sirrah* A page· carried his master's purse; cf. 1. 2. 231, since when Quick. had contributed £10.

372. *how men of merit...after* Sheer swank; but it has deceived the very elect, among them Maurice Morgann.

385–8. *O run, Doll...come, Doll?* (Vaughan) Q. assigns the whole as a single speech to *Hoſt.* i.e. Quickly; F. omits all after 'run, good Doll', as if the prompter found Sh.'s intentions impenetrable; Dyce and mod. edd. read 'She comes blubbered' as a S.D. But this leaves Quick. bidding Doll 'come' and 'run' from her at the same time. It can hardly be doubted that the 'comes' belong to the impatient Bard. at the door, while 'she comes blubbered' (v. G.), as Collier saw, is an excuse for the delay. Poss. the end of the sc. got crowded into the foot of an MS. page.

3. 1.

For the omission of this scene in some copies of Q., v. pp. 121–3.

S.D. Q. 'Enter the King in his night-gown alone'. For 'alone' cf. 1. 2, head-note. For 'night-gown' v. G.

1. *Warwick:* (F.) Q. 'War.'.

4–31. *How many...a crown* Cf. *Hen. V*, 4. 1. 247 ff. Both speeches owe much to Sidney's sonnet, 'Come, sleep, O sleep' (*Ast. & Stella*, 39). But for their germ v. *C.W.* iii. 115 (of the K. after Shrewsbury):

But now the king retires him to his peace,
A peace much like a feeble sickemans sleepe,
(Wherein his waking paines do neuer cease
Though seeming rest his closed eyes doth keepe)
For ô no peace could euer so release
His intricate turmoiles, and sorrowes deepe,
But that his eares, kept waking all his life,
Continue on till death conclude the strife.

5–6. *O sleep...soft nurse* Developed in *Macb.*
2. 2. 36–40; cf. Sidney, *op. cit.*

9. *smoky cribs* hovels without chimneys.

10. *uneasy* uncomfortable.

12. *perfumed chambers* Well-to-do Elizabethans,
dreading fresh air, perfumed their rooms to dispel
mustiness; cf. *Ado*, 1. 3. 55.

14. *lulled...melody* Cf. 4. 5. 3, *M.N.D.* 4. 1. 82 ff.

15. *dull* 'drowsy' and 'stupid'.   *li'st* Q. 'li'fte'.
vile common, low-born.

16. *leav'st* (F.) Q. 'leaueft'.

17. *A watch-case...bell* Much debated. I think
Sh. likens 'the kingly couch', with its 'canopy of costly
state' and wakeful occupant, first to a watch-case
(v. G.), usually of gold or silver and elaborately
ornamented, in wh. lies the watch that sleeplessly tells
every minute of the night and strikes every hour; and
then, intensifying the image, to a watch-tower from
wh. the unsleeping bell-man sounds the tocsin of public
danger or state alarm. Cf. the elaborate clock-simile,
Ric. II, 5. 5. 50–60.

18. *mast* (F.) Q. 'maffe'. 'A typographical error'
(Shaaber).

19. *seal up* For quibble v. G. Poss. the ship-boy
aloft reminds Sh. of the hovering falcon. For 'ship-
boy' cf. *Hen. V*, 3 Prol. 8; *K. John*, 4. 3. 4.

23–4. *hanging...clouds* Cf. *Temp.* 1. 2. 3–5. Surely
a poet who writes thus had been at sea in a storm!

24. *deafing* (Vaughan) Q. 'deaffing' F. 'deaff'ning'.
Cf. *K. John*, 2. 1. 147 and v. G.

26. *partial* Contrast Sidney, *op. cit.* 'Th' indifferent judge between the high and low'.

thy (F.) Q. 'them'. Perhaps a 'correction', v. next note.

27. *sea-boy* (F.) Q. 'ſeaſon'. Prob. a 'correction' of some missp. of 'seaboy', 'wet season' having an imagined relevance to the context.

30. *Then, happy low, lie down* (F.) Q. 'then (happy) low lie downe'.

32. S.D. Q. gives a second entry for the mute 'Blunt' at 5. 2. 42 (v. note).

36. *letters* (F.) Q. 'letter'. Cf. 'letters' (l. 2).

41. *yet* Goes with 'but'.   *distempered* indisposed.

45–56. *O God...and die* Malone cites *Son.* 64. Cf. Elton, *Essays and Addresses,* 1939, p. 30, for a comment on the imagery.

46. *revolution of the times* changes time will bring in due course.

51. *chances mock* (Rowe) Q., F. 'chances mockes'. [1961.]

53–6. *O, if this...die* F. omits, perhaps because it seemed 'profane and sceptical to the serious-minded' clerical censor (Shaaber). Cf. p. 116.

55. *passed* Q. 'paſt', i.e. passed by, escaped (without knowing it at the time). Cf. *Oth.* 1. 3. 167.

57–79. *'Tis not ten...amity* These details, which have no basis in Hol., and are often in conflict with Sh.'s account in *Ric. II* (5. 1. 51–68), illustrate his subordination of historical fact to the claims of drama.

66. *Nevil* The only Neville to be Earl of Warwick was 'the king-maker' (1428–71), who figures in *Hen. VI,* whence no doubt Sh. took the name.

72–4. *Though then...to kiss* This is not inconsistent with the confession at 4. 5. 184–6, v. next note.

73. *necessity...state* i.e. the dignity of the crown was so debased (by Richard; cf. 'carded his state', *1 Hen. IV,* 3. 2. 62) that I was of necessity compelled etc.

80–5. *There is a history...intreasured* The normal classical and renaissance doctrine of history as
a store-house of 'examples', by which great men in
the present can learn from the experience of those
in the past, while their lives in turn will admonish
posterity. Cf. Plutarch's *Lives* and *The Mirror for
Magistrates*.

81. *natures or* (Q.) F. 'nature of' wh. all edd. read,
though Q. makes good sense; 'natures' (v. O.E.D. 2)=
characters. Surely Sh. is thinking of Plutarch?

83–5. *the main...intreasured* Cf. *Macb.* 1.3.58 ff.,
and (for the imagery) Clemen, *Sh.s Bilder*, pp. 257–8;
v. G. 'main chance'.

84. *who* (Q.) F. 'which'. Cf. 'winds, Who'
(ll. 21–2), and Franz, § 335.

85. *beginnings* (F.) Q 'beginning'.

86. *hatch and brood of time* Cf. *Ham.* 3.1.169.

87–8. *by the necessary form...guess* i.e. inevitably
from the look of things then K. Richard might have
made a safe guess.

91. *should* would be able.   94. *cries out on* ad-
monishes.

103. *Glendower is dead* Hol. (iii. 536) dates this
1408–9. For 'instance' v. G.

104. *this fortnight ill* This seems to mark the period
of time since 1.2.104–10, when we first heard of the
K.'s illness.

107. *inward* domestic.   *out of hand* done with.

108. *unto the Holy Land* Cf. *1 Hen. IV*, 1.1.19–27,
101–2. The motif, there dropped, is here resumed, to
prepare us for the death in the Jerusalem Chamber.

3.2.

S.D. Theobald read 'Justice Shallow's seat in
Gloucestershire'. The scene is far from the road to
the north; but if P John and "the dozen captains"

are in a hurry, Fal. is not, and the route he takes enables Sh. to give us a glimpse of life in his own district. F. W. Fortescue considers the picture of the taking-up of soldiers (cf. 2. 1. 186–7) as 'prob. little exaggerated', v. *Sh. Eng.* i. 124 ff.

1. *come on* (Qa, F.) Qb. 'come on ſir,' Qb, reset from Qa, lacks independent authority; cf. p. 121 note.

2. *early stirrer* early riser.

9. *a black ousel* 'Mock-modest disparagement' (Cowden Clarke). Qu. Elizabeth being fair, Elizabethan gentlemen preferred blondes; v. G. 'ousel'. *ousel* Q. 'wooſel'.

10. *By yea and no* v. note 2. 2. 129–30.
dare say suppose.

11–14. *at Oxford...inns of court* Ox. and Camb. to some extent functioned like the mod. 'public schools': Sidney went to Ox. at 13; Southampton to Camb. at 12, and was 3 years later entered at Gray's Inn. The law colleges of London provided 'the university life' for most gentlemen's sons, were 'at the height of their glory in Eliz.'s reign', and 'were very exclusive, admitting none except "gentlemen of blood"' (*Sh. Eng.* i. 408–10).

15. *Clement's Inn* Not one of the four exclusive Inns of Court, but an 'Inn of Chancery' wh. admitted students unable to get into the others (*Sh. Eng.* i. 411), e.g. 'lusty Shallow'.

17. *You were...then* Whence we infer that Shal. often told these 'stories of his London days' (Cowden Clarke); cf. l. 211, and v. G. 'lusty'.

20–2. *Doit...Pickbone...Squele* Suggesting insignificance (v. G. 'doit'), parsimony, and cowardice; ironical names for 'swinge-bucklers'.

22. *Cots'ole man* Q. 'Cotſole man'. F. 'Cot-ſal-man'. Cf. *Wives*, 1. 1. 84 (F. 'Cotſall'), *Ric. II*, 2. 3. 9 (Q. 'Cotſhall'). Cotswold man.

24. *bona-robas* (F.) Q. 'bona robes'.

26–7. *page...Norfolk* Reed (Var. '78) declared this based on the facts of Oldcastle's life, citing Weever's biography, *The Mirror of Martyrs* (1601); a point constantly repeated even to-day (e.g. by J. Q. Adams, *Life of Sh.* 1923, p. 227, n. 4), though, as A. Wright showed in 1897 (Clar. *1 Hen. IV*, p. xx), 'Weever's authority is apparently nothing more than the play itself, and is perfectly worthless'.

28. *This...cousin* (Qa, F.) Qb. 'Coofin, this fir Iohn'. Cf. note 3. 2. 1.

30. *see* (Q.) Old pret., v. Franz, § 166.

31. *break...head* Prob. at single-sticks; cf. l. 66.

Scoggin's Q. 'Skoggins', F. 'Scoggans'. There were two men, (i) John Scoggan, fl. 1480, fool at Ed. IV's court, whose apocryphal *Jests* were pub. 1565; (ii) Henry Scoggin or Scogan, gentleman, poet, Chaucer's friend, and tutor to Hen. IV's sons, who d. 1407, and who, as Stow reports (*Survey of London*, ed. Kingsford, i. 241) sent a ballad to the young prince [Hal] and his brother 'being at supper amongst the Merchantes of London in the Vintry', so that he may have been mentioned in the orig. *Henry IV*. But Sh. need not have had either man in mind, since 'scoggin' (v. O.E.D. 'scoggery', 'scoggin', 'scogginism') meant in 16th and 17th c. 'coarse buffoon' or 'scurrilous jester'.

33. *Sampson Stockfish* The juxtaposition of names is ludicrous; v. G. 'stockfish'.

fruiterer While the 'crack' Fal. is chastising 'Scoggin' at the palace gates (v. G. 'court') 'lusty' Shal. is giving battle to a costermonger's boy. Cf. the contemptuous reference to costermongers, 1. 2. 167.

39. *as the Psalmist saith* Cf. 'as ancient writers do report', *1 Hen. IV*, 2. 4. 407.

40. *How...Stamford fair?* Cf. G. 'Stamford' 'how'=what's the price of? *Stamford* (F.) Q. 'Samford'.

42. *Double* Suggesting extreme old age.

46. *John a Gaunt* belonged to the golden age of the long bow, with wh. we won in succession Crécy, Poitiers, and (later) Agincourt.

48–9. *clapped...half* 'It is difficult to say whether
Shal. is praising Double for feats worthy of a champion
or simply making himself ridiculous' (Shaaber). But the
account seems to represent excellent shooting. Cf. *Sh.
Eng.* ii. 383: 'To hit the clout with a forehand shaft at
twelve score [yards, the length of a normal archery
range] was a fine performance', since for long distances
a lighter arrow was loosed, at a curved trajectory;
v. G. 'clout', 'forehand shaft'. *a fourteen*=over a
fourteen.

52. *Thereafter...be* Acc. to their condition. 'Good'
is emphatic.

54. S.D. 'and one with him' (Q.), F. 'and his Boy'.

57. *Good morrow* etc. Assigned to *Shal.* by F., to
Bard. by Q. in some copies, and continued to *Sil.*
in other copies. Cf. p. 121 note. The courtesy is foreign
to Bard. (cf. note 2. 2. 99); it is not for Sil. to welcome
newcomers; 'honest gentlemen' displays Shal.'s usual
penetration: I think F. is right.

61. *good* (Qa, F.) Qb omits; cf. note 3. 2. 1.

62. *commends him* sends his kind regards; cf. note
2. 2. 124–5.

65. *greets me well* is very polite (cf. O.E.D.
'well', 2c).

66. *backsword-man* fencer at single sticks—a pren-
tice-boy's accomplishment; cf. *Sir Thom. More*, 2. 1. 12.

68–79. *accommodated...good command* Cf. Jonson,
E.M.I. (1616), 1. 5. 126–8, and *Discoveries* ('CXLII
§ 2 Perspicuitas') 'the perfumed termes of the time, as
Accommodation' etc. The word is evidently new to
Shal.; on his side, Bard. is baffled by 'phrase'.

accommodated (F.) Q. 'accommodate'. Cf. ll. 70ff.

75. *Pardon* (Qa, F.) Qb 'Pardon me'.

76. *this* (Qa, F.) Qb 'this good'. Cf. note 3. 2. 1.

78–9. *word...command* Bard. has heard of 'words
of command', though O.E.D. gives no ex. earlier
than 1639.

80–1. *is...whereby* Q. 'is, beeing whereby,'.

83. *just* true.

85–6. *like well* (Q.) Cf. G. and 'well-liking'.

89. *Surecard* (F.) Q. 'Soccard', v. G., i.e. Master Absolute Winner. 'Mischievously applied...to the still unknown, but evidently unimpressive Sil.' (Herford).

90. *cousin Silence* Qa 'coſen Scilens', Qb 'cooſin Silens'. Qa repeats this sp. of the name in ll. 92, 211, 212, and gives 'Scil.' as a prefix in l. 94. Cf. p. 119 and 5. 3 head-note.

95. *Fie...weather* A broad hint from a thirsty soul.

96. *provided* 'The levy is...taken from parish to parish by local constables.' Fortescue (*Sh. Eng.* i. 124).

97. *sufficient* fit for service.

107. *of good friends* of respectable people; v. G. 'friend'. Relevant to domestic, hardly to military, service, esp. under Fal.

114. *Prick him* (F.) Q. 'Iohn prickes him' (a S.D.). Clearly Sh. wrote 'Iohn pricke him' intending 'Iohn' as a prefix (=*Fal.*), and the compositor misunderstood.

115. *pricked...enough* worried enough (by the parish constables, cf. note l. 96); v. G. 'prick (ii)'.

and you (Q.) F. 'if you' Cap. etc. 'an you'.

116. *dame* mother.　　　119. *go out* go to the wars.

121–2. *spent...Spent!* consumed...Killed!

124. *th' other* the others.

127. *cold* (*a*) cool-headed; cf. 5. 2. 98, (*b*) cowardly.

132–5. *Thy...father's substance* A difficult passage full of quibbles with obsolete implications. I paraphrase:

Your mother's son! That's probable enough, and the very image of your father; which is as much as to say that what is a son (sun) to the female is but a shadow (=image) to the male. Indeed, a mother's son is often enough merely the shadow (=delusive image) of her husband, because there is precious little of his substance in him.

For 'male' = begetter, v. 3 *H. VI.* 5. 6. 15 n.

Cf. *Ham.* 2. 2. 260–7, and G. 'shadow', 'much'.

137. *serve* With quibble on the mil. sense.

138–9. *for we...muster-book* It was common for captains to increase their own pay by drawing that of dead men. Cf. *Sh. Eng.* i. 124, and G. 'shadow (iii)'.

138. *to fill* (F.) Q. 'fill'.　　145. *ragged* v. G.

147. *his apparel* (F.) Q. 'apparell'.

147–8. *is built...upon pins* i.e. only keeps hanging on his back because it is held together with pins. Fal. uses the language of carpenters, who built up the wooden frames of Eliz. houses, and fastened them together with 'pins' or pegs. Cf. G. 'stand upon'.

149. *prick...more* Here 'prick'=fasten with pins.

150. *you can do it* etc. i.e. Brilliant! sir, brilliant!

157. *pricked you* v. G. 'prick (v)'.

158. *battle* battle-line.

160. *do my good will* do my best; cf. *Cor.* 1. 9. 18.

164. *magnanimous* valiant.

168–9. *put him to* v. G. and Schmidt, 'put to' a4.

170. *thousands* i.e. of lice (in his rags).

172. *bound to* obliged to.

177–8. *prick...roar again* Alluding to the 'pricking' (goading) of young bulls at a 'baiting'; cf. *1 Hen. IV*, 2. 4. 257 (note), and G. 'again'.

prick me (F.) Q. 'pricke'—the compositor is pressed for room.

186. *gown* v. G. 'night-gown'.

188. *for thee* (*a*) in your place, (*b*) for your death.

189–90. *Here...four* Shal. reckons six, five alone have been called, and Fal. eventually (ll. 259–67) only takes three. Prob. Sh. did not notice these inconsistencies, or knew his audience would not.

192–3. *I cannot tarry dinner* Fal. never seems to need food; cf. *Fortunes*, p. 27.

196. *the windmill* A conspicuous object in 'Seynte Georges Feeldes' (v. G.) as depicted on Norden's Map of London (1600), with a couple of men fighting a duel close by. (For particulars of the map, v. note *Ham.*

5. 2. 222 S.D.) The present passage shows that it served as a brothel.

197–8. *No more...no more of that* (F.) Q. 'No more of that mafter Shallow'. The Q. is prone to omission, and the repetition suggests a roguish dig in the ribs.

200. *Jane Nightwork* Cf. Jonson, *E.M.O.* 5. 8. 30–2, 'I ma'rle what peece of nightwork you have in hand...is this your Pandar?'

206. *a bona-roba* i.e. one of the smarter whores, cf. G.

210. *Clement's Inn* Q. (uncorr.) 'Clemham'—an odd misprint.   211. *That's...ago.* Cf. note l. 17.

218–19. *Hem, boys!* The topers' cry of encouragement; cf. note 2. 4. 29 and *1 Hen. IV* 2. 4. 16 (note).

222–3. *four Harry...crowns* A bucolic way of saying '£2 in French crowns' (*écus*), a common coin (v. *Sh. Eng.* i. 342). 'Harry' (v. G.) used by anachronism for the reign of Henry IV.

228. *Go to* Cf. ll. 233, 245 and G.

229. *old* (F.) Q. omits.

232. *forty* i.e. 40s. Cf. Jonson, *Poetaster*, 3. 4. 165.

235. *we owe...death* Prov., cf. *1 Hen. IV*, 5. 1. 126; Apperson, p. 478.

236. *so* good!

236–7. *No man's...prince* Shaaber cites *F.V.* sc. x. 7, 'I am fure he is not too good to ferue ȳ king'; and there are other links between the two scenes.

237–8. *he that dies...next* Prov. Cf. Apperson, p. 140, *Temp.* 3. 2. 129, *Cymb.* 5. 4. 160–1.

243. *three pound* 'The fourth being his profit on the transaction' (Herford).

245. *Go to, well* Come, that's good!

249. *Shadow* (F.) Q. 'Sadow'.

250–52. *for you...come unto it* This has caused trouble. But Fal. is quibbling on 'service': (*a*) military, (*b*) domestic, such as Mouldy renders his 'dame', and (*c*) the kind of service the parish bull gives; cf. 2. 4. 48 'serve bravely' and G. 'serve (b)'.

come unto it 'reach the age of puberty...attain full growth' (Schmidt); v. G.

256. *tell me* The 'me' is emphatic.

258. *assemblance* appearance.

260–1. *charge...discharge* load...fire.

261. *with...hammer* with the speed and rat-a-tat of a metal-worker's hammer; cf. ll. 282–3.

262–3. *come off...bucket* lift his caliver up and down swifter than a man can hoist with a brewer's crane. Cf. G. 'gibbet', 'bucket'. The bucket is the beam of the crane or gibbet.

265. *with...aim* with as good a chance of hitting; v. G. 'aim'.

268. *spare...ones* don't give me the large ones.

270. *Hold* Here! take it! Cf. *Two Gent.* 4. 4. 125. *traverse* Meaning doubtful; v. G.

thus, thus, thus (F.) Q. 'thas, thas, thas'. Cf. MSH. pp. 108–9.

273–4. *O, give...shot* 'The tallest and strongest men were always preferred for the pike and the little nimble men for the musket' (*Sh. Eng.* i. 115). For 'shot' v. note ll. 281–4.

274. *Well said* Bravo! well done! Cf. 5. 3. 10.

275. *Scab* v. G. Quibble on 'wart'.

277. *He is...craft's master* He doesn't make a job of it.

278. *Mile-end Green* v. G. and *All's Well*, 4. 3. 266 (note).

279–80. *Sir Dagonet in Arthur's show* Dagonet, Arthur's fool, was no doubt the butt of this show; v. G. 'Arthur's show' and *Sh. Eng.* ii. 385–6.

280. *quiver* v. G. (nothing to do with archery).

281–4. *manage...a' come* Describes the usual practice of the 'shot', or musketeers, who, drawn up in solid squares together with the pikemen, fired from the front and then doubled round to the rear to reload (cf. *Sh. Eng.* i. 115).

282–3. *rah-tah-tah...bounce* The rattle of the loading (i.e. 'rat-a-tat', cf. note l. 261), and the bang of firing; v. G. 'bounce'.

286. *will* (F.) Q. 'wooll'.

290. *give...coats* Fortescue (*Sh. Eng.* i. 124) objects that Fal. and Bard. could not cart supplies of 'coats' for recruits about with them. Sh. does not raise the problem of transport; what he suggests is that here is yet another source of profit.

295–6. *Master Shallow* (F.) Q. omits.

297. *I have...word* I need say no more.

300. *On Bardolph* etc. Q. assigns this and what follows to 'Shal.' Shaaber suggests that the Q. 'Shal.' belongs to the 'exit' of the previous line.

301–2. *fetch off* fleece.

304. *lying* A vice Fal. esp. abhorred; cf. *1 Hen. IV*, 5. 4. 144–5.   *starved* v. G.

306. *Turnbull Street* v. G.

307. *duer...tribute* i.e. wh. the hearer gets more certainly than the Sultan his rigorously exacted tribute.

308–9. *like a...cheese-paring* Being very thin, Banbury cheeses consisted chiefly of rind. Cf. *M.W.W.* 1. 1. 120.

310. *radish* (F.) Q. 'reddiſh'.

312. *so forlorn* such a 'misery'.   *thick* v. G.

313. *invisible* (Rowe) Q., F. 'inuincible'. Minim-error, i.e. misread 'inuinsible', a recog. sp. of 'invincible'. Cf. MSH. pp. 106–7.

313–15. *yet lecherous...mandrake* The decorous F. omits; cf. p. 116 and G. 'mandrake' with J. W. Lever in *R.E.S.* 1951, pp. 120–1. [1961.]

315. *ever* (F.) Q. 'ouer'.

316. *overscutched huswives* well-whipped whores; cf. 5. 4. 5 (note), Jonson, *Barth. Fair*, 4. 5. 78, and G. Implying that Shal. had consorted, not with bona-robas, but with the lowest of the profession.

carmen whistle Carters and ploughmen were noted

whistlers; cf. Jonson, *Barth. Fair*, 1. 4. 75 ff., Milton, *L'Allegro*, l. 64, and *Life in Sh.'s England*, p. 277 (top).

318. *fancies...good-nights* Musical terms, v. G. The point, I take it, is that they were impromptu compositions.

Vice's dagger Dagger of lath, for the stage; v. G. 'Vice', *1 Hen. IV*, 2. 4. 133, *Tw.Nt.* 4. 2. 123 (note), *Hen. V*, 4. 4. 75–7.

319–20. *talks...Gaunt* The 'talk' (3. 2. 46) occurs before Fal.'s entry; but what matter? Cf. note ll. 189–90.

321. *the Tilt-yard* At Westminster. John of G. again figures as patron of manly sports; cf. l. 46.

322. *burst*=broke.   *crowding*=thrusting.

323. *marshal's men* officials in charge of the tournament.

324. *beat his own name* i.e. beat a 'gaunt'; cf. *Ric. II*, 2. 1. 73 ff.

trussed (F.) Q. 'thruſt'. I adopt the more pregnant reading, wh. makes the eel-skin serve as a cloak-bag; v. G. 'truss', and for 'eel-skin' *1 Hen. IV*, 2. 4. 242 (note), *K. John*, 1. 1. 140–1. Cf. pp. 116–17.

325–6. *treble hautboy* v. G. Requires a very long narrow case; cf. 'bow-case', *1 Hen. IV*, 2. 4. 245. Perhaps Shal. also has a high piping voice.

326. *a court* a palace; cf. l. 31.

326–7. *has...beefs* Cf. *Ham.* 5. 2. 87–90.

328–9. *a philosopher's two stones* i.e. twice as profitable as the Philosopher's stone (v. G.); with the inevitable quibble, cf. *Tim.* 2. 2. 113–18.

329–31. *If the young dace...at him.* Hitherto misunderstood. Fal. contrasts slow-witted Shal. with the dace, liveliest and most active of the carp family, and says: 'If an old pike can catch a nimble young dace, a fortiori...'. For 'bait' (=a meal) v. *Troil.* 5. 8. 20, *1 Hen. IV*, 4. 1. 98–9 (note).

4. 1.

S.D. Q. 'Enter the Archbiſhop, Mowbray, Bardolfe, Hastings, within the forrest of Gaultree.'
Repeats the list of 1. 3, omitting 'Fauconbridge' who
was not then used; 'Bardolfe' (=L. Bard.) is not used
here. F. omits 'Bardolfe' but adds 'Weſtmerland'
(who enters l. 24) and 'Coleuile' (who enters in 4. 3).
The naming of the locality, unusual in Sh., perhaps
implies arboreal stage-properties (cf. *Eliz. Stage*, iii.
89), which were probably also required for the almost
contemp. *As You Like It.* The ancient royal forest of
Galtres, said to comprise 100,000 acres, stretched
north of York; it was enclosed and cut up after the
Act of 1670. For 'clad in armour' v. 4. 2. 8, 'an iron
man'.

15–16. *the hazard...meeting* 'the fearful hazard
of meeting' (Shaaber).

17–18. *the hopes...pieces* The metaphor shifts:
(i) the hopes are drained to the bottom (cf. *1 Hen. IV*,
4. 1. 49–50), (ii) and so split like a ship on the rocks.

23. *the just proportion* the very estimate.

24. *sway on* v. G.

S.D. Q., F. 'Enter Weſtmerland.'

28. *Duke of Lancaster* Cf. note 1. 3. 82.

30. *What...coming?* What is the purpose of your
mission?

Then, my lord (F., Q. corr.) Shaaber notes that the
phrase was first overlooked by the Q. compositor and
then inserted on the same line as the next verse, in
order to avoid resetting the type; a clear instance of
correction from the MS.

34. *rags* (S. Walker) Q., F. 'rage'. 'Rags', as Greg
notes (*Aspects*, p. 159), 'allows a more precise meaning
for "guarded" (i.e. trimmed) and supplies a parallel
antithesis to the "boys and beggary" of the next line'.

36. *appeared* (Pope) Q., F. 'appeare'. Cf. MSH. p. 109, and above, p. 117.

42. *by a civil peace* by the existence of orderly temporal government.

44. *good letters* scholarship (literae humaniores).

45. *investments* v. G. 'Formerly all bishops wore white [i.e. the rochet] even when they travelled' (Hody, *Hist. of Convocations*, 1701, p. 141).

figure (F.) Q. 'figures'.

47. *translate* A quibble, v. G. and cf. *M.N.D.* 3.1.114.

50. *Turning...graves* 'As "books" result from the exercise of the graceful "speech of peace", so "graves" from the exercise of the "boist'rous tongue of war"' (Herford).

52. *point of war* Musical term, v. G.

55–79. *And with...wrong* Q. omits; v. pp. 119–21.

57. *And...bleed for it* Cf. *Ric. II*, 1.1.153–7 for the word-play.

60–1. *I take not...peace* Something is prob. lost between these two lines, since as it stands l. 60 is contradicted by ll. 64–6, in wh. the Archb. speaks like a 'physician'.

64. *rank*=surfeited.

67. *in equal...weighed* Cf. *Ham.* 1.2.13.

69. *griefs* v. G.

71. *shore* (Vaughan) F. 'there'. The reading is graphically easy (*t:ʃ+e:o* misprint), fits well with 'stream of time' (=general trend of affairs) and 'torrent of occasion' (=tide of emergency; cf. *K. John*, 4.2. 125ff.), and introduces a favourite image of Sh.'s; cf. *Hen. V*, 4.1.282, 'the high shore of this world'; *Macb.* 1.7.6; *K. John*, 2.1.335–40, etc. and Spurgeon, *Sh.'s Imagery*, pp. 91–6. Warburton proposed 'sphere' and Theobald 'chair'.

83. *of...instance* of which we have examples every moment.

84. *Hath* Cf. 4.2.37; Franz, § 156.

91–2. *this...rebellion* this forged deed, rebellion;
v. G. 'book'.

93. *And...edge*   95. *To brother...cruelty* (Q.
uncorr.) Both lines omitted in Q. (corr.) and F. Much
discussed, v. Shaaber. Alice Walker (*Library*, Sept.
1951, pp. 115–16), though admitting that ll. 94–6 are
'awkwardly expressed,' makes an ingenious attempt to
explain them, and suggests that ll. 93, 95 were left out of
Q. in mistake for ll. 101–03, which might well have been
included with the cut of 37 ll. that follows (v. next
note). The 'import' of ll. 94–6 is intelligible, since
'brother general' = his brothers, the common people,
and 'brother borne...cruelty' refers to the death of
L. Scroop (v. *1 H. IV*, 1. 3. 267–8). But it is hardly
'clear' and I cannot think that Sh. meant to leave the
speech so syntactically confused. Note too, the Arch.
makes no direct reply to West.'s questions, while 'redress'
in l. 97 refers to nothing he says. [1952.]

103–39. *O my...the king* Q. omits; cf. pp. 119–21.

104–5. *Construe...indeed* Judge the present state
of affairs according to the conditions that determine
them, and you will be forced to admit....

109–10. *an inch...build* Cf. note 1. 3. 41–62.

110–12. *were you...father's* Nothing of this in Hol.

114. *need* Cf. note 1. 3. 78.

115. *the state* the state of affairs.

116. *force* (Theobald) F. 'forc'd'. Cf. MSH. p. 109.

119. *Their...spur* The neighs of their coursers
clamouring for the spur to set them off; v. G. 'dare'.

120. *arméd...charge* lances at rest (ready for the
encounter).

127. *Then threw...lives* Cf. *Caes.* 3. 2. 195.

128. *dint* v. G.   135. *borne...out* v. G.

136. *in a...voice* with one accord.

139. *indeed* (Thirlby) F. 'and did'.

145–6. *set off* v. G.   *think* suggest.

151. *ken* v. G.   154. *battle* v. G.

161. *A rotten...handling* Prov. Apperson, p. 539.
case lit. = box.

163. *In...virtue of* as plenipotentiary for.

164–5. *absolutely...stand upon* give a final opinion on the conditions we shall have to insist upon.

166. *intended...name* 'implied in his title of general' (Herford).

172. *insinewed* (Capell 'ensinew'd) Q. 'enfinewed', F. 'infinewed'.

173. *by...form* in true legal form; v. G. 'substantial'.

174–5. *present...confined* immediate execution of our demands, which are restricted to ourselves and our grievances, i.e. are of limited scope.

175. *and to our* (F.) Q. 'and our'.

176. *our awful banks* i.e. 'the banks of our obedience' (Sh.'s Addition to *Sir T. More*, l. 39). Cf. note 4. 1. 71.

180. *And either* (Thirlby) Q., F. 'At either'. Cf. p. 117.

185. *Fear you not that: if* (Pope) Q., F. 'Feare you not, that if'. Cf. p. 117.

187. *consist* insist.　　189. *valuation* reputation.

193. *were...love* even were we faithful to the king till death. For 'royal faiths' cf. 'royal minds', *Hen. VIII*, 4. 1. 8.

198. *such picking* 'I cannot but think this line is corrupted' (J.). I conj. 'search-picking', i.e. picking over objects already sifted in a 'search' or sieve, and thus doubly selected, which would hark back to the winnowing image in ll. 194–6.　　*dainty*=finicking.

199–200. *to end...life* i.e. that as soon as he rids himself of one foe two greater ones appear among the survivors.

201. *tables* v. G.

207–9. *His foes...friend* Cf. *Matt.* xiii. 29 and ll. 194–6 again.

211. *him on* Collier suggests 'her man'; 'hir man' with a space before the 'a' might be thus misread (minim+*a* : *o* misprint).

215. *wasted* v. G.　　216. *late* former.

219. *offer...hold* attack but not grip.

222–3. *like a broken...breaking* Cf. *Oth.* 2. 3. 328–31.

226. *just distance* half-way. Cf. Hol. iii. 530, 'iuſt in the midwaie betwixt both the armies'.

228. S.D. Q. reads 'Enter Prince Iohn and his armie' at l. 226, and F. 'Enter Prince Iohn' here, but neither mark a fresh scene (first introduced by Pope) and the action is clearly meant to be continuous, the two armies being drawn up on either side of the stage and the principals meeting in the centre.

4. 2.

8. *Than* (F.) Q. 'That'.

an iron man (*a*) in armour; cf. Hol. iii. 529, 'the archbiſhop comming foorth amongst them clad in armor', (*b*) merciless; cf. *1 Hen. IV*, 2. 3. 50.

talking F. and edd. omit. Perhaps 'an iron man talking' is contrasted with the priest talking to his flock, or 'man talking' may be a misprint of another word.

10. *the word to sword* Cf. *M.W.W.* 3. 1. 41. The word-play depends on a similarity of sound now lost.

11–12. *that sits...favour* For a close parallel in Nashe v. *1 Hen. IV*, p. 195.

15. *In shadow* Alluding to 'sunshine', l. 12 (Shaaber).

17. *the books of God* Cf. G. 'book' and 2. 2. 44–5.

18–22. *the speaker...workings* The Speaker in the Tudor H. of Commons, though formally elected, was nominated by the Crown and acted both as interpreter of the Commons to the monarch and as mouthpiece of the monarch's will to the Commons. Cf. Cheyney, ii. 187–92, 197.

19. *imagined* (Rowe) Q., F. 'Imagine'. Cf. MSH. p. 109, and p. 117.

20. *opener...intelligencer* v. G. and cf. note ll. 18–22.

21. *the grace, the sanctities* i.e. the Divine presence and the celestial hierarchy. Sh. is thinking of monarch and court (cf. note ll. 18–22). 'About him all the Sanctities of Heaven / Stood thick as stars' wrote Milton (*P.L.* iii. 60), sublimating Sh.

22. *workings* minds v. G.

24. *Employ* (F.) Q. 'Imply'.

26. *ta'en up* levied; cf. 2. 1. 187.

27. *zeal* 'with a play on seal' (Herford); cf. *K. John,* 2. 1. 477–9 (note).

28. *substitute* deputy.

30. *up-swarmed* A word of Sh.'s coining. Cf. 2 *Hen. VI,* 3. 2. 125–7.

33. *in common sense* as all can see.

34. *monstrous form* malformed shape, (or) abnormal course. Of a tree or plant misshapen by its environment.

37. *hath* Cf. note 4. 1. 84.

39. *Whose...asleep* Sh. does not 'confound' Argus with Hydra, as some assert; he passes from one tale to the other in the same construction to suit his ends.

44–9. *And...generation* Develops the Hydra-metaphor (Arden): cf. G. 'generation'. A prophecy of the Wars of the Roses.

46. *theirs* their 'supplies' (=reinforcements, reserves).

47. *success of mischief* a succession of misfortunes; cf. *Wint.* 1. 2. 394.

48. *this* (F.) Q. 'his'. F. is 'much better' (Shaaber).

52–3. *Pleaseth...articles* Seeing a wrangle impending, West. politely brings P. John back to business (after Capell).

53. *far forth* For the redundant 'forth' cf. *Temp.* 1. 2. 177 and Franz, § 429.

60–5. *If this...amity* Hol. (iii. 530) attributes the proposal to West.

67–9. *I give...army* (F.) Q. continues ll. 67–8 to *Bishop* and gives ll. 69–71 to *Prince*: a mistake difficult to explain.

73–7. *if you knew* Spoken with double meaning.

117. *and such…yours* (F.) Q. omits. Cf. p. 116.

122. *these traitors* (F.) Q. 'this traitour'.

123. *Treason's…breath* Critics dispute whether Sh. means us to approve or condemn P. John's trickery. We can be sure that to the majority of his audience rebellion was 'as the sin of witchcraft', with which it was impious to keep faith. If Sh.'s humanity out-topped this, that is his secret.

4. 3.

S.D. Capell read 'The same. Another part', and edd. follow, though the action is once again continuous. The Colevile episode anticipates *Hen. V*, 4. 4, itself derived from the old play (*teste F.V.* sc. xvii). All Hol. (iii. 530) tells us is that a 'sir Iohn Colleuill of the Dale' was beheaded at Durham (not York, cf. l. 72).

1. *condition* rank.

8. *a dale deep* (Tyrwhitt). Cf. *R.E.S.* July, '51, p. 219. The jest hitherto unexplained, turns on 'dale' = pit; v. G.

14–15. *do observance to* do homage for, kneel and beg.

17. *in that thought* i.e. as to the hero of Shrewsbury; cf. *Fortunes*, pp. 89, 110.

18–20. *I have…my name* i.e. I am known everywhere by my belly (cf. *1 Hen. IV*, 2. 4. 517); 'school (= shoal) of tongues' recalls the tongues painted on the belly of Rumour (Ind. head-note). Fal. is bragging of his European fame.

22. *undoes me* ruins me, i.e. I might be a woman!

23. S.D. Q. 'Enter Iohn Weſtmerland, and the reſt. Retraite.' The last word should rightly come after West. has had time to 'call in the powers' (l. 25), e.g. just before l. 70 when he returns to announce 'retreat

is made'. Poss. added later and inserted opposite the wrong entry for West.

26–9. *Now, Falstaff...back* Shows that Fal. has only just arrived; cf. 'pure and immaculate valour' (l. 37) and *Fortunes*, p. 86.

30. *but it should be thus* 'if it were not thus' (Schmidt).

31. *I never...but* I always knew that...
check reproof.

34–5. *the very...possibility* i.e. he has stretched possibility to its farthest limits. [The account that follows goes farther!]

35–6. *foundered...posts* As fresh horses were provided every ten miles (v. G. 'post'), Fal. claims to have traversed at least 1800 miles. But perhaps he 'foundered' several posts at each stage; cf. 'horseback-breaker' (*1 Hen. IV*, 2. 4. 240–1).

37. *pure and immaculate* In contrast with 'travel-tainted'; cf. note ll. 26–9.

40. *that* so that; cf. l. 118.

hook-nosed 'The medallion portrait of Caesar in North's trans. of Plutarch...shows, in profile, a nose with a hook' (Shaaber).

41. *Rome* (F. and most edd.) Q. 'Rome, there Cosin'. Johnson printed 'Rome there, Caesar' wh. is poss., as is 'then Caesar' (=at that time Caesar), and there are other guesses. Mine is 'Ju. Caesar', misread 'thr. Cosen'.

45. *booked* i.e. by the chroniclers in the Prince's train.

47. *particular* one all to myself. The Eliz. ballad was a broadside, and often decorated with a cut 'on the top on't', a popular tune being suggested for its singing. Cf. *Wint.* 4. 4. 181–200, 256–309, and *Sh. Eng.* ii. ch. 29.

49. *show...two-pences* i.e. look sham beside me. Gilded two-penny pieces (silver) often passed as half-crowns (gold), which were about the same size.

51. *cinders of the element* Contemptuous term for
stars; cf. *Caes.* 3. 1. 63.

53. *of the noble* like myself.

54. *mount* receive promotion.

55–7. *heavy...thick* bad...dim (with a quibble),
v. G.	60, 61, 71. *Colevile* A trisyllable.

66–7. *I know not...gratis* A. E. Morgan (p. 38)
notes that, omit the word 'gratis', as F. does, and
we get two lines of blank verse in keeping with the
context.

73. *Blunt* The only time he is addressed in the
text; cf. notes 1. 1. 16; 3. 1. 32.

79–81. *My lord...report* The orig. verse here
shows clearly. Note the rhymes 'court'—'report'.
F. adopts verse-lining, but without initial capitals;
Q. prints as prose. Cf. *Library*, June 1945, pp. 14–16.

81. *stand* v. G.	*pray* (F.) Q. omits.

82–3. *Fare...deserve* (F.) Q. as prose.

in my condition Fal.'s reference to 'dukedom' (l. 85)
shows that he takes 'condition' as=rank, i.e. he interprets the Prince as haughty. But this is wilful distortion;
what the P. means, I think, is 'Out of my kindness of
heart'; cf. G. 'condition'.

84. *had but* (F.) Q. 'had'. Cf. p. 116.

85. *dukedom* Cf. note 1. 3. 82.

88–9. *come...proof* turn out well; v. G. 'proof'.

89–90. *thin drink...fish-meals* For parallel from
Nashe v. *1 Henry IV*, p. 196.

93. *inflammation* being 'lit up' by drink.

93–9. *A good sherris-sack...wit* This seems to be
suggested by a passage in T. Bright's *Treatise of Melan-
cholie*, 1586, ch. xvii, pp. 99–100, which also inspired
Jonson's description of jealousy in *E.M.I.* (Q.), 1. 4.
206 ff., first acted Sept. 1598. For words like 'crudy',
'vapours', etc. v. G.

99–101. *The second...blood* etc. Cf. Jente, No. 32,
'Good wine engendreth good blood'.

104. *parts extremes* Q. 'partes extreames', i.e. the extremities of the body. All edd. follow F 3 'parts extreme'.

105. *as a beacon gives warning* i.e. of invasion.

106. *this...man* A common notion with Sh. Cf. *Lear*, 3. 1. 10–11; *Cor.* 2. 1. 68–9; *Caes.* 2. 1. 67–9; *K. John*, 4. 2. 245 ff.

106–7. *vital...spirits* v. G.

110–13. *So that...and use* For parallel in Nashe v. *1 Hen. IV*, p. 196.

112. *hoard...devil* Alluding to the belief that mines, and buried treasure of all kinds, were guarded by devils; cf. *What Happens in 'Hamlet'*, p. 81.

112–13. *commences...act* Quibbling on the use of these words (v. G.) at universities in connection with the taking of degrees; a point for law-students, mostly from Ox. and Camb. Cf. note 3. 2. 11–14.

116–17. *manured...fertile* Consult G.

117. *drinking...good store* Cf. *F.V.* ii. 97, 'the young Prince...called for wine good store'.

119. *humane* secular (i.e. excluding divinity).

123. *The army...gone* Bardolph speaks verse.

125. *esquire* Said with a grin, being superfluous after 'Master'.

126–7. *I have him...with him* i.e. I have already begun working upon him, and soon I'll turn him to good use; v. G. 'temper', 'seal'.

127–8. *Come away* Come along!

4. 4.

S.D. Entries based on Q. Clarence 'as Sh. could have seen in the chronicle (Hol. iii. 515) was at that time in France' (Ax p. 87). *The Jerusalem Chamber* (G. and 4. 5. 232–40) is in Westminster Abbey, as Hol. (iii. 541) relates, but since everything in the scene suggests the palace, Theobald and edd. down to Camb.

located it there, and it is poss. Sh. himself so imagined it. I follow Camb's. non-committal 'Westminster'.

3–4. *We will...sanctified* Scarcely intelligible to an audience which has not *1 Hen. IV*, 1. 1. 18–29, fresh in mind.

5–7. *addressed...substitutes...invested...level* v. G.

12–13. *Humphrey...brother* Q., F. as prose. Prob. the only 'mislining' of the sort common to both texts (Shaaber).

12–49. *Humphrey...care and love* 'Grounded upon a conversation between the K. and P., recorded by Stowe [*Annals*, A.D. 1413]; in which the former puts the latter on his guard against the machinations of Clarence'. T. Davies, *Dramatic Miscellanies*, 1784, i. 314 (cited Shaaber).

23. *brothers...boy* F. 'Brothers:...(Boy)' Q. 'brothers,...boy:'.

30–5. *For he is gracious...day* Prepares us for the atonement with the L. C. Justice and the rejection of Fal.

30. *observed* Cf. ll. 36, 49, G., and 4. 3. 15.

32. *Open as day* generous as the daylight (cf. *Matt.* v. 45).

melting (F.) Q. 'meeting'. Q. give poss. sense, e.g. 'meeting the needs of charity' (Furnivall); but 'melting' (='compassionate'; cf. G., *Oth.* 5. 2. 349, and *1 Hen. IV*, 2. 4. 117) leads on to 'flint' in l. 33.

33. *he's* (F.) Q. 'he is'.

flint i.e. at once very hard and, when struck, giving out angry sparks. The image is developed in *Caes.* 4. 3. 111–13.

34. *humorous* capricious, sudden, violent and unexpected.

35. *flaws...day* icy squalls at daybreak. 'Flaw in Scotch is a storm of snow' (Boswell, Var. 1821), and Home Guards in Scotland know all about 'flaws congealéd in the spring of day'.

39. *line* (F.) Q. 'time'. Either reading might be

misread as the other. I accept F. as (*a*) more pregnant than the commonplace 'time', and (*b*) leading on to 'whale'. Arden objects that it 'presents a metaphor which is ill-sorted with the simile of the stranded whale'. But that is how Sh.'s trains of images often move: 'line and scope' suggests fishing and fishing suggests whales. Cf. *Ham.* Introd. pp. xxxviii–ix.

40. *a whale on ground* i.e. aground. Stone (p. 156) finds the source of this simile in an account by Hol. (iii. 1259) of the stranding of a whale in Kent in 1574. But it is more likely that Sh. and his audience had heard talk of 'the Whale of Berckhey, or the great fish which stranded or came on shoare at Berckhey in Holland, the third of February 1598' (v. D. C. Collins, *Handlist of News pamphlets 1590–1610*, 1943, p. 40); v. G. 'confound', 'working'. Cf. *M.W.W.* 2. 1. 57.

43–8. *A hoop...gunpowder* An interesting amalgam of diverse images: hooped barrel (cf. note 2. 3. 54), vial of blood (cf. *Ric. II*, 1. 2. 11–12, 16–19), strong poison and 'rash' gunpowder, cf. *Rom.* 5. 1. 60–5).

52. *canst...that* (F.) Q. omits. Cf. p. 116.

54. *Most...weeds* Prov.; v. Apperson, p. 39, 'The best ground is the dirtiest'—*Euphues* (Bond i. 251). 'An indication from Sh. how we are to regard the P.'s way of life' (Clemen, p. 253).

58–66. *The blood...decay!* Expanded in 4. 5. 119 ff. Consult G. for 'unguided', 'rotten', 'riot', 'rage', 'lavish', 'affection', 'opposed', 'decay'.

67. *look beyond* v. G.

68–78. *The prince...advantages* This should, I think, be regarded as Sh.'s own apologia; cf. notes ll. 30–5, 54, and *1 Hen. IV*, 1. 2. 187 ff.

75–8. *cast off...advantages* . 'cast off' suggests clothes, and the image follows of a tailor using old clothes as the pattern for new ones; cf. *Wint.* 4. 4. 379–80.

77. *other* (Q.) F. (+edd.) 'others'.

79–80 *'Tis. . .carrion* i.e. he is not likely to give up his pleasures, corrupt though his companions be. Perhaps Sh. remembers *Judges* xiv. 8 ff.

92. *the haunch of winter* i.e. the 'back-winter'= return of winter in spring. Cf. Nashe (McKerrow, iii. 165, 'backewinters or frostes that nippe it in the blade').

93. *lifting...day* sunrise, cf. l. 35.

94. *heaven* (F.) Q. 'heauens'.

99. *shrieve* (Q.) F. 'Sherife'. A monosyllable, as in Sh.'s Addition to *Sir Th. More*, ll. 41–5, and prob. also at *1 Hen. IV*, 2. 4. 496, 505.

104. *mete...terms* (Alice Walker), Q. 'wet... termes'. F. 'write...letters'—an obvious makeshift by the prompter. Cf. A.W. *Text Prob.*, p. 117. [1961.]

118–20. *Th'incessant...break out* Cf. *Library*, June 1945, p. 5, for close parallel in *C.W.*

120. *and will break out* (F.) Q. omits; cf. p. 116.

121. *fear me* frighten me. Monstrous births and unaccountable natural phenomena were considered sure indications of the impending death of kings. Cf. Introd. *K. John*, p. xvi.

122. *Unfathered heirs* Prob. offspring without human fathers; cf. G.

123. *The seasons change* etc. Cf. 'The seasons alter' etc., *M.N.D.* 2. 1. 107 ff. *as* as if.

125. *The river...ebb between* Hol. (iii. 540; Stone, p. 158) notes: 'In this yeare [1411]...were three flouds in the Thames, the one following vpon the other, and no ebbing betweene.'

130. *apoplexy* Cf. notes 1. 2. 105, 108–15.

132. *softly, pray* (F.) Q. omits, v. p. 116.

4. 5.

S.D. No S.D. or break of any kind in Q. and F. Capell read 'Attendants, and Lords, take the King up; convey him into an inner Room, and lay him upon a Bed'. Camb. first marked a change of scene and

I follow their S.D. Capell's S.D. describes what prob.
happened on the Elizabethan stage (the 'inner room'
=the inner-stage); and the audience was then certainly
intended to imagine a change of scene. The objections
to the use of the inner-stage, urged by some, are met
by supposing that once the King was laid in bed the
latter was trundled or carried on to the outer stage
which thus became part of the 'inner room'.

1–4. *Let there...room* In the corresponding sc. of
F.V. the K. bids his lords 'Draw the Curtaines and
depart my chamber a while, And cause some Musicke
to rocke me a sleepe' (viii. 10–11). Continuity of
stage-arrangement with the old play is evident.

3. *music...spirit* Cf. *Lear*, 4. 7. 16, and *Univ. of
Edinburgh Journal*, 1942, pp. 223–5.

13. *altered* (F.) Q. 'vttred'—*a:u* error.

15–16. *Not so...sleep* (F.) Q. prints as prose.

20. *sit and watch* 'Regarded as an office of love'
(Arden).

21–47. *Why doth...left to me* Cf. *Fortunes*,
pp. 78–9.

24. *ports* i.e. the eyes, shut (like city-gates) at
night.

25. *sleep* Most edd. take as imperative. I agree
with Deighton and Shaaber who take it as an exclamation. 'What, does he actually sleep with it now? Yet
not so soundly' etc.

28. *the watch of night* 'the whole night' (Craig).

29. *pinch* v. G.

31. *scald'st* (Q., F.) By attraction with 'dost'
(l. 29), v. G.

with safety=whilst giving safety.

32–3. *downy...down* Q.,F. 'dowlny (F. 'dowl-
ney')...'dowlne'. For this double correspondence of
Q. and F. v. Alice Walker in *R.E.S.* July '51, p. 221.
H. Bradley (*Sh. Eng.* ii. 573) notes 'dowlne' as 'a
curious confusion' between 'dowle' (cf. *Temp.* F.
3. 3. 65) and 'down'. [1952]

32. *stirs not* Such a temporary suspension of breathing is known to doctors (cf. *Sh. Jahrbuch*, xvi. 88; cited Shaaber).

38. *of the blood* i.e. that drain the blood; cf. note 2. 3. 46.

39. *nature* v. G.

42. *immediate* Cf. *Ham.* 1. 2. 109.

43. *Lo, where* (Q.) F. 'Loe, heere', wh. all edd. follow; cf. l. 89.

44–6. *and put...from me:* Cf. *F.V.* viii. 74, 'And he that seekes to take the Crowne from my head, Let him looke that his armour be thicker then mine, Or I will pearce him to the heart, Were it harder then brasse or bollion'.

49. *how fares your grace?* (F.) Q. omits; cf. p. 116.

51–2. *We left...by you* (F.) Q. prints as prose.

64. *See, sons* etc. Addressed to the sons in the audience as much as to the princes about him.

68. *thoughts* v. G. and cf. 'thoughtful', l. 72.

70. *piled* (F.) Q. 'pilld'.

71. *strange-achievéd* Meaning disputed, v. G. I think it=hard-won, or 'won by extraordinary exertions' (Kittredge).

73. *arts...exercises* 'The two branches of a polite education in the 16th c.' (Arden); cf. *Troil.* 4. 4. 80; *A.Y.L.* 1. 2. 67.

74. *culling* (F.) Q. 'toling' (omitting 'the virtuous sweets'). I conj. that Sh. wrote 'coling' (an old sp.) and that the Q. compositor both misread it 'toling' (cf. MSH. p. 111), and overlooked 'the virtuous sweets' (cf. p. 116) which probably offered a problem in Sh.'s MS. since its inclusion appears to have disturbed the lineation in F. for the rest of the speech. But ll. 74–7 probably represent an unresolved tangle' in Sh.'s MS.: cf. Shaaber, and Greg, *Edit. Prob.*, ix.

76. *thighs with...honey packed,* (Dyce). F. 'thighs ...honey'. Q. 'thigh...honey'. [1961.]

78. *murdered* Seemingly by the bee-keeper.

79. *yields* (Q., F.) The subj. being 'engrossments', Rowe and most edd. read 'yield'. But cf. 1. 3. 108; 4. 1. 84; 4. 3. 99, and Franz, §§ 673, 679 (3rd pers. plur. in *s*).

81. *have* (Ridley) Q. 'hands', F. 'hath'. Q. may be explained as 'haue' misread 'hand' and corrected to 'hands' (cf. MSH. pp. 106–9).

83. *kindly* filial. Cf. *Ham.* 1. 2. 65.

85–7. *tyranny...eye-drops* Suggested by the story of the tyrant Alexander of Pherae being moved at the *Troades* of Euripides, cited in my Additional Notes on *Ham.* (2. 2. 562–3), v. North's *Plutarch*, ii. 323, Tudor Translations. Sidney also refers to it in his *Apologie* (ed. Arber, p. 45), but not in connexion with Hecuba, as Hamlet does.

90. *Depart the chamber* Cf. *F.V.* viii. 10, 'depart my chamber' (v. note ll. 1–4).

93. *by thee* Either 'with you' or poss. 'in your opinion' (selon toi), Schmidt.

99. *so weak a wind* Referring to his dying breath (Clemen, p. 100).

103. *sealed my expectation* confirmed my worst fears.

106. *daggers...thoughts* Cf. *1 Hen. IV*, head-note 3. 2, and note 5. 4. 51–7.

107. *Whom* (Q.) F. 'Which'. Cf. 3. 1. 21–2, 84 and Franz, § 335.

whetted...heart Cf. *M.V.* 4. 1. 123; *Ric. III*, 4. 4. 227.   108. *hour* Q. 'hower'. A dissyllable.

115. *compound...dust* Cf. *Ham.* 4. 2. 6; *Son.* 71. 10.

118. *form* law and order. Cf. Sh. Add. to *Sir T. More*, l. 146, 'gyve vp yoʳ sealf to forme'.

128. *gild...guilt* A frequent Sh. quibble; cf. *Macb.* 2. 2. 56.

132. *flesh his tooth* gratify his lust; cf. *1 Hen. IV*, G. and 5. 4. 129.

133. *civil* i.e. of civil war; cf. 'civil wounds', *Ric. II*, 1. 3. 128.

134–5. *riots...riot* civil disorder...moral disorder.

136–7. *O, thou...inhabitants* Cf. *Troil.* 1. 3. 121–4 and *Fortunes*, p. 80.

140. *dear and deep* sore and heartfelt. A chiasmus.

143–4. *And He...yours!* Cf. *F.V.* viii. 57 'And liue my Lord and Father, for euer'—which looks like a 'reporter's' version.

affect v. G. and 'affection', l. 172.

147–8. *Which...bending* i.e. my 'duteous spirit' teaches my obedience to assume this humble posture. 'Obedience' lit.=kneeling, and 'inward'=from the heart, sincere.

149–55. *God witness...thinking you dead* Cf. *F.V.* viii. 47–50, 'I came into your Chamber...and finding you...dead to my thinking, God is my witnesse'.

152. *wildness* unregenerate state.

158–9. *The care...father* Cf. 4. 4. 118–20.

160. *worst of* (F.) Q. 'worſe then'—prob. a 'correction'. Cf. p. 121 note.

161. *carat* Q. 'karrat', F. 'Charract' (cf. *Err.* 4. 1. 28 (F.) 'charect'). *is* (F.) Q. omits.

162. *med'cine potable* v. G.

166–8. *try...quarrel* v. G. 'try'.

168. *true inheritor* rightful possessor. Cf. *F.V.* viii. 53–4, 'who might better take it then I after your death?' In the old play the P. asserts what he merely hints in Sh.

169. *infect* Carrying forward the ideas of ll. 158–64.

170. *swell...strain* Sh. has perhaps music in mind, v. G. 'strain'.

177. *O my son!* (F.) Q. omits, v. p. 116.

178. *put it in* (F.) Q. 'put in'.

179. *win* (Q.) F. 'ioyne', a misreading of 'wynne' (Collier).

181. *Come...bed* Cf. *F.V.* viii. 62, 'But come neare my sunne'.

182. *latest counsel* Cf. Stow, *Annals*, 'King Henry his counsell to his sonne' (marginal heading).

183–6. God knows...my head Cf. *F.V.* viii. 70–1,
'For God knowes my sonne, how hardly I came by it,
And how hardly I haue maintained it'; and Hol.
(iii. 541; Stone, p. 158), 'What right I had to it God
knoweth'.

185. met v. G.   *188. opinion...confirmation* v. G.
189. soil A quibble.
195. fears v. G.
196. answerèd v. G.
199. Changes the mood Begins a new phase.
mood (Q., F.) v. G. All edd. but Arden read
'mode'. Sh. quibbles.

purchased v. G. 'Purchase' (=booty) wh. Hudson
suggests is attractive; cf. *1 Hen. IV*, 2. 1. 91.

201. successively by right of succession. Cf. Hol.
iii. 541 (Stone, p. 158) 'Well...if you die King,
I will haue the garland'; v. G. 'garland'. 'Every
usurper snatches a claim of hereditary right as soon
as he can' (Johnson).

204. my friends (Tyrwhitt) Q., F. 'thy friends'.
Cf. p. 117; Camb. and most edd. read 'my friends'.
Either Sh. wrote 'thy' in error or Q. and F. coincide
in a misprint. I cannot doubt that 'my' is correct:
(i) it carries on the 'me—thee' antithesis of the previous
lines, (ii) it refers back to Hal's 'noble change' (l. 154)
which involves the rejection of his own friends and
the taking over of his father's, false as well as true (cf.
Hen. V, 2. 2. 29–31).

206–9. By whose fell...them off The slight ob-
scurity belongs to the sick K.'s mind, wh. passes from
the thought of the supporters of his dynasty in general
to that of the rebellious nobles in particular, whose
'cutting off' is the subject of both Parts; after which
he reverts to the remainder, the poss. treachery of
whom is revealed in *Hen. V*, 2. 2. The 'friends' of a
usurper are all potential foes.

212–15. Therefore...former days Cf. *C.W.* iii. 127,
'To thee is left to finish my intent' [the crusade]:

Who to be safe must neuer idly stand;
But some great actions entertaine thou still
To hold their mindes who else will practise ill.

214. *action hence borne out* Cf. 4. 4. 88, 'hence'=
abroad.

218. *How...forgive* Cf. note ll. 183–6.

220. *My gracious liege* Q. omits, v. p. 116.

221–4. *You won...maintain.* Cf. ll. 44–6 and note.

224. S.D. Q. 'enter Lancaſter'.

228–9. *But health...trunk:* Cf. *Son.* 73, 1–4. The
quibble in 'trunk' is obvious.

229. *thy sight* seeing you.

230. *My worldly business* i.e. my life.

233. *swoon* (F4) Q. 'ſwound'—old sp.

234. *Jerusalem* v. G. and head-note 4. 4. Nothing
about it in *F.V.*, but both Stow and Hol. mention it
and the prophecy connected with it. Cf. also Wylie,
iv. 103–4.

5. 1.

On the alternation of the scenes here v. *Fortunes*,
pp. 114 ff. The al fresco setting after supper in 5. 3,
the mention of 'red wheat' at l. 14, and Hinckley Fair
at l. 22 suggest late August as the season (cf. Madden,
p. 381).

11. *precepts* writs. The business of the self-important
Davy is more urgent than his master's.

12. *again* moreover.

hade land (Q.) F. 'head-land' wh. all edd. (ex.
Arden) follow; v. G. The terms mean much the same
thing.

14. *red wheat* App. also called 'red Lammas' and
sown in August wet weather in the Cotswolds (cf.
Madden, p. 381, O.E.D., and Prothero in *Sh. Eng.*
i. 352).

18. *cast* i.e. checked.

20. *link to the bucket* chain for the yoke.

22. *Hinckley* (F.) Q. 'Hunkly'—a minim error; cf. MSH. pp. 106–7. Hinckley Fair (v. G.) was held on 26 Aug.

24. *answer it* pay for it.

25. *short-legged hens* Better table-birds than long-legged ones (Arden).

26. *tine* (F.) Q. 'tinie', v. G. F.'s 'durior lectio' is prob. correct.

28–9. *A friend...purse.* Prov.; cf. Apperson, p. 237 and *Euphues* (v. Bond ii. 227, ll. 26–7).

32. *marvellous* Q. 'maruailes'—a Sh. spelling, cf. MSH. p. 115.

33. *Well conceited* very witty; cf. *M.W.W.* 1. 3. 24.

35–6. *William Visor...of the hill.* Since R. W. Huntley pointed out (*Gloss. Cotswold Dialect*, 1848) that a Vizard was living in 1612 at Dursley, of which Woodmancote or Woncote is a suburb, and that a family named Purchase or Perkis lived at Stinchcombe Hill near by in the 16th c., these identifications have been widely accepted. But Malone identified 'Won-cot' with Wilmcote a mile from Stratford (cf. *Shrew*, Ind. ii. 21) which seems equally, if not more likely, and there is a 'Hill' in Stratford also.

40–50. *I grant...wrong* The country J.P. was the constant butt for dramatists at this time; cf. *Fortunes*, pp. 111–12 and Cheyney, ii. ch. xxxvii.

44. *and if* (F.) Q. 'and', poss. for 'an', wh. Ridley reads. 46. *but a very* (F.) Q. omits.

50–1. *Look about* 'look after the guests' (Arden), or poss. 'look sharp'.

56. *tall* v. G. Ludicrously addressed to Page, who is a very small boy (cf. note 1. 2. 1, and 'my little soldier', 5. 3. 32).

63. *semblable coherence* close correspondence.

64. *observing of* (F.) Q. 'obſeruing'. Balances 'conversing *with*' (l. 65); v. G. 'observe'.

67–8. *so…conjunction* 'joined in so intimate a union' (Arden).

in consent in chorus; cf. *Hen. V*, 2. 2. 22.

70. *with the imputation…near* by affecting to be (or giving out that I am) intimate, etc.

73–5. *It is…company* i.e. Evil communications corrupt good manners. Dangerous doctrine for Fal.! Cf. *Fortunes*, pp. 115–16.

78. *four terms* = twelve months.

actions 'There is something humorous in making a spendthrift compute time by the operation of an action for debt' (Johnson). The jest seems designed for inns-of-court students.

79. *intervallums* v. G.

80. *a sad brow* a grave face.

82. *laugh…laid up!* Cf. *M.V.* 1. 1. 80; *Tw.Nt.* 3. 2. 76–7.   *ill laid up!* not properly folded up.

5. 2.

S.D.   Q. 'Enter Warwicke, duke Humphrey, L. chiefe Iuſtice, Thomas Clarence, Prince Iohn, Weſtmerland.' Here the Q. entries seem to be 'massed' (cf. p. 150) but prob. Sh. jotted down the names before making up his mind when they were to appear (Shaaber). N.B. Q. gives 'Enter Iohn, Thomas, and Humphrey' at l. 13.

3. *Exceeding well* Cf. *A. & C.* 2. 5. 33, *Wint.* 5. 1. 30.

16. *of he* (Q.) F. 'of him'. Shaaber cites *Temp.* 2. 1. 27.

18. *strike sail* Like a noble argosy brought to by pirates.

34. *swims…quality* goes against the current of your nature. Cf. G. 'quality'.

38. *ragged* v. G.

forestaled Q. 'foreſtald'. Edd. cite 'a forestal'd

remission', Massinger (*Duke of Milan*, 3. 1. 152; *Bondman*, 3. 3. 169) and interpret 'a remission forestalled (or refused in advance)'. But A. K. McIlwraith (T.L.S. 19 Jan. 1933, p. 40), pointing out that all readings have only one *l*, suggests 'forestaled'=staled beforehand (by the ignominy of having to beg for it), wh. gives the best meaning in all three instances.

42. S.D. Q.'s entry for Blunt provides his majesty with a gentleman in-waiting.

44. *new and gorgeous garment* The metaphor is exemplified by the royal robes he wears, which contrast with the deep black of the others.

46. *mix* (F.) Q. 'mixt'. Prob. 'mixe' misread 'mixd' and set up as 'mixt'. (Shaaber).

48. *Amurath* In 1574 Amurath IV of Turkey strangled his brothers on his accession; and Mahomet his successor did the like in 1596.

52. *deeply* with deep seriousness. Cf. note 4. 5. 140.

53. *wear...heart* Cf. *Ham.* 1. 2. 85–6; 3. 2. 71.

61. *By number* i.e. give you an hour of happiness for every tear.

62. *otherwise* (Q.) F. 'other'. Cf. *1 Hen. VI*, 1. 3. 10.

64–121. *You are...wise directions* The legend here drawn upon is a combination of two versions: (*a*) by Th. Elyot (*Boke of the Governour*, 1531), and (*b*) by Redmayne (*Chronicle*, c. 1540), repeated respectively by Stow and Hol. I feel sure Sh. went direct to Elyot. Cf. *Library*, June 1945, pp. 7–9.

72. *washed in Lethe* Cf. *Tw.Nt.* 4. 1. 62; *Ric. III*, 4. 4. 250–1. But Lethe was for drinking not immersion. Poss. Sh. took the latter notion from Dante, whom Beatrice immerses in Lethe (*Purg.* 31. 101) as R. K. Root points out (*Class. Myth. in Sh.*, Yale Studies, xix). See Shaaber. But Dante is forced to drink also.

73. *use the person* assume the character; v. G. 'person'.

85–90. The queries (Q., F.) are ignored by most edd.

86. *your awful bench* the court of King's Bench, as Elyot and Stow (but not Hol.) mention.

90. *in a second body* in another person.

102. *right Justice* (Q., F.) i.e. justice itself. Edd. read 'right, justice,' taking 'justice' as a vocative.

103. *Therefore...sword* Neither Elyot nor Stow mention a confirmation of office but the latter has a marginal note 'William Gascoigne was Chiefe Iustice of the Kings bench from the sixt of Henry the fourth till the third of Henry the fift', wh. prob. suggested the idea to the old dramatist, since *F.V.* anticipates Sh. here; cf. sc. ix. 193–6.

108–12. '*Happy...Justice*' A paraphrase of the K.'s speech in Elyot; *F.V.* has nothing corresponding.

115. *remembrance* In the legal or official sense; cf. G. and 'remembered' (l. 142).

123–5. *My father...I survive* Cf. *Romans*, vi. 4–6, wh. perhaps suggested the idea to Sh. Cf. also 4. 5. 189–90 and *Hen. V*, 1. 1. 25–7. By 'My father' the P. means of course his corpse.

125. *spirits* (Q., F.) F3 'spirit' wh. all edd. follow. Cf. *Ham.* 3. 2. 56; *Ant.* 5. 2. 173. 'Spirits' (=disposition, character) is contrasted with 'affections'; v. G. and cf. *Romans* i. 26, 'vile affections'. The K.'s 'spirit' in the theol. sense is not in question; that is with God. *sadly* soberly.

128. *Rotten opinion* Alluding to the noisome breath of public scandal; v. G. *who* Cf. 4. 5. 107 (note).

130. *proudly* Cf. *M.N.D.* 2. 1. 91, 'Have every fretting river made so proud'. After 'blood' there is also a suggestion of 'proud'=lustful; cf. *V.A.* l. 260.

132. *the state of floods* 'the majesty of the ocean' (Schmidt, Onions).

135–7. *let us choose...nation* Cf. Hol. iii. 543, 'he chose men of grauitie, wit, and high policie, by whose

wise counsell he might at all times rule to his honour
and dignitie'.

136–7. *go...rank* walk abreast.

141–2. *accite...state* summon all the great men
of the land.

5.3.

S.D. Q. 'Enter ſir Iohn, Shallow, Scilens, Dauy,
Bardolfe, page.' F. 'Enter Falſtaffe, Shallow, Silence,
Bardolfe, Page, and Piſtoll'. For Q.'s 'Scilens' (which
occurs 13 times in the scene) v. p. 119. Pope read
'Gloucestershire', Theobald 'Shallow's Seat in Glou-
cestershire', and Capell 'Glostershire. Orchard of
Shallow's House. Tables under an Arbor'.

3. *caraways* Steevens cites Cogan, *Haven of Health*,
1584, 'We are wont to eate carawaies or biskets or
some other kind of comfits or seedes together with
apples, thereby to breake winde ingendred by them'.

3–4. *come, cousin* This, repeated l. 16, directs the
attention of the audience to the desperate plight of Sil.

6–7. *a goodly...a rich* (F.) Q. 'goodly...rich'.

10. *well said* cf. note 3.2.274.

11. *serves...uses* is most serviceable (and so saves
his parsimonious master much in wages).

17–23. *Ah, sirrah!...merrily* Q., F. print as
prose. In 'Ah sirrah!' Sil. is addressing himself; cf.
A.Y.L. 4.3.165; *Rom.* 1.5.31, 128. No ballad
original has been discovered for the song.

23. *ever among* all the while (v. O.E.D. 'among',
B1).

27. *Sweet sir, sit* Davy now takes upon him as
host, and 'impertinently asks Bard. and the Page who,
according to their place, were standing, to sit down'
(Johnson). My S.D. has the backing of Kemble (v.
Sprague, p. 93).

29–30. *what...in drink.* Prov. saying (Arden);
cf. Lodge's *Rosalynde* (ed. Greg), p. 23; Heywood,
1 Fair Maid of the West, 2.1; *Histriomastix*, 2.1.223.

30–1. *but you...all* But you must excuse our poor entertainment; and take the will for the deed. The conventional apology of a host.

34–6. *Be merry...wag all* Q. prints as prose; F. as verse, ''Tis merry...wag all' is prov.; v. Apperson, p. 414.

36. *wag* (F.) Q. 'wags'. Cf. note 4. 5. 79. But I think Q. here misprints, if only on grounds of euphony.

41. *merry* Here prob. = tipsy.

46. S.D. Capell, 'to Bard.' Cf. note l. 27. Silence overhears.

47–9. *A cup...long-a* Q., F. print as prose.

48. *thee* Q., F. 'the'. A common sp. of 'thee'.

51. *An* (Capell) Q. 'and', F. 'If'.

51–2. *now...the night* Cf. 2. 4. 364–5.

55–6. *Till...bottom* Q., F. as prose.

55. *let it come* i.e. come round again. A drinking-party formula; cf. 'let it pass', and *2 Hen. VI*, 2. 3. 65.

56. *a mile to the bottom* i.e. 'to the bottom, if it were a mile' (Herford).

59. *tine* F. 'tyne', Q. 'tiny'. Cf. note 5. 1. 26.

61. *caballeros* Q. 'cabileros', F. 'Cauileroes'. Shal. uses the Sp. form.

62. *once* one day.

64. *crack...together* i.e. split a quart. Not a very ample invitation, which Bard. is quick to enlarge.

67. *By God's liggens* F. omits, v. p. 116 and G. 'liggens'.

68. *will not out* will not drop out, i.e. get dead drunk, and so desert the company—an act of treachery among topers. Cf. *Ant.* 2. 7. 36.

68–9. *A' will not out, a'. 'Tis* Q. 'a wil not out, a 'tis', F. 'He will not out, he is'. The Q. ''tis' is retained by taking the second ''a' as emphatic duplication; cf. *Lear*, 2. 2. 104, 'he cannot flatter, he' and Franz, § 298. For ''Tis' = 'he is' cf. 2. 1. 3, 'Is't a lusty yeoman?'

74. S.D. Capell and Camb. 'To Silence, seeing him take off a bumper'.

75–8. *Do me...not so?* Q., F. print as prose. Cf. G. 'do'.

75–7. *Do me...Samingo.* Malone cites *Yorkshire Tragedy* (1608) i. 93 ff., 'They call it knighting in London when they drink upon their knees', and Arden notes that in Nashe's *Summer's Last Will* (McKerrow, iii. 267) Bacchus 'dubs Will Summer with the black Iacke' as he kneels drinking before him and a chorus sings:

> Mounsieur Mingo for quaffing did surpasse
> In Cup, in Can, or glasse.
> God Bacchus doe him right
> And dubbe him Knight.

Thus 'Samingo'=a corruption of 'Sir Mingo' (identity unknown).

87. *What wind...hither* Prov.; v. Apperson, p. 690.

91. *but* except. Sil. takes 'greatest' for 'biggest'.

92. *Barson* Sugden identifies with Barcheston (local pron. 'Barson'), a village on the Stour, ten miles from Stratford, and suggests that Goodman Puff was some 'notoriously fat man whom Sh. remembered from his Stratford days'. This identification lends support to 'Woncot'=Wilmecote (5. 1. 36).

93–8. *Puff...price* Q., F. print as prose. As 'puff'=swaggerer, Pist. assumes that Sil. insultingly compares Fal. with some braggart; hence the retort of 'coward'.   *i'thy* Q. 'ith thy', F. 'in thy'.

99–100. *a man of this world* 'an ordinary mortal' (Arden).

101–8. *A foutre...lap* (F.) Q. as prose.

102. *Africa* where the gold comes from.

103–4. *O base...thereof* As Pist. refuses to speak 'like a man of this world', Fal. adopts the style of an African king; v. G. 'Cophetua'.

105. *And Robin...John* A ballad-snatch, contemptible stuff to 'high-brow' Pistol.

106. *Helicons* i.e. the Muses (or true poets, like
himself). Pist. had given much thought to the delivery
of his news.

108. *lay thy head...lap.* send thy wits to the devil.

109. *I know...breeding* Shal. goes carefully with
one from court.

116. *Besonian* (Q.) F. 'Bezonian', v. G. A deliberate insult to one 'in some authority'.

118–22. *A foutre...Spaniard* (F.) Q. as prose.

118. *A foutre...office* On the death of a king a
J.P.'s office terminated.

121. *do this* He makes the offensive gesture; v. G.
'fig'.

124. *As nail in door* Prov.; v. Apperson, p. 137.

127. *double-charge* Quibbling on his name; cf.
2. 4. 106–8 note.

129–30. *knighthood* (F.) Q. 'Knight'.

139. *Let us...horses* i.e. 'press' them in the K.'s
name, and so avoid the expense of hiring 'posts' (v. G.).

141. *woe...justice!* Note this follows the reconciliation scene; cf. *Fortunes*, pp. 117–18.

142–4. *Let...days* (F.) Q. as prose.

142. *Let vultures...also* i.e. in hell. Cf. *M.W.W.*
1. 3. 84. A tag of the Marlowe-Greene drama, derived
from *Aeneid*, vi. 597–9.

143–4. *Where...days* i.e. others may sigh for the
good old days, we have them before us. Cf. *Shrew*,
4. 1. 129. *they?* (F.) Q. 'they:'.

5.4.

S.D. Q. 'Enter Sincklo and three or foure officers'.
I adopt the Camb. S.D. For 'Beadles' v. G. Sincklo
(alias Sinckler) is the name of a small-part actor in Sh.'s
company; also found in S.D.s at *3 Hen. VI* (F.) 3. 1
(passim), *Shrew* (F.), Ind. i. 88, the 'plot' of *2 Seven
Deadly Sins* (a play acted c. 1590–1 by the Admiral's

and Strange's men, cf. Greg, *Eliz. Dram. Documents*,
pp. 12 ff.), and the Ind. to Marston's *Malcontent*
(1604). A. Gaw plausibly identifies him with the
'mere anatomy' for whom Sh. in succession created
the Apothecary in *Rom.*, Robert Falconbridge in
K. John, Starveling in *M.N.D.* and this 'famished
correctioner', 1 Beadle. The appearance of actors'
names in a dramatic text used to be taken as an indication of prompt-book orig. (cf. Pollard, *Sh. Folios* etc.
p. 44; Chambers, *Wm. Sh.* i. 379 f.). But we now
'see the hand of the author himself writing a particular
part with a particular actor in view' (p. 40, Greg,
Editorial Problem). Moreover, in the present instance
Shaaber (p. 493) points out that 'it would be a most
defective prompt-book indeed that failed to warn the
prompter of...essential entrances' like those of Doll
and Quickly, which Q. omits. Cf. p. 119.

1–7. *No, then...about her* We are, I think, to
imagine the arrest has just taken place. Quick. still
struggles against it and 1 Beadle explains to her that
Doll is the main culprit.

2. *I might die...hanged* i.e. that he might be
hanged for her murder; cf. ll. 14–15.

4. *The constables* etc. Q. prints '*Sincklo*' or '*Sinck.*'
as prefix to this and all 1 Beadle's other speeches.

5. *whipping-cheer* i.e. the hospitality of Bridewell.
Doll is being carried off to be whipped as a notorious
whore; cf. 3. 2. 316 note, T. Heywood, *Royal King*,
2. 2, 'Send him to Bridewell ordinary; whipping cheer
is best for him', and Jonson, *Barth. Fair*, 4. 7. 58 (to
Alice, 'the punk of Turnbull'), 'You know where
you were taw'd (=thrashed) lately, both lash'd and
slash'd you were in Bridewell'. *enough* (F.) Q. omits.

7. *about her* Either 'in her company' or 'because
of her'.

8. *Nut-hook* v. G.　　9. *come on* v. G.

tripe-visaged i.e. sallow, 'pock-marked' (Dr F. Fra-
ley *ap*. Shaaber); cf. 'paper-faced' (l. 11).

10. *the child* Some have supposed the child real and Fal. the father. This is just what Quick. wishes the officers to believe. But ll. 16–17 tell us what the pregnancy amounts to.

13–14. *he would* (F.) Q. 'I would'. All edd. follow F., I think rightly.

14–15. *I pray...miscarry* She means 'may not miscarry'. Another attempt to frighten the beadles; cf. l. 2.

18–19. *the man...you* Clearly in Fal.'s absence Doll has been more successful in provoking Pistol to bloodshed than she was in 2. 4. Cf. *Fortunes*, pp. 107, 118.

20. *thin...censer* Variously explained as (i) like a figure on the lid of a perfume-pan (v. G. 'censer'), or (ii) wearing a cap like a 'censer'. No. (i) seems the more likely; cf. the ridicule of the face and figure of Holofernes in *L.L.L.* 5. 2 and of R. Falconbridge in *K. John*, 1. 1. 138 ff.

21. *blue-bottle* Beadles, like mod. policemen, wore blue coats, the uniform of servants.

22. *correctioner* i.e. whore-beater. App. a word of Doll's coinage, from 'house of correction', i.e. Bridewell.

24. *she knight-errant* Cf. *1 Hen. IV*, 1. 2. 24 (note). A quibble on night-errant (sinner by night) seems patent.

26. *of sufferance comes ease* Prov.; v. Apperson, p. 608. But she means 'suffering', not 'tolerance'.

31. *atomy* v. G. She means 'anatomy'=skeleton.

32. *rascal* Cf. note 2. 4. 40.

5. 5.

Q. and F. give different arrangements for this scene, set out on p. 118, and all edd. have followed that of F. I follow Q.'s, which has never been understood, though it is implicit in the dialogue of the Strewers, who speak of the hour the service is to finish and yet imply that their job requires the utmost dispatch. 'The trumpets have sounded twice' says 2 Strewer, whereupon (in Q.) they sound a third time, 'and the King and his train pass over the stage', i.e. entering from a side door, they move across the freshly strewn rushes into the inner-stage, which stands for the Abbey. Locality, occasion and time are all fixed with absolute precision, and beautiful economy. By dispensing with the first procession, F. leaves the prelim. dialogue in ruins. 'Dispatch, dispatch' is deleted, but the urgency in 'More rushes, more rushes' and 'The trumpets have sounded twice' remains, unexplained and pointless. That the whole ceremony should be imagined as taking place during the 35 ll. of dialogue between the K.'s first entry and his second is entirely in accordance with Eliz. stage-conventions. Cf. the meeting of the K.'s council at 1. 3. 122 of *Ric. II.*

5. *Robert* (F.) Q. omits.

6. *do you grace* show favour to you.

I will leer upon him Cf. *The Brut* (1479), ed. F. W. D. Brie (E.E.T.S.), p. 594:

[They] that were attendant to his misgovernaunce... supposed that he would have promoted them to great offices. And trusting hereupon, they were the homelier and bolder unto him, insomuch that when they were come before him, some of them winked on him and some smiled, and thus they made nice semblance unto him. But for all that the Prince kept his countenance full sadly.

11. *new liveries* i.e. uniforms with royal badges to denote that they were the K.'s servants. Would this have cost £1000?

15, 17, 19. *It doth so* etc. Q. gives all three speeches to *Pist.*; Hanmer and mod. edd. all to *Shal.* Q. is probably wrong about 15 since Fal. is addressing Shal. I follow F., which shows the two men paying obsequious court to Fal., now 'one of the greatest men in this realm' (5. 3. 89).

23–4. *It is best, certain. But to travel* etc. F.'s distribution. Q. gives the whole to Shal.

28. *obsque* (Q., F.) Whether Sh. intended Pist. to blunder or himself wrote the 'a' like an 'o' (as he often did) cannot be determined. 'Semper idem' is a motto, used by Qu. Eliz., and 'absque...est' is prob. another (=without this, i.e. our seeing him, there is nothing).

29. *all in every part* (F.) Q. 'in euery part'. Another motto or prov. phrase signifying absolute identity; in full 'all in all and all in every part'.

31–8. *My knight...but truth* (Capell) Q., F. as prose.

35. *Haled* (Camb.) Q. 'halde', F. 'Hall'd', Pope, etc. 'hauled'. O.E.D. agrees with Pope, since 'hall'd' is a 16th c. sp. of 'hauled'. But Q. 'halde' surely= haled. The two words are the same in origin, but Pist. would affect the more poetical or archaic form.

36. *mechanical* v. G. Eliz. constables were working-men when not on duty.

37. *ebon den* Bombast for 'hell'.

38. *in* i.e. in Bridewell.

40. S.D. Q. 'Enter the King and his traine'. F. 'The Trumpets sound. Enter King Henrie the Fift, Brothers, Lord Chiefe Iustice'. Cf. head-note.

42–3. *royal imp of fame* Arden cites Peele, *Alcazar*, l. 412, 'the impe of roiall race'.

45–7. *My lord...heart!* The K. tries to avoid the encounter, but Fal. brushes the L.C.J. aside. Cf. *Fortunes*, p. 121, and art. by H. H. Stewart, *Notes and Queries*, ii, 1 July 1916 (cited Shaaber, p. 591), which suggests that 'My lord...vain man' is spoken aside ('vain'=silly).

48–73. *I know thee not...set on* Cf. *Fortunes*, pp. 120–3.

48. *I know thee not* The words of the Bridegroom to the foolish virgins, *Matt.* xxv. 10–12.

51. *surfeit-swelled* For Nashe parallel v. *1 Hen. IV*, p. 196. 53. *hence* henceforth. Cf. *L.L.L.* 5. 2. 812.

54–5. *Leave...other men* Warburton notes that the word 'gormandizing...unluckily presenting him with a pleasant (=humorous) idea, he...is just falling back into Hal' in an allusion to Fal.'s bulk, when he pulls himself up and 'resumes the thread of his discourse'.

64–71. *Till then...advancement* Here are four points: (1) banishment on pain of death, (2) a ten-mile limit, (3) an allowed competence, (4) possibility of a return to favour after reformation. All but no. (3) are reflected in *F.V.* (sc. ix. 58–64); all but no. (4) in Hol. (iii. 543), and all but no. (2) in Stow (*Annals*, Hen. V, 1413).

68. *evils* (Q.) F. 'euill'.

71–2. *Be it...my word* The order which leads to the arrest that takes place at l. 92.

73. *Set on* What flint-like finality! Cf. 4. 4. 33.

74. *I owe...pound* 'It would be interesting to know whether Sh.'s Fal. said this like a Stoic accepting the facts of life, or with an inward chuckle, delighted to think that he had at all events taken £1000 off the foolish Justice' (Bradby, *Short Studies in Sh.* 1929, p. 66). Critics are divided. Cf. *Fortunes*, p. 126.

88. *A colour...die in* With a quibble on 'dye'.

89. *Fear no colours* Prov.; v. Apperson, p. 207; *Tw.Nt.* 1. 5. 5–6 and G. there.

90. *Lieutenant Pistol* None but Dyce and Shaaber have noticed 'Pist.'s sudden promotion', a point that could be made quite clear to the audience if the title were well stressed. Promotion is all Fal. has to give.

91. S.D. Q. 'Enter Iuſtice and prince Iohn'. F. gives no entry. But the L.C.J. must have gone out with 'the train' at l. 73, if only to fetch the officers for the arrest. Some suppose that he would wish to keep an eye on Fal., lest he should escape. Why should he? How could he? 'His womb, his womb' made escape impossible.

92. *carry...to the Fleet* v. G. 'Fleet'. Usually interpreted as an act of vengeance (by the L.C.J.) or spite (by the K.), because it is forgotten that this prison was very different in Tudor times from what it became after 1641. Fal. was being treated with no cruelty or indignity, but merely undergoing a temporary detention for the purpose of an enquiry, following on the order at ll. 71–2. This is shown (1) by the fact that the whole 'company' is arrested, (2) by the words 'I will hear you soon', and (3) by the contradiction between a permanent imprisonment and the terms of the banishment. Cf. *Fortunes*, pp. 118–20.

95–6. *I...away* (F.) Q. as prose.

97. *Si fortuna...contenta* Cf. note 2.4.177. Whether by accident or design the motto is here quoted in a different form.

98–100. *I like...provided for* By giving this comment to the 'sober-blooded boy' (4. 3. 86) Sh., many hold, wished to underline the ungenerous treatment that Fal. had received. On the contrary, I think, Sh. merely puts into the mouth of the last speaker of the play the abiding impression he desires to leave with us, viz. of a 'fair proceeding'. Cf. *Fortunes*, p. 127.

106–8. *ere this...France* Prepares the way for *Hen. V.*

107. *civil swords* Cf. 'civil blows', 4. 5. 133.

108. *I heard a bird so sing* Prov.; cf. Apperson, 'Bird' 3.

110. *Come, will you hence?* 'I fancy any reader, when he ends this play, cries out with Desdemona, "O most lame and impotent conclusion!"' (Johnson). Does this refer to the last scene or the last line? Malone thought the latter and compared it with similar endings in other of Sh.'s plays, while Steevens added that these may 'have proved as satisfactory to our ancestors as the moral applications and polished couplets' that terminated the plays of the neo-classical dramatists (Var. 1821, pp. 239–40).

Epilogue

I follow the Q. text. F., wh. all other edd. follow,
ends par. 1 with 'infinitely' and transfers the con-
cluding words (with the omission of 'I') to the end
of par. 3, though whether for theatrical or literary purposes seems doubtful. One thing may, I think, be said
with certainty: that all 3 paragraphs were never spoken
together on the stage, since the reference to 'a displeasing play' in par. 1 was obviously written for a
special occasion and since pars. 2 and 3, following the
prayer for the Queen, were as obviously written for
another one; though they must always have been
prefaced with at least the opening sentences of par. 1
(down to 'marring' perhaps) if they were to make
sense. Pope et seq. head the whole 'Spoken by a
Dancer'; v. 17 ff. n.

1. *fear* stage-fright (pretended).   *curtsy* Q. 'cur-
sie'; bow.

4–5. *what I have...making* This reads as if spoken
by the author, as indeed all par. 1 might be.

6. *I doubt* I fear.   7. *to the venture* i.e. I'll
risk it.

8. *a displeasing play* All sorts of guesses, but no
evidence.

11. *break* (*a*) break my promise, (*b*) am bankrupt.

13–15. *I commit...infinitely* The language of a
bankrupt debtor to his creditors who might send him
to prison.

bate me...you some i.e. accept this indifferent play
as part payment.

15–16. *and so...Queen* The speaker kneels osten-
sibly to ask pardon of the audience, and then, waggishly,
protests it is to pray for the Queen. Such prayers are
often to be found at the end of printed interludes, but
the fashion was seemingly going out in the public
theatres about the end of the 16th c. Cf. Creizenach,
p. 277; Chambers, *Eliz. Stage*, ii. 550.

17 ff. This is of course spoken by a dancer.

18. *light* (*a*) easy, (*b*) nimble.

21–4. *All the gentlewomen...assembly* This suggests a court audience and that the speaker had already won popularity with the ladies. Had he played the little Page? *seen before* (F.) Q 'feene'.

25–7. *If you...Sir John in it* Here is a definite promise, perhaps at court, that Fal. should figure in *Henry V*. Cf. *Fortunes*, pp. 5, 123–5.

29. *die of a sweat* Generally taken as alluding to the plague (cf. *Meas.* 1.2.81) or venereal disease, and there may be a glance at these. But the main point, as Shaaber notes, is that Fal., who 'sweat to death' on Gad's Hill, will do so again at Agincourt.

30–1. *for Oldcastle...not the man* Sh.'s famous apology for the misuse of Old.'s name is spoken jestingly. I cannot believe it was uttered on the stage while the matter was still dangerous. Cf. *Library*, June 1945, pp. 12–13.

30. *died a martyr* (F.)   Q. 'died Martyre'. Cf. J. C. Maxwell in *N. & Q.* cxcv (1950), 314. [1961.]

GLOSSARY

Note. Where a pun or quibble is intended, the meanings are distinguished as (*a*) and (*b*).

ABATE, (*a*) diminish, (*b*) blunt; 1. 1. 117

ACCITE, (i) summon; 5. 2. 141; (ii) induce (with a quibble on i); 2. 2. 58

ACONITUM, poisonous extract of wolf's bane or monk's hood; 4. 4. 48

ACT, thesis maintained by candidate for a university degree; 4. 3. 113

ADDRESSED, ready for action; 4. 4. 5

AFFECT, desire; 4. 5. 144

AFFECTION, (i) desire, lust (cf. *Lucr.* 500); 4. 4. 65; 5. 2. 124; (ii) inclination; 2. 3. 29; 4. 5. 172

AGAIN. Indicating intensity of action (cf. *Merch.* 3. 2. 204); 3. 2. 178

AGATE, tiny figure cut in agate for a ring or brooch; 1. 2. 16

AGGRAVATE, blunder for 'mitigate'; 2. 4. 156

AIM, (i) guess; 3. 1. 83; (ii) target; 3. 2. 265

ALECTO, one of the furies; 5. 5. 37

AMONG, 'ever among' = all the while; 5. 3. 23

ANCIENT, standard-bearer, corruption of 'ensign'; 2. 4. 65, 78, 106, 146, 168

ANGEL, gold coin (= 6s. 8d.), showing St Michael slaying the dragon; 1. 2. 162–3

ANSWER, 'to his answer' = to answer the charge in the courts; 2. 1. 31

ANSWER (vb.), (i) make amends; 2. 1. 129; 5. 1. 24; (ii) repel; 4. 5. 196

APE, (i) figure of fun; 2. 2. 70; 4. 5. 122; (ii) fool. A term of affection (cf. *1 Hen. IV*, 2. 3. 79); 2. 4. 213

APPLE-JOHN. Ripened *c.* St John's Day (midsummer) and eaten two years later, when shrivelled, thus typifying an aged lover; 2. 4. 2–5

APPREHENSIVE, swift to understand; 4. 3. 96

ARGUMENT, theme; 4. 5. 198; 5. 2. 23

ARTHUR'S SHOW. 'The Ancient Order of Prince Arthur and his Knightly Armory' (v. Shaaber) gave an annual exhibition of archery at Mile End Green (q.v.) after processing the streets; 3. 2. 280

ASSEMBLANCE, appearance; 3. 2. 258

ATOMY, atom (cf. *A.Y.L.* 3. 2. 230). But here prob. blunder for 'anatomy' = skeleton; 5. 4. 31

ATONEMENT, reconciliation; 4. 1. 221

ATTACH, seize, arrest; 2. 2. 4; 4. 2. 109

AWFUL, commanding reverence; 4. 1. 176; 5. 2. 86

BACKSWORD-MAN, fencer at single-stick; 3. 2. 66

BAFFLE, treat with contempt (cf. *1 Hen. IV*, G.); 5. 3. 107

BAIT, food, a little meal (O.E.D. 4); 3. 2. 330

BAND, bond; 1. 2. 31

BARBARY HEN, guinea fowl (a euphemism for 'prostitute', cf. *Oth.* 1. 3. 317); 2. 4. 94

BARTHOLOMEW BOAR-PIG, young porker fattened for sale at Bartholomew Fair, held every 24 Aug. at West Smithfield; 2. 4. 229

BASKET-HILT. Lit. hilt formed of steel plates curved like a basket, but often a contemptuous epithet for a poor swordsman, poss. because the style was old fashioned; 2. 4. 126

BATE (sb.), strife, quarrel; 2. 4. 248

BATE (vb.), let off, remit; ep. 13

BATTLE, battle-line; 3. 2. 158; 4. 1. 154, 179

BEADLE, parish officer, who did the whipping (esp. of rogues and whores) for the constable (cf. *2 Hen VI*, 2. 1. 136ff.); 5. 4. 1 (S.D.)

BEAR, (i) (a) carry, (b) endure; 1. 2. 222; (ii) bear in mind; 2. 2. 17; (iii) forbear, bear with; 5. 3. 31; (with quibble) 2. 4. 57

BEAR'ARD, either 'bear-ward' or 'bear-herd'; 1. 2. 167

BEAR DOWN, overwhelm; 1. 1. 11

BEAR IN HAND, delude, 'lead on'; 1. 2. 35

BEAR OUT, (i) carry the day; 4. 1. 135; (ii) carry through

a campaign; 4. 4. 88; 4. 5. 214; (iii) back up; 5. 1. 45

BEAVER, face-guard of helmet; 4. 1. 120

BED-HANGER, bed-curtain (cf. O.E.D. 'hanger' 2 a); 2. 1. 145

BEEF, fat ox (cf. *1 Hen. IV*, G.); 3. 2. 327

BEETLE, 'three-man beetle' = wooden mallet requiring three men to wield it, used for driving in piles, etc.; 1. 2. 224

BEFORE! forward! on!; 4. 1. 228

BEING (conj.), seeing that; 2. 1. 186

BELIE, tell falsehoods of; 1. 1. 98

BESEEK, dial. form of 'beseech'; 2. 4. 156

BESONIAN. Lit. raw needy recruit, from It. *bisogno* = need, (hence) beggar, rascal; 5. 3. 116

BESTOW (reflex), acquit oneself; 2. 2. 168

BIGGEN or biggin, night-cap; orig. cap worn by the order of Béguines; 4. 5. 27

BLESS (reflex), express surprise. Lit. say 'God bless me!' (cf. O.E.D. 10); 2. 4. 90

BLOOD, mood, humour; 2. 3. 30; 4. 4. 38

BLOODY, bloodthirsty; 1. 1. 127, 159; 4. 1. 34 (cf. 1. 3. 22, 'bloody-faced')

BLUBBER, disfigure with weeping; 2. 4. 387

BLUNT, dull; *ind.* 18

BONA ROBA, high-class courtesan. It. *buona roba* = good stuff; 3. 2. 24, 206

BOOK, (i) object of study; 2. 3. 31; (ii) document (cf. *1 Hen.*

IV, G.); 4. 1. 91; (iii) good
graces. Lit. account-book;
2. 2. 45; 4. 2. 17

BOOK-OATH, Bible-oath; 2. 1.
102

BORNE, laden, freighted (C.
Clark); 2. 4. 361

BOTTLE-ALE (adj.). °Abusive
epithet of uncertain meaning: prob. 'cheap' (Shaaber);
cf. *Tw.Nt.* 2. 3. 30 (note);
2. 4. 126

BOUNCE, bang; 3. 2. 283

BRAWN, 'boar fattened for the
table' (O.E.D.); 1. 1. 19

BREATHE, (i) rest; 1. 1. 38;
(ii) endow with breath;
4. 1. 114

BRISK, not flat (of wine); 5. 3.
47

BUCKET, beam or yoke for
carrying or hoisting; 3. 2.
263; 5. 1. 20

BUCKLE, bend under pressure;
1. 1. 141

BUNG, a cant word among
thieves for 'purse'; 2. 4. 123

BURN, infect with syphilis
(Schmidt; O.E.D. 14 e); 2.
4. 336

CABALLERO, Sp. gallant, good
fellow; 5. 3. 61

CALIVER, light musket; 3. 2.
269, 271

CALM, blunder for 'qualm';
2. 4. 35

CANDLE-MINE, tallow-maga-
zine; 2. 4. 299

CANKERED, tarnished; 4. 5. 71

CANNIBAL, blunder for Han-
nibal; 2. 4. 162

CANVASS, toss; 2. 4. 222

CASE (in good), well-to-do;
2. 1. 105

CAST, reckon; 1.1.166; 5.1.18

CATASTROPHE, posterior (jocular); 2. 1. 60

CAUSE, (i) case, (O.E.D. 10); 1.
3. 26; (ii) charge; 2. 1. 110;
4. 1. 190

CENSER, perfume-pan (? with
figure of a man cut out on
lid); 5. 4. 20

CERTIFICATE, licence, patent
(v. note); 2. 2. 119

CHAMBER, (a) small cannon,
(b) of uncertain equivocal
meaning; 2. 4. 50

CHANNEL, gutter; 2. 1. 47

CHARACTER, (a) sign, (b) letter
of the alphabet; 1. 2. 177

CHEATER, 'tame cheater' =
cant term for card-sharper's
decoy duck; 2. 4. 92

CHECK (sb.), reproof; 4. 3. 31;
(vb.) reprove; 1. 2. 192

CHOPT or chapped, dried up;
3. 2. 274

CLAW, scratch gently; 2. 4. 258

CLOSE WITH, make peace with;
2. 4. 325

CLOUT, the mark in archery,
i.e. a square piece of canvas
with a small white circle on
it, in the centre of which
stood the 'pin', a wooden
peg; 3. 2. 48

COCK, 'by cock and pie', a
trivial oath; 5. 1. 1

COLOUR, pretence; 1. 2. 242;
5. 5. 87–9

COME, 'come in' = return to
the firing-line; 3. 2. 282;
'come off' = retire; 2. 4.
48, 49; 'come on' = an
interjection implying rebuke
(Schmidt); 5. 4. 9; 'come
to proof' = turn out well;
4. 3. 88; 'come unto it' =
reach the age of puberty
(cf. *Ham.* 4. 5. 59; *Troil.*
1. 2. 90); 3. 2. 252

COMMENCE, take the university degree of Master; 4. 3. 112

. COMMODITY, profit; 1. 2. 244

COMMON, (a) low-bred (dog), (b) vulgar (people); 1. 3. 97

COMMOTION, rebellion; 2. 4. 360; 4. 1. 36, 93

COMPANION, fellow. Contemptuous; 2. 4. 89, 118'

CONCEIT, intelligence; 2. 4. 240

CONCEIVE, understand; 2. 2. 112

CONDITION, (i) social position; 4. 3. 1; (ii) natural disposition; 4. 3. 82; (iii) circumstances of the time; 3. 1. 78; 4. 1. 101; 5. 2. 11

CONFIRMATION, legal validity (O.E.D. 4); 4. 5. 188

CONFOUND, destroy, waste; 4. 4. 41

CONSIGN, set the seal; 5. 2. 143

CONSTRAINED, against one's will; 1. 1. 196

CONTINENT, (a) contents, (b) land-surface; 2. 4. 284

CONTINUANTLY, blunder for 'incontinently' = at once; 2. 1. 26

CONVERSATION, conduct; 5. 5. 101

CONVERSE WITH, associate with; 5. 1. 65

COPHETUA, African king, only known in the ballad, 'K. Cophetua and the Beggarmaid', L.L.L. 4. 1. 65, Rom. 2. 1. 14, Ric. II, 5. 3. 80, and Jonson, E.M.I. 3. 4. 56 ('as rich as K. Cophetua'); 5. 3. 104

COURSE, phase; 4. 4. 90

COURT, palace; 3. 2. 31, 326

COVER (vb.), lay the cloth; 2. 4. 10

CRACK, pert boy; 3. 2. 32

CROSS, (a) silver. All. Eliz. silver coins bore a cross, (b) punishment, adversity; 1. 2. 222

CRUDY, curdled; 4. 3. 96

CURRENT, genuine (alluding to 'current coin'); 2. 1. 120

CURRY WITH, flatter; 5. 1. 71

CURTSY, bow (by either sex); 2. 1. 123; Ep. 1

CUTTLE. Doubtful; may mean (i) cut-throat, (ii) cut-purse, or (iii) cuttle-fish, spewing black fluid; 2. 4. 125

DALE, pit (O.E.D. 'dale' 2, 'dell' 1). Cf. Piers Plowman, Prol. l. 15 'depe dale' (= hell), and Kyd, Sp. Trag. 3. 11. 21, 'a hugy dale of lasting night'; 4. 3. 6

DAME, mother; 3. 2. 116, 230

DAMN, ruin (cf. Yorkshire Trag. 2. 28, 'he that has no coyne is damnd in this world'); 2. 4. 337

DARE, defy; 4. 1. 119

DEAD, deadly pale; 1. 1. 71

DEAF (vb.), drown one sound by another; 3. 1. 24

DEAFNESS, numbness (cf. O.E.D. 'deaf' 4; Cor. 4. 5. 239); 1. 2. 115

DEAR, grievous; 4. 5. 140

DEBATE, quarrel; 4. 4. 2

DEBUTY, i.e. deputy of the ward (v. 1 Hen. IV, G.); 2. 4. 81

DECAY, ruin; 4. 4. 66

DEGREE, (i) stage of life; 1. 2. 228, (ii) rank; 4. 3. 6

DETERMINE, put an end to; 4. 5. 81

DIFFERENCE, battle (cf. K. John, 3. 1. 238); 4. 1. 181

DINT, force; 4. 1. 128

Do, 'do one right' = do the proper thing by one; 5. 3. 74

Doit, Dutch coin = ½ farthing. A name; 3. 2. 20

Dole, (a) dolour, (b) distribution; 1. 1. 169

Draw, (i) assemble; 1. 3. 109; (ii) withdraw; 2. 1. 148; (iii) drag; 2. 4. 288

Drawer, tapster; 2. 2. 171; 2. 4. 96, 287

Drollery, comic picture in the Dutch manner; 2. 1. 143

Drooping, i.e. where the sun sets; *Ind.* 3

Dry (of a hand). A supposed sign of failing virility (cf. *Tw.Nt.* 1. 3. 75 note); 1. 2. 177

Dull, (i) blunt (cf. *Merch.* 2. 7. 8); 1. 1. 118; (ii) drowsy, sluggish; 3. 1. 15; 4. 3. 95; 4. 5. 2

Easy, unimportant; 5. 2. 71

Element, sky (cf. *Tw.Nt.* 3. 1. 59); 4. 3. 51

Endeared, bound by ties of affection; 2. 3. 11

Enforcement, propulsion (cf. 'enforced', 4. 1. 71); 1. 1. 120

Engaged to, involved in; 1. 1. 180

Enrage, make frenzied; 1. 1. 144, 152

Ensinewed, knit by strong sinews; 4. 1. 172

Ephesian, boon companion (v. note); 2. 2. 148

Exion, blunder for 'action'; 2. 1. 29

Faitor, rogue (a high falutin' word); 2. 4. 154

Fancy, fantasia, musical impromptu; 3. 2. 318

Fang, grip. A name; 2. 1. 1

Favourable, kindly; 4. 5. 2

Fear (sb.), danger; 1. 1. 95; 4. 5. 195; (vb.) (i) frighten; 4. 4. 121; (ii) 'fear no colours' = have no fear. Lit. fear no foe; 5. 5. 89

Fertile, fertilizing; 4. 3. 117

Fetch off, fleece; 3. 2. 301

Fig (vb.), insult with a gesture of the thumb known as 'the fig of Spain'; 5. 3. 121

Figure, (a) design, (b) 'figure of the house' = horoscope; 1. 3. 43

Flap-dragon, 'a small combustible body fired at one end and floated in a glass of liquor, which an experienced toper swallowed unharmed, while still blazing' (D'Israeli, *Curiosities of Literature*); 2. 4. 245

Fleet, prison of the Star Chamber and Chancery Courts, generally used for distinguished persons temporarily detained by the Crown; after 1641 became a prison for debtors, bankrupts, etc.; 5. 5. 92

Fly-bitten, fly-specked; 2. 1. 145

Foin, thrust (a) with the sword, (b) in an equivocal sense; 2. 1. 16; 2. 4. 230

Forehand shaft, arrow designed for shooting point blank (v. note); 3. 2. 49

Forestaled, already stale (v. note); 5. 2. 38

Forgetive, creative, inventive (cf. *Ham.* 4. 7. 88); 4. 3. 97

FORSPENT, exhausted; 1. 1. 37

FOUTRE, indecent Fr. word used as term of contempt; 5. 3. 101, 118

FRANK, sty; 2. 2. 145

FRENCH CROWN, écu (= 4s.); 3. 2. 222

FRIENDS, relatives (cf. *A.Y.L.* 1. 3. 62); 3. 2. 107

FRONT, confront; 4. 1. 25; 4. 4. 66

FUB or fob, put off with false promises; 2. 1. 33

FULL POINT, full stop; 2. 4. 180

FUSTILARIAN, 'nonce-word, comic formation of "fustilugs" = fat frowzy woman' (O.E.D.); 2. 1. 60

GALEN (A.D. 129–199), physician to Marcus Aurelius, and voluminous author, whose writings dominated medical practice until mod. times; 1. 2. 115

GALL, supposed seat of envy, hatred, and malice; 1. 2. 173

GALLOWAY NAG, lit. a small Scottish horse. Nag = prostitute; cf. *Willobie his Avisa*, 1594 (sig. *4v), 'they may for an angell...haue hired nagges to ride at their pleasure'; 2. 4. 186–7

GARLAND, crown; 4. 5. 201; 5. 2. 84

GENERATION, issue; 4. 2. 49

GIBBET (vb.), hoist with a crane (cf. O.E.D. 'gibbet' sb. 3a, citing Dee, 1570, 'All Cranes, Gybbettes and Ingines to lift up'); 3. 2. 262

GIDDY, unstable, 1. 3. 89; 3. 1. 18; 4. 5. 213

GIVE, 'give out' = assert; 4. 1. 23; 'give way' = allow free scope; 2. 3. 2; 5. 2. 82

GLASS, model (cf. 'mirror', *Hen. V*, 2 ch. 6); 2. 3. 21, 31

GLOBE, (a) world, (b) 'complete or perfect body' (O.E.D. 1 b); 2. 4. 284

GO TO! Get along with you! Exclamation denoting 'contemptuous concession' (O.E.D.); 3. 2. 228, 233, 245; 5. 1. 50

GOODNIGHT, serenade; 3. 2. 318

GOOD YEAR, 'what the good year!' = what the dickens!; 2. 4. 57, 173

GOWN, v. *night-gown*; 3. 2. 186

GRAFF, graft; 5. 3. 3

GRATE ON, vex, annoy; 4. 1. 90

GRAVY, sweat (cf. Apperson, pp. 269–70, 'fry in one's own grease'); 1. 2. 160

GRAY'S INN, one of the Inns of Court; 3. 2. 34

GREEN (WOUND), fresh; 2. 1. 97

GREEN-SICKNESS, kind of anaemia affecting young women; 4. 3. 91

GRIEF. A word of wide meaning, including pain, worry, grievance, and sorrow; *Ind.* 13; 1. 1. 144, 211; 1. 2. 113; 4. 1. 69, 73, 110, 142; 4. 2. 36, 59; 4. 4. 56; 4. 5. 141, 203

GROAT, silver coin = 4d.; 1. 2. 231

GROUND, 'get ground of' = get the better of (cf. *vantage*); 2. 3. 53

GUARD (sb.), (a) trimming, (b) band, defence; 1. 1. 148

HA? eh?; 1. 1. 48

HADE LAND, unploughed strip, used as boundary and means of access between two portions of a field; 5. 1. 12

HAIR, the least bit; 1. 2. 23

HALF-FACED, hatchet-faced. Lit. with face as thin as the profile on a coin (cf. *K. John*, 1. 1. 94); 3. 2. 263

HALF-KIRTLE, skirt (v. *kirtle*); 5. 4. 23

HARRY TEN SHILLING, half-sovereign, *temp.* Henry VII or VIII; 3. 2. 222

HAUTBOY, oboe; 3. 2. 326

HAVE, (i) 'have at' = here's for…; 1. 2. 189; (ii) 'have away', get rid of; 3. 2. 187

HEAD, armed resistance, armed force; 1. 1. 168; 1. 3. 17, 71

HEAT, climax of a battle; 4. 3. 24

HEAVY, (i) (*a*) ponderous, (*b*) dejected; 1. 1. 118–21; (ii) profound;. 2. 2. 172; 4. 5. 38; (iii) bad, wicked; 4. 3. 55; (iv) sorrowful; 5. 2. 14, 24, 25, 26

HECTOR, bravest of Trojans; 'hectoring' not ascribed to him before 2nd half of 17th c. (v. O.E.D.); 2. 4. 216

HEMPSEED, i.e. tiny boy destined for the gallows; 2. 1. 58

HILDING, worthless; 1. 1. 57

HINCKLEY, town *c.* 30 miles N.E. of Stratford; its fair (horses, cattle, sheep and cheese) held on 26 Aug.; 5. 1. 22

HIREN, i.e. Irene, mistress of Sultan Mahomet II and later beheaded by him (heroine of Dr Johnson's play, *Irene*); 2. 4. 154, 171

HOLLAND, fine linen fabric, first made in Holland; 2. 2. 23

HUNT COUNTER, follow the trail backwards; 1. 2. 88

HURLY, tumult; 3. 1. 25

HUSBAND (sb.), husbandman, steward; 5. 3. 12; (vb.) till; 4. 3. 116

HUSH (vb.), lull; 3. 1. 11

HUSWIFE, hussy; 3. 2. 316

ILL-BESEEMING, apparently evil; 4. 1. 84

ILL-SORTED, in bad company; 2. 4. 144

IMBRUE, shed blood (an old-fashioned word; cf. *M.N.D.* 5. 1. 352); 2. 4. 192

INCISION, bloodshed. Surgical term used bombastically; 2. 4. 192

INDIFFERENCY, moderate size; 4. 3. 21

INDITE, blunder for 'invite'; 2. 1. 27

INFINITIVE, blunder for 'infinite'; 2. 1. 24

INSTANCE, example, proof; 1. 1. 56; 3. 1. 103; 4. 1. 83

INTELLIGENCER, one who carries information; 4. 2. 20

INTEND, (i) incline; 1. 2. 8; (ii) indicate; 4. 1. 166

INTERVALLUM, vacation at the law-courts; 5. 1. 79

INVEST, (i) clothe with authority; 4. 4. 6; (ii) endue; 4. 5. 72

INVESTMENT, vestment; 4. 1. 45

INWARD, (i) domestic; 3. 1. 107; (ii) sincere; 4. 5. 147

INWARDLY, secretly; 2. 2. 47

JEALOUSY, suspicion; *Ind.* 16

JERUSALEM CHAMBER, hall at W. front of Westminster Abbey built near end of 14th c. and now used as the Chapter House; so called from three texts referring to Jerusalem inscribed about the fire-place (Sugden); 4. 4. S.D.; 4. 5. 234

JEWEL, (a) brooch, (b) darling (cf. *M.W.W.* 3. 3. 40; *Oth.* 1. 3. 195); 1. 2. 18

JOINED-STOOL, stool made by a joiner; 2. 4. 246

JUGGLER, buffoon; 2. 4. 125

JUST, true, exact, equal; 3. 2. 83; 4. 1. 23, 226

JUVENAL, youth. Jocular; 1. 2. 19

KEECH, lump of animal fat. A name; 2. 1. 93

KEEPER, sick-nurse; 1. 1. 143

KEN, 'within a ken' = within sight; 4. 1. 151

KICKSHAW, fancy dish (Fr. quelque chose); 5. 1. 26

KINDLY, filial; 4. 5. 83

KINDRED, posterity; 2. 2. 26

KIRTLE, coat and skirt; 2. 4. 273

LA! exclamation calling attention to an emphatic statement; 2. 1. 154

LAND SERVICE, military (as opposed to naval) service; 1. 2. 133

LARGELY, abundantly; 1. 3. 12

LAVISH, licentious; 4. 4. 64

LAVISHLY, with excess; 4. 2. 57

LAY DOWN, formulate; 1. 3. 35

LEATHER-COAT, russet apple; 5. 3. 43

LEER, look lovingly; 5. 5. 6

LEMAN, sweetheart; 5. 3. 48

LEVEL, 'level to our wish' = ready for action; 4. 4. 7

LIGGENS, 'by God's liggens'. An oath of unexplained meaning; 5. 3. 67

LIGHTEN, enlighten, make wise; 2. 1. 196

LIKE WELL, be in good condition; 3. 2. 85–6

LINE, reinforce (from within). A tailoring term; 1. 3. 27

LINK, chain; 5. 1. 20

LIVER, supposed seat of the passions; 1. 2. 173; 5. 5. 31

LODGE (vb.), harbour; 4. 5. 207

LODGING, room; 4. 5. 233

LOOK, (i) 'look beyond' = misjudge; 4. 4. 67; (ii) 'look through' = become visible; 4. 4. 120; (iii) 'look up' = cheer up; 4. 4. 113

LOOSELY, (a) carelessly, (b) wantonly; 2. 2. 8; 5. 2. 94

LOW COUNTRIES, lower regions (cf. *Err.* 3. 2. 137); 2. 2. 22

LUSTY, (a) merry (cf. *K. John,* 1. 1. 108), (b) lascivious (cf. *Oth.* 2. 1. 304); 3. 2. 17

MAIN CHANCE, general probability. A term in the game of 'hazard'; 3. 1. 83

MAKE, (i) gather together; 1. 1. 168, 214; (ii) make out; 1. 2. 76; 2. 4. 40; (iii) 'make shift' = contrive (with quibble on 'shift' = shirt); 2. 2. 22

MALMSEY, strong sweet red Spanish wine; 2. 1. 38

MALT-WORM, orig. weevil found in malt, hence = toper; 2. 4. 332

MAN (vb.), attend; 1. 2. 16, 52

MANDRAKE, wanton manikin. Lit. a poisonous plant (genus *Mandragora*) associated by the Greeks and Hebrews (v. *Gen.* xxx. 14 ff.) with desire, because of its whitish root 'divided into two or three parts resembling the legs of a man with other parts ... adjoining thereto' (Gerarde, *Herball*, 1597); 1. 2. 14; 3. 2. 315

MAN-QUELLER, murderer; 2. 1. 52

MANURED, tilled (by hand); 4. 3. 116

MARE, nightmare; 2. 1. 78

MARK, (i) (*a*) sum of 13*s.* 4*d.*, (*b*) score; 2. 1. 31; (ii) conspicuous object on land or sea serving as a guide to travellers; 2. 3. 31

MARSHAL, officer in charge of tournaments; 3. 2. 323

MARTLEMAS. Reference to Martlemas beef or pork, i.e. slaughter of beasts, etc. about 11 Nov. (St Martin's day) for salting and winter consumption; an annual event until improvement of crops in 18th c. enabled man to feed cattle all the year round; 2. 2. 100

MATE, fellow (contemptuous); 2. 4. 120

MEANS, 'in our means' = with our available resources; 1. 3. 7

MECHANICAL, belonging to the working class; 5. 5. 36

MEDICINE POTABLE, i.e. 'aurum potabile', drug containing gold, supposed of supreme life-giving property, closely akin to the 'philosopher's stone' (q.v.); 4. 5. 162

MEET, receive reward, punishment, etc. (O.E.D.); 4. 5. 185

MESS, small quantity; lit. what a person needs for a single course; 2. 1. 95

METE, (*a*) measure, (*b*) appraise; 4. 4. 77, 104

METTLE, (*a*) spirit, (*b*) metal; 1. 1. 116; 5. 3. 40

MILE-END GREEN (now Stepney Green), used as drill-ground and for fairs and shows; 3. 2. 278

MODEL, builder's plan; 1. 3. 42

MODEST, restrained; 5. 5. 102

MOE, more (in number); 1. 2. 4

MOOD, (*a*) mode = musical key, (*b*) frame of mind; 4. 5. 199

MORE AND LESS, high and low; 1. 1. 209

MORROW, morning; 3. 1. 32–3

MUCH, (i) exclamation indicating scoffing incredulity; 2. 4. 127; (ii) 'precious little'; 3. 2. 134

MURE, wall; 4. 4. 119

MUSE, marvel; 4. 1. 167

MUTTON, (*a*) sheep's flesh, (*b*) loose woman (v. note); 2. 4. 344

NATURE, natural affection (cf. *Ham.* Introd. p. xxxiii); 4. 5. 39, 65

NAVE, hub (of a wheel); 2. 4. 254

NEAF, fist; 2. 4. 182

NEAR, (i) closely; 4. 5. 212; (ii) intimate with; 5. 1. 70

NEW-DATED, a few days old; 4. 1. 8

NICE, (i) trivial, foolish; 1. 1. 145; 4. 1. 191; (ii) punctilious; 2. 3. 40

NIGHT-GOWN, dressing-gown; worn for warmth, indoors and out, on all occasions— except warfare; 3. 1 (S.D.)

NOBLE, gold coin = 6s. 8d.; 2. 1. 153

NOISE, band of musicians; 2. 4. 11

NUT-HOOK, cant variant of 'catchpole', i.e. beadle or constable; 5. 4. 8

OBSERVANCE, 'do observance to', submit oneself; 4. 3. 15

OBSERVE, pay respect to, humour; 4. 4. 30, 36, 49; 5. 1. 64

OCCUPY, 'have to do with sexually' (O.E.D. 8); cf. *Rom.* 2. 4. 105. This meaning led to the almost complete disappearance of the word from print in the 17th and 18th c.; 2. 4. 143

O'ERPOST, shirk or escape responsibility for (a crime); 1. 2. 148

OFFEND, (a) harm, (b) wound; 2. 4. 112

OFFER, (i) propose; 1. 2. 41; (ii) attack; 4. 1. 219

OLD, grand, fine (colloq.); 2. 4. 20

OMIT, neglect; 4. 4. 27

ONCE, some time; 5. 3. 62

OPENER, interpreter; 4. 2. 20

OPINION, reputation (gen. scandalous); 4. 5. 188; 5. 2. 128

OPPOSED, hostile; 4. 4. 66

OPPOSITE, adversary; 4. 1. 16

OSTENTATION, exhibition; 2. 2. 49

OUCH, (a) 'boss of gold set with diamonds' (Pope), (b) scab; 2. 4. 47

OUSEL, blackbird; 3. 2. 9

OVERSCUTCHED, whipped repeatedly or all over (v. note, and G. 'beadle'); 3. 2. 316

OWE, own; 1. 2. 4

PAGAN, harlot (cf. note 2. 4. 222); 2. 2. 152

PANTLER, pantry man (pantry = orig. bread-room); 2. 4. 236, 313

PARCEL, item; 4. 2. 36

PARCEL-GILT, silver ornamented with gilt; 2. 1. 87

PART (sb.), action; 4. 5. 63

PART (vb.), depart; 4. 2. 70

PARTITION, distinction; 4. 1. 196

PAUL'S, i.e. the nave of (old) St Paul's Cathedral, a public resort where business of all kinds was carried on; 1. 2. 50

PERSON, character, function (cf. *M.N.D.* 3. 1. 56); 5. 2. 73

PHILOSOPHER'S STONE, the goal of alchemy, which when discovered would turn all metals to gold and give immortality to those who drank it as a potable; 3. 2. 329

PICKING, fastidious; 4. 1. 198

PIKE. For the quibble v. *Ado*, 5. 2. 21 (and G.); 2. 4. 49

PINCH, pain, torment; 1. 2. 227; 4. 5. 29

PLACE, 'hold one's place' = keep to one's station; 2. 2. 105

PLOT OF SITUATION, site; 1. 3. 51

POINT, tag or lace for fastening clothes together; 1. 1. 53; 2. 4. 128

POINT OF WAR, 'short phrase sounded on an instrument as a signal' (O.E.D.); 4. 1. 52

POLICY, craft; 4. 1. 148

Post (sb.), (i) post-horse. Provided for hire at 2½*d*. a mile, and at stages *c*..10 miles distant, on all main highways; *Ind.* 4; 4. 3. 36; (ii) courier, travelling by such stages; *Ind.* 37; 1. 1. 214; 2. 4. 353

Post (adv.); 2. 4. 373

Pottle, two quarts; 2. 2. 76; 5. 3. 66

Power, armed force; 1. 1. 133, etc.

Precept, writ; 5. 1. 11

Present (vb.), represent; 5. 2. 79

Present (adj.), immediate; 4. 1. 174; 4. 3. 72

Presently, at once; 2. 1. 177; 2. 4. 368

Prick, (i) prick off a name on a list; 2. 4. 330; 3. 2. 114, 177, 180; (ii) provoke, worry; 3. 2. 115; (iii) choose; 3. 2. 117; (iv) fasten with pins; 3. 2. 149; (v) dress; 3. 2. 157

Privy-kitchen, kitchen for cooking a monarch's personal food; 2. 4. 331

Proface, formula of welcome in eating or drinking = 'may it do you good'; 5. 3. 29

Profit, be an apt pupil; 2. 2. 82

Project (in), in prospect; 1. 3. 29

Proof, 'come to proof' = turn out well; 4. 3. 89

Proper, (i) belonging (to); 1. 3. 32; (ii) own; 5. 2. 109

Proportion, number (of troops); 4. 1. 23

Propose, imagine; 5. 2..92

Proudly, with unrestrained vigour (v. note); 5. 2. 130

Purchase (vb.), legal term = 'acquire otherwise than by inheritance' (O.E.D.); 4. 5. 199

Push, thrust, onset; 2. 2. 37

Put to, put to a trade or occupation; 3. 2. 168–9

Quality, (i) disposition; 5. 2. 34; (ii) rank; 4. 1. 11; (iii) attainment; 1. 3. 36; 5. 5. 70

Quantities, lengths (of wood); 5. 1. 60

Quean, shrew; 2. 1. 47

Question, 'in question' = under summons; 1. 2. 58

Quick, lively; 4. 3. 97

Quit, cleared, absolved, well said; 2. 4. 340; 3. 2. 238

Quittance, requital; 1. 1. 108

Quiver (adj.), nimble; 3. 2. 280

Quoit (vb.), pitch spinning through the air; 2. 4. 188

Rabbit = the young animal; 'coney' = mod. rabbit; 2. 2. 83

Rage, lust (cf. *Ham.* 3. 3. 89); 4. 4. 63

Ragged, (i) rough, dilapidated; *Ind.* 35; 1. 1. 151; (ii) 'full of rough or sharp projections' (O.E.D.); 3. 2. 145; (iii) beggarly; 5. 2. 38

Rampallian, 'riotous strumpet' (Steevens); 2. 1. 59

Rash, sudden and violent in operation; 4. 4. 48

Reason, cause for complaint; 4. 1. 191; 'in reason' = naturally; 2. 2. 48

Recordation, remembrance; 2. 3. 61

Red lattice, betokening an ale-house; 2. 2. 77–8

Remembrance, lit. 'note or entry serving as a record' (O.E.D.); 5. 2. 115

RESCUE (sb.), 'forcible taking of a person out of legal custody' (O.E.D.); 2. 1. 55

RIGOL, ring, circlet; 4. 5. 36

RIOT, (i) wantonness (cf. G. *1 Hen. IV*); 4. 4. 62; 4. 5. 135, (ii) insurrection; 4. 5. 134

ROAD, harlot (fig.); 2. 2. 165

ROTTEN. Commonly in Sh. 'applied to unwholesome vapour etc.' (Onions); 4. 4. 60; 5. 2. 128

ROYAL (sb.), 10s. piece; 1. 2. 24; (adj.), splendid, princely; 1. 2. 22

RUDE, violent; 1. 1. 159; 3. 1. 20

RULE, 'in military rules' = in the conduct of war; 2. 3. 30

SACK, Spanish wine (cf. note *1 Hen. IV*, 1. 2. 3–4); 1. 2. 194, etc.

SAINT GEORGE'S FIELD (more often 'fields') lay between Southwark and Lambeth; 3. 2. 196

SALTNESS, asperity; 1. 2. 96

SAMINGO, v. note; 5. 3. 77

SAVING YOUR (reverence, manhood, etc.), without offence to your, etc.; 2. 1. 26–7

SCAB, scurvy fellow; 3. 2. 275

SCALD, scorch; 4. 5. 31

SCALY, of scale-armour; 1.1.146

SEA-COAL, sea-borne coal from Newcastle; 2. 1. 88

SEAL, (a) lit. with wax, (b) come to terms with; 4. 3. 127

SEAL UP, (i) quibble on 'seel' = sew up a hawk's eyes; 3. 1. 19; (ii) confirm; 4. 5. 103

SECOND, subordinate; 5. 2. 90

SECT, profession (as elsewhere in Sh.); 2. 4. 36

SEMBLABLE, similar; 5. 1. 63

SERVE, (a) in the wars, (b) ''cover the female', of bulls, etc. (cf. O.E.D. 'serve' 52 and *Meas.* 3. 2. 117); 2.4.48

SET OFF (p.part.), ignored; 4. 1. 145

SET ON, instigate; 2. 1. 151

SETTLED, congealed, stagnant; 4. 3. 101

SHADOW, (i) Lat. *umbra*, i.e. hanger-on; 2. 2. 158; (ii) likeness; 3. 2. 133; (iii) dead man's name in the muster-book; 3. 2. 138

SHAPE (sb.), image (cf. *M.N.D.* 5. 1. 16); 4. 3. 98

SHAPE (vb.), (i) conceive; 1. 2. 170; 4. 4. 58; (ii) decree (O.E.D. 21 a); 3. 2. 331

SHERRIS SACK, sherry, 'sack' (q.v.) from Xeres; 4. 3. 94

SHIFT, change one's clothes; 5. 5. 22

SHOT, musketeer; 3. 2. 274

SHOVE-GROAT SHILLING, smooth Ed. VI shilling which came to be preferred to the groat for the game of shovel-board, forerunner of mod. shove-halfpenny; 2. 4. 188

SIGHT, visor; 4. 1. 121

SIGN OF THE LEG, boot-maker's shop-sign; 2. 4. 247

SIGNORIES, estates; 4. 1. 111

SIMPLY, absolutely; 4. 3. 21

SINGLE, feeble (cf. *Macb.* 1. 3 140); 1. 2. 180

SLIGHT, trifling; 2. 1. 143

SLOPS, wide baggy short breeches, often costing £10 to £100 (Linthicum, p. 209); 1. 2. 29

SMITHFIELD, London cattle and horse market.down to 1855; 1. 2. 48

SMOOTH, easy, accommodating, well-fitting; *Ind.* 40; 2. 1. 28; 2. 4. 248

SMOOTH-PATE, sleek round-head; 1. 2. 37

SNARE, noose. A name; 2. 1. 5

SNEAP, snub; 2. 1. 121

SOBER, calm, moderate; 4. 3. 78

SOBER-BLOODED, calm, lacking in passion; 4. 3. 86

SOON AT NIGHT, 'towards evening' (Onions); 5. 5. 91

SORT, rank, class; 1. 2. 6

SORTANCE, 'hold s. with' = suit; 4. 1. 11

SOUTH, the S.W. wind; 2.4. 360

SPENT, (*a*) consumed, (*b*) done with; 3. 2. 121–2

SPIRITS, (i) faculties; 1. 1. 198; (ii) sentiments (cf. *Macb.* 1. 5. 27); 5. 1. 63, 66; (iii) disposition, character (cf. *Ham.* 3. 2. 56); 5.2.125; (iv) 'vital spirits' (q.v.)

STAB, 'with an obscene double meaning' (Schmidt; cf. *Caes.* 1. 2. 277); 2. 1. 13

STAMFORD (Lincs.) held 3 fairs p.a. (Feb., Lent, Aug.) when 'a price was set on live stock that remained current in the country round till the next fair' (Unwin, *Sh. Eng.* i. 312); 3. 2. 40

STAND, act, behave as (cf. *Cor.* 2. 3. 198); 3. 2. 221; 4. 3. 81

STAND TO, (i) stand by; 2. 1. 64; (ii) 'stand to it' = act stoutly; 2. 1. 4

STAND UPON, (i) depend upon; 3. 2. 148; (ii) insist upon; 1. 2. 36; 4. 1. 165

STARVED, miserable, emaciated; 3. 2. 304

STEWED PRUNES. A dish of

these stood in the window of a brothel; 2. 4. 141

STEWS, brothel, specially one in Southwark, the name (acc. to Fuller) being derived from 'stews' or fish-ponds once there; 1. 2. 52

STICK, (i) hesitate; 1. 2. 22; (ii) shine steadfastly like a jewel on a person or a star in the sky (cf. *Ham.* 5. 2. 255; *Ant.* 5. 2. 79); 2. 3. 18

STOCKFISH, dried cod fish, beaten before cooking (cf. *Meas.* 3. 2. 106). A name; 3. 2. 33

STOMACH, (i) courage; 1. 1. 129; (ii) appetite; 4. 4. 105, 107

STOP, (i) one's mouth = satisfy; 1. 2. 41, (ii) one's ear = deafen, 1. 1. 78–9

STRAIN, (*a*) pitch, (*b*) excessive feeling; 4. 5. 170

STRANGE, foreign; 4. 4. 69

STRANGE-ACHIEVÉD, hard-won (?). Other proposals: (i) acquired by foreign trade; (ii) wrongly gotten, (iii) gained for others to enjoy; 4. 5. 71

STRATAGEM, (i) device to effect surprise (military term); 2. 4. 20; (ii) deed of violence (= loose extension of i); 1. 1. 8

STRAY, stragglers. Lit. strayed cattle; 4. 2. 120

STRIKE SAIL, yield (as to a pirate); 5. 2. 18

STUDIED, (*a*) diligent, (*b*) inclined; 2. 2. 8

STUDY (sb.), mental application; 1. 2. 114

SUBSTANTIAL, well-established, valid; 4. 1. 173

SUBSTITUTE (sb.) deputy; 4. 2. 28; 4. 4. 6; (vb) appoint deputy, 1. 3. 84

SUCCESS, a succession; 4. 2. 47

SUGGESTION, evil prompting; 4. 4. 45

SUPPLY, reinforcement; 1.3. 12, 28; 4. 2. 45

SURE (with vbs. 'hold,' 'guard'), harmless; 2. 1. 25; 4. 3. 73

SURECARD, lit. winning card; thus a person bound to succeed; 3. 2. 89

SURGERY (vb.), have wounds or sores dressed; 2. 4. 49

SWAY ON, advance; 4.1. 24

SWINGE, thrash; 5. 4. 21

SWINGE-BUCKLER, blusterer; lit. shield-beater; 3. 2. 23

TA, thou (dialect); 2. 1.58

TABLES, writing tablet, notebook; 2. 4. 265; 4. 1. 201

TAKE ON (or upon), pretend, profess; 2. 2. 112; 4. 1. 60

TAKE UP, (i) cope with; 1. 3. 73; (ii) obtain goods on credit (cf. *Ado* 3. 3. 172); 1. 2. 39; (iii) raise, levy; 2. 1. 186; 4. 2. 26

TALL, fine (fellow), doughty; 3. 2. 62; 5. 1. 56

TALLOW, dripping, animal fat rendered down; 1. 2. 156

TASTE (sb.), test, trial, lit. sample (cf. *Ham.* 2. 2. 436); 2. 3. 52; (vb.) experience; 4. 2. 116

TEMPER, (a) melt, soften (like wax; cf. *V.A.* 565); (b) come to proper frame of mind; 4. 3. 126

TEMPERALITY, 'Humorous misuse of temper' (O.E.D.), frame of mind; 2. 4. 23

TENNIS (cf. *Hen. V*, 1. 2. 254 ff.). The orig. game played in an enclosed court or house, not mod. 'lawn tennis'; very popular with gallants in Tudor and Stuart London, but already so in Paris of 14th c., and 'tennis' said to derive from 'tenez' (= take!); 2. 2. 19

TERM, proportion; 4. 4. 104

TESTER, sixpence; 3. 2. 275

TEWKESBURY, where the best mustard came from; 2.4.240

THICK, (i) 'speak thick', i.e. so quickly that the words are slurred; 2. 3. 24; (ii) dim; 3. 2. 312; 4. 3. 57

THOUGHT, care, worry; 4. 5. 68

THOUGHTFUL, anxious; 4. 5. 72

TIDY, prime, plump; 2. 4. 228

TILLY-FALLY (or 'tilly-vally'), hoity-toity, fiddlesticks!; 2. 4. 79

TIME, (i) age; 1. 2. 96; (ii) life; 2. 2. 140; (iii) present or existing circumstances (cf. *Ham.* 4. 7. 110); 1. 3. 70, 110; 2. 3. 3; 4. 1. 70, 104

TINE, obs. or W. country dial. for 'tiny'; always found with 'little'; 5. 1. 26; 5. 3. 59

TINGLING, 'pins and needles' in a limb 'gone to sleep' (?); 1. 2. 110

TISICK, i.e. phthisic, consumptive cough. A name; 2. 4. 81

TO-NIGHT, last night (cf. *M.V.* 2. 5. 18); 2. 1. 168

TOOTH, appetite; 4. 5. 132; 'i'the teeth', in the face; 5. 3. 94

TOSS IN A BLANKET, 'rough irregular mode of punishment' (O.E.D.); 2. 4. 219–20

Town, village; *Ind.* 33; 2. 2. 156

Trade, traffic; 1. 1. 174

Train, troops; 4. 2. 93

Translate, (*a*) i.e. from one speech to another, (*b*) transform (*M.N.D.* 3. 1. 114); 4. 1. 47

Traverse, mil. command of doubtful meaning; either 'traverse your ground' (i.e. advance or retire; O.E.D. 3) or 'alter the position of your gun so as to take aim' (O.E.D. 8; earliest quot. 1628); 3. 2. 270

Treble hautboy (v. *hautboy*). The smallest of Eliz. reed instruments; 3. 2. 325–6

Trick, fashion, habit, way (cf. *Meas.* 5. 1. 501); 1. 2. 211

Trigon, 'fiery Trigon', astrol. term = 'triple combination of the three signs of the Zodiac—Aries, Leo, Sagittarius—all of the same hot and dry quality' (*Sh. Eng.* i. 460); 2. 4. 264

Trim (vb.), deck out (cf. *1 Hen. IV*, G.); 1. 3. 94

Troop (vb.), march; 4. 1. 62

Truncheon (vb.), cudgel (with a captain's truncheon); 2. 4. 137

Truss, pack, bundle up; 3. 2. 324

Trust, reliance (cf. *Rom.* 3. 2. 85); 1. 3. 100

Try, ascertain the rights of a dispute or quarrel by test or endeavour (O.E.D. 5 c); 4. 5. 166

Turnbull Street, Clerkenwell, 'the most disreputable street in London, a haunt of thieves and loose women (Sugden); 3. 2. 306

Turn on (reflex.), (*a*) blunt the edge, (*b*) turn in flight; 1. 1. 118

Undo, ruin; 2. 1. 23; 4. 3. 22; *Ep.* 4

Unequal, unjust; 4. 1. 102

Unfathered, unnaturally begotten (e.g. by demons or fairies, cf. Spenser, *F.Q.* III. iii. 13); 4. 4. 122

Unguided, anarchic; 4. 4. 59

Unpay, undo; 2. 1. 118

Unseconded, unsupported; 2. 3. 34

Untwind, obs. form of 'untwine' (O.E.D.); 2. 4. 195

Utis (or 'utas'), high-jinks. Lit. 'octave' of a festival, (hence) festival, fun; 2. 4. 20

Vail, let fall; 'vail stomach' = lose heart; 1. 1. 129

Vain, vainglorious; 4. 5. 171

Vantage, opportunity; 2. 3. 68; 'vantage of ground' = favourable position; 2. 1. 79; 2. 3. 53

Vapours, injurious 'exhalations supposed to be developed' in the stomach (O.E.D. 3); 4. 3. 96

Vaward, vanguard; 'in the v. of' = in advance of; 1. 2. 174

Venture (sb.), ship or cargo of a merchant venturer; 2. 4. 60; *Ep.* 7, 11; (vb.) risk cargo at sea; 1. 1. 181, 183, 185

Vice, (i) grip; 2. 1. 22; (ii) jester or buffoon in a morality play; 3. 2. 318

VITAL SPIRITS. 'Certain subtle highly-refined substances or fluids (distinguished as *natural*, *animal*, and *vital*)' were 'supposed to permeate the blood and chief regions of the body' (O.E.D.); 4. 3. 106–7 (cf. 2. 3. 46)

WAIT, follow, attend; 1. 2. 15, 55; 2. 1. 183

WANTON, (i) effeminate; 1. 1. 148; (ii) frivolous; 4. 1. 191

WARDER, ceremonial staff; 4. 1. 125

WASSAIL CANDLE, large candle made to last out the night at a wassail or festivity; 1. 2. 156

WASTE (sb.), something destroyed (cf. *Son.* 12. 10); 1. 3. 62; (vb.) (i) destroy, efface; 4. 5. 216; (ii) spend, use up; 4. 1. 215

WATCH, time when watchmen are on duty; 4. 5. 28

WATCH-CASE, 'a hinged case or cover of an old-fashioned watch, enclosing the watch proper' (O.E.D. 2); 3. 1. 17

WATCHFUL, wakeful; 4. 5. 25

WATCH-WORD, pass-word, private sign; 3. 2. 218

WATERWORK, 'imitation tapestry, painted in size or distemper' (O.E.D.), prob. from Holland or Germany; 2. 1. 144

WEN, tumour; 2. 2. 104

WHEESON, Whitsun (dialect); 2. 1. 89

WILD-MARE, see-saw; 2. 4. 246

WORK OUT, 'preserve to the end' (O.E.D.); 1. 1. 182

WORKING, (i) exertion; 4. 4. 41; (ii) operation; 4. 5. 206; 5. 2. 90; (iii) operation of the mind (cf. *Ham.* 2. 2. 137 note); 4. 2. 22

WORLDLING, inhabitant of the world (cf. *A.Y.L.* 2. 1. 48); 5. 3. 101

WORLDLY, of this world; 4. 5. 230

WOT, wilt; 2. 1. 57

WRATH, impetuous ardour; *Ind.* 30; 1. 1. 109

WRATHFUL, impetuous; 3. 2. 163

WRITE DOWN, delineate; 1. 2. 176; 5. 2. 128

WRITE MAN, attain manhood; 1. 2. 26

WRONG, injury, loss; *Ind.* 40; 2. 2. 95; 5. 1. 50

YEA-FORSOOTH, (*a*) eschewing blasphemy, like a puritan (cf. note 2. 2. 129–30), (*b*) ready in compliance, like a tradesman; 1. 2. 35

YEOMAN, assistant to a constable; 2. 1. 3

ZEAL, religious zeal; 2. 4. 327; ditto with a quibble on 'seal'; 4. 2. 27